IREDELL COUNTY PUBLIC LIBF
www.iredell.lib.nc.us

SO-AHH-860

Conservative Bias

UNIVERSITY PRESS OF FLORIDA

Florida A&M University, Tallahassee
Florida Atlantic University, Boca Raton
Florida Gulf Coast University, Ft. Myers
Florida International University, Miami
Florida State University, Tallahassee
New College of Florida, Sarasota
University of Central Florida, Orlando
University of Florida, Gainesville
University of North Florida, Jacksonville
University of South Florida, Tampa
University of West Florida, Pensacola

Conservative Bias

How Jesse Helms Pioneered the Rise of Right-Wing Media
and Realigned the Republican Party

BRYAN HARDIN THRIFT

University Press of Florida
Gainesville · Tallahassee · Tampa · Boca Raton
Pensacola · Orlando · Miami · Jacksonville · Ft. Myers · Sarasota

Copyright 2014 by Bryan Hardin Thrift
All rights reserved
Printed in the United States of America. This book is printed on Glatfelter Natures Book,
a paper certified under the standards of the Forestry Stewardship Council (FSC). It is a
recycled stock that contains 30 percent post-consumer waste and is acid free.

This book may be available in an electronic edition.

19 18 17 16 15 14   6 5 4 3 2 1

Library of Congress Cataloging-in-Publication Data
Thrift, Bryan Hardin, author.
Conservative bias : how Jesse Helms pioneered the rise of right-wing media and
realigned the Republican Party / Bryan Hardin Thrift.
pages cm
Includes bibliographical references and index.
ISBN 978-0-8130-4931-1 (alk. paper)
    1. Helms, Jesse—Political and social views. 2. Republican Party (U.S. : 1854–)—
History. 3. Mass media—Political aspects—United States. 4. Conservatism—United
States—History—20th century. 5. Television broadcasting of news—Objectivity—
United States. 6. Legislators—United States—Biography. 7. United States—Politics and
government. I. Title.
E840.8.H44T47 2014
328.73'092—dc23   2013029232

University Press of Florida
15 Northwest 15th Street
Gainesville, FL 32611-2079
http://www.upf.com

And all is for my wife, Rebecca

Contents

Figures

Acknowledgments

Many people helped to make this book possible. Nina Silber, Diana Wylie, Sarah Phillips, and Robert Dallek read early drafts. Ella Howard also offered me valuable assistance. Not only did the project begin in a Bruce Schulman seminar, but his advice and gentle criticism guided it through every stage. He suffered through multiple drafts of every chapter, seeing potential where others may have seen incoherence.

This book would not be possible without the senator's papers at the Jesse Helms Center in Wingate, North Carolina, and the aid of archivist Jo Jackson, who facilitated my use of an unprocessed collection. I also want to thank archivist Albert Nasan of the Jimmy Carter Library and the staff of Wilson Library at the University of North Carolina at Chapel Hill.

A part of chapter 1 was published as "Jesse Helms's Politics of Pious Incitement: Race, Conservatism, and Southern Realignment in the 1950s" in *The Journal of Southern History* 74, no. 4 (November 2008): 887–926. I want to thank the anonymous reviewers for the journal as well as editor John Boles and managing editor Randall Hall.

Daniel Williams offered a thorough reading of the manuscript, as did anonymous readers of the University Press of Florida. I am also grateful for the guidance of editor Sian Hunter at the University Press of Florida and copy editor Jonathan Lawrence.

Tougaloo College awarded me a faculty fellowship in 2009, which provided research funds and a reduced course load at a critical point. I am grateful to the college and to my colleagues, especially Candace Love Jackson, William Woods, Jim Brown, and Ernie Limbo. I received the 2003 Angela and James Rallis Memorial Award from the Humanities Foundation at Boston University, and the Boston University History Department supplied additional support through the Engelbourg Fellowship in 2002 and 2003.

I am grateful to Jay Eller and Bryan Marshall; to my in-laws, Debbie and Freddie Scott; and to my parents, Jean and Jerry Thrift, for putting up with me during my research at the Jesse Helms Center. I am also grateful to Sandy and Craig Lewis for bearing a similar burden during my research at the Jimmy Carter Library. My parents deserve many additional thanks for all the ways they supported my ambitions, beginning with the value they placed on education.

Finally, I dedicate this book to my wife, Rebecca Elizabeth Hardin-Thrift, for reasons too numerous to list, but especially for the reminder that there is more to life than work.

Introduction

Jesse Helms's Politics of Pious Incitement

In the American South, a region where cultural conservatism and segregation coexisted with loyalty to the Democratic Party and wide support for liberal economic policies, Jesse Helms became a pivotal figure in advancing the conservative movement of the 1950s and 1960s. From the 1940s to the early 1970s his career immersed him in politics and mass media: city editor of the *Raleigh Times*, news director for WRAL radio, editor of the *Tarheel Banker*, administrative assistant to Senator Willis Smith, and starting in 1960, vice president of WRAL television. In Washington, D.C., as Smith's assistant, the young Helms developed a national vision for conservative power. He recognized that conservative southern Democrats had more in common with western and midwestern Republicans—like Richard Nixon, Robert Taft, and Joseph R. McCarthy—than with liberal Democrats. A national conservative party, however, would require southern realignment. In 1953 Helms left Washington for a private-sector job promoting free enterprise. His new position afforded him a chance to advocate realignment.

Although his critics have often painted Helms as a fringe figure, such depictions represent wishful thinking rather than a serious appraisal of his influence. True, Helms—a polished, well-connected extremist in a banker's suit—expressed views associated with the fringe during the postwar decades. But Helms helped conservatives win a majority, first in North Carolina and then nationally. He believed the liberal consensus was shallow, mainly an elite phenomenon. The problem was how, with a moderate to liberal media, the right could reach these voters. He found solutions. By the 1970s, no one could doubt Helms's centrality to the conservative movement. He signed a fund-raising letter for the Moral

Majority, and the dollars streamed in. His National Congressional Club supplied Ronald Reagan with money and ideas during his 1976 and 1980 campaigns. In his autobiography, Bill Clinton charged that Helms lay behind Kenneth Starr's appointment as a special prosecutor to investigate Clinton's activities.[1]

Even before his election to the U.S. Senate, then, Helms had become a significant figure in American political history. There were two reasons for this. First, he forged a new form of southern conservatism that made it possible for movement conservatives, grounded in the South and the Republican Party, to gain power. He rooted conservatism in private enterprise as the vanguard of a modern, progressive society—one that could simultaneously provide prosperity and maintain traditional values. Avoiding discussions of "race purity" yet never criticizing racists, Helms made white supremacy "safe" for conservative campaigning. His commentaries united conservatives: working class with country club, Democrats with Republicans, small-government advocates and do-anything-to-win anticommunists with segregationists and conservative Christians.

Second, Helms pioneered the attack on the "liberal media" and, most important, the building of conservative media. While he was vice president of WRAL-TV in Raleigh, Helms's commentaries and news department undermined Democrats, advanced conservatism, and challenged the forces advocating change. His commentaries made him something new—a conservative TV personality—and represented the culmination of a career as a media insider. Helms intended to use WRAL's influence to elect conservatives. His news department and commentaries anticipated Fox News' barely disguised conservative advocacy. Risking WRAL's broadcast license, he defied the Federal Communication Commission's Fairness Doctrine for the conservative movement. His commentaries and news department molded the 1960s anti-liberal backlash in North Carolina into a powerful voter coalition supporting conservative Republicans.

A Movement Conservative

Since Reagan's victories in the 1980s, historians have investigated the rise of the New Right. They found its origins in the conservative movement of the 1950s and 1960s and the leadership of William F. Buckley Jr. and Senator Barry Goldwater of Arizona. With the foundation of *National Review* in 1955, Buckley built a conservative alternative to mainstream media and a movement culture. In his books, magazine, and media appearances he attacked liberal elites in politics, academia, and the media while espousing a populist religious traditionalism. Buckley's magazine brought together disparate conservative elements: traditionalist Catholics and Protestants, libertarian advocates of private enterprise and small government, and anticommunists demanding victory over communism abroad and conformity at home. He used his magazine to distance the movement from the most objectionable elements of the right, most notably the John Birch Society (JBS) and southern segregationists. But Buckley was measured in his criticism, because conservatives needed the votes and energy of southern whites and JBS members. His criticism of the JBS centered on Robert Welch. And he defended the South's segregation with limited-government ideology.[2]

Goldwater was conservatives' "knight on a white horse" saving them and the Republican Party from Eisenhower's modern Republicanism. In his landslide loss to Lyndon Johnson, Goldwater captured the Republican Party for movement conservatives. Perhaps even more vital, he convinced millions of voters—segregationists, religious traditionalists, and fervent anticommunists—that they were conservatives and the GOP was their party. The most significant of the voters newly willing to vote Republican were southern whites. Goldwater, and later Reagan, gave the movement a western image of rugged individualism, but it was the swing in the white southern vote that really made conservatism viable. The white South's realignment was not merely racial backlash. Affluent white suburbs in the South resembled Republican enclaves in other regions. But without backlash and Republican willingness to exploit it, realignment would not have happened.[3]

With their focus on presidential elections rather than the conservative movement, Dan T. Carter and Thomas Byrne Edsall and Mary D. Edsall posited a top-down model, with presidential candidates Richard Nixon and Alabama governor George C. Wallace leading the way. In Carter's view, Wallace's national campaigns exported Deep South politics to the rest of the country; Nixon's southern strategy simply stole the governor's fire.[4] In this narrative, the Wallace and Nixon campaigns molded a cross-class white constituency for conservatism that depended on racial anxiety, hostility to cultural elites, anticommunism, and rejection of big government. This meant not only a new conservatism but also a southernization of American public life.

Matthew D. Lassiter and Kevin M. Kruse have challenged this top-down, Deep South version of southernization and examined the grass-roots constituency for conservatism in the Sun Belt South. Lassiter and Kruse complicate southern class relationships, demonstrating that, rather than unifying whites, integration debates exacerbated class conflict. The white working class resented the safely segregated middle-class suburbs. The key actors in Lassiter's and Kruse's narratives are working- and middle-class white southerners who organized grassroots resistance to busing and neighborhood integration in rapidly growing Sun Belt cities such as Charlotte and Atlanta. Although opposition to desegregation began with massive resistance and explicit racism, these activists advocated an ideal of color-blind individualism that obscured their defense of racial and class discrimination. In this bottom-up model, white flight gave birth to modern conservatism: private schools, the tax revolt, and the rejection not only of big government but also of public space. The basis of southernization and the shift of the nation's politics rightward was not a simple model of racial backlash but rather a convergence in the interests of residentially segregated suburbs in all regions.[5]

More recently, Joseph Crespino and David Farber have pushed the history of modern conservatism back before the Goldwater campaign and before the *National Review*. Farber begins his history with Senator Robert Taft's challenge to Roosevelt's New Deal. Taft defended business against New Deal efforts to regulate capitalism and use federal power to ensure the security of the American people. In his 1938 Senate campaign, Taft was the first American politician to use the term "conservative" to describe his views. He championed individual economic liberty over federal regulation and claimed moral superiority for the conservative cause. Crespino establishes the importance of Strom Thurmond's 1948 Dixiecrat challenge to President Truman for modern conservatism. Thurmond, he shows, even in 1948 was simultaneously "one of the last Jim Crow demagogues" and "one of the first Sunbelt conservatives." Anticipating the future of conservative campaigning, he mixed racial politics with anticommunism and advocated pro-business, anti-labor policies. Once elected to the Senate, Thurmond supported Republican president Dwight Eisenhower more than did any other Democrat and second among all senators. In 1964 Thurmond switched parties to support Republican nominee Goldwater, and in 1968 his endorsement helped Nixon win southern votes.

Thurmond and Taft are remembered as leaders of the old right, but the modern Republican right owes them a debt.[6]

Helms's career in North Carolina confirms Lassiter and Kruse's argument that the conservative movement took shape in the Sun Belt South. His positions at the North Carolina Bankers Association and WRAL-TV linked him with two of the industries most responsible for transforming the state. At the Bankers Association and WRAL, he made a career as a booster of free enterprise. An early advocate of private schools, Helms listened to suburban concerns in the growing Sun Belt city of Raleigh—taxes, annexation, and desegregation. He also made a major contribution toward solving the class divide among southern whites. His ideological experiments in his WRAL-TV commentaries unified eastern North Carolina whites—working class with country club, suburban with rural—and shaped grassroots anger over taxes and Supreme Court decisions on school prayer into winning issues.

Although Helms was sympathetic to Wallace, Thurmond, and other segregationist candidates, and just as racist, his national experience led him to conclude that an overly racist defense of an unchanging segregation would not only make a national conservative party difficult but also cause it to fail. Both Thurmond and Wallace spoke to white audiences outside the South, and both hoped to be national leaders, but they depended on the rawest racial politics. Thurmond in 1948 repeatedly raised the threat of "racial intermingling" to defend segregation and used the "n-word" in his first speech as the Dixiecrat presidential candidate. A decade and a half later, Wallace relied on warnings of racial "amalgamation" and insisted on "segregation forever." Both reminded white southerners of the humiliations of the Civil War and Reconstruction. Thurmond was still warning of amalgamation in 1960.[7]

Helms shared a great deal with fellow southern Democrats Wallace and Thurmond. He pushed North Carolina Democrats toward massive resistance and advocated segregated private schools in a 1955 editorial. Yet Helms differed from Wallace and Thurmond in key ways. He described private schools as "private enterprise" and did not threaten his readers with race-mixing. In fact, he eschewed racist epithets altogether and never raised the threat of race-mixing in his commentaries. He considered reminders of the Lost Cause a threat to realignment. Privately, Helms expressed anxiety about interracial couples, but his public silence on the issue demonstrates the extent to which he considered it a political liability. In his third week on the air at WRAL, he made a rare mention of the subject, but only to deny the importance to the South of "intermarriage of the races."[8] He understood that segregationists would think of race-mixing whether he mentioned it or not. He identified with the white southerners most committed to segregation and knew that conservatives had to have their votes. He often failed to hide his distaste for African Americans in commentaries, and few rivaled his ability to fire up segregationist voters. Despite these qualifications, his shifts in racial rhetoric are important for two interconnected reasons. First, growing numbers of southern whites in Sun Belt suburbs rejected being labeled racist and opposed the most overtly racist politics. Helms, for example, believed that segregationist candidate I. Beverly Lake lost the 1960 Democratic primary battle for governor in North Carolina because his racial views were "too strong." Second, toning down their racism was necessary for southern conservatives to gain acceptance in the conservative movement. But as Buckley's *National Review* made clear, a little bit was enough. Conservatives outside the South were willing to put up with a lot to gain white southern votes.[9]

Helms was in the perfect place to reconfigure southern racial politics and build support for the new conservatism. WRAL broadcast from Raleigh, which, along with Durham and Chapel Hill, formed the Triangle, the quintessential Sun Belt metropolis. But WRAL's broadcast area also included many Black Belt counties in eastern North Carolina. White voters in these counties supported Democrats' liberal economic policies, but they were segregationists and committed to disenfranchisement. In the 1950 runoff between Willis Smith and the more liberal Frank Porter Graham, voters in these counties switched to Smith once race became the central issue.

Unlike Wallace and Thurmond, Helms had two decades without the pressure of running for major political office to reformulate racial politics and experiment with conservative advocacy in his commentaries. Although Helms won two city council elections during the 1950s, the stakes were low: his two terms on the council were another opportunity to experiment. Although Helms focused his racial attacks on allegations that at least nominally applied to specific individuals, such as immorality, crime, and communism, his WRAL commentaries held African Americans collectively responsible for these charges. Still, Helms used racial politics more to convince whites to vote conservative than to defend the racial status quo. He advocated flexibility in defense of segregation while hoping the white South allied with a national conservative party could have the final say in how much change occurred.

Helms, Wallace, and Thurmond all favored to varying degrees the low-tax, pro-business strategies that southern state governments pursued to attract industry. Helms differed from Wallace in his rejection of the New Deal and unreserved embrace of conservative pro-business, anti-labor policies. As a state legislator, governor, and presidential candidate, Wallace combined New Deal economic policies with racial and cultural conservatism. Wallace opposed Alabama's right-to-work legislation: any suggestion that unions were legitimate was anathema to Helms. Even Thurmond—two decades older than Wallace and Helms—began his career favoring New Deal spending and courting the favor of labor unions; he only gradually adopted the free-enterprise advocacy so emblematic of the modern Republican right.[10]

Finally, Helms advocated an uncompromising commitment to laissez-faire, traditionalism, and anticommunism. In the depth and breadth of this ideological commitment to conservatism, Helms differed from Wallace, Nixon, and to a lesser extent Thurmond. In his ideological commitment, Helms had more in common with movement conservatives like Goldwater and Buckley. Helms found the moderation of the Eisenhower administration and Vice President Nixon in his 1960 presidential campaign frustrating. In the 1950s, Helms advocated that Nixon push for realignment of the South with the GOP and believed he was an electable conservative. But Nixon was never a movement conservative. Wallace remained a southern Democrat all his life. Thurmond's conservative politics evolved in the heat of his political campaigns. Between 1946 and 1960 he ran for statewide office in South Carolina five times in addition to his 1948 presidential bid.[11] Helms spent two decades developing his politics before his first Senate campaign.

Helms recognized that if forming national conservative alliances meant accepting change, it at least allowed a ditch-to-ditch fight rooted in an ideology of limited government. A conservative party dependent on southern white votes would reverse the white South's political isolation, increase southern influence on the nation, and preserve white privilege. Helms did not just want southern conservatives to join the Republican Party; he wanted the most conservative party possible. His desire for a pro-business, anti-tax party that would enforce traditional religious values was just as strong as his urge to protect the South's racial arrangements. He wanted a party so conservative that it could make criticism of the private sector unacceptable, undermine spending on the public sector, and adopt a unilateral foreign policy. Voters needed to fear their government and the world to make this party viable.

When he returned to Raleigh from Washington in 1953, Helms spent the rest of the decade as executive director of the North Carolina Bankers Association and editor of its magazine, the *Tarheel Banker*. At the Bankers Association, his main job was promoting banking and free enterprise. Free-enterprise boosterism allowed him to advocate conservatism while fulfilling the aims of the Bankers Association. Helms developed a populist attack on the mainstream media, began reformulating southern racial politics, and urged realignment while defending the Eisenhower administration. Because bankers' interests were his main concern, Helms was often circumspect regarding politics until late in the decade. The anxiety of the Little Rock crisis, his election to Raleigh's city council, and growing involvement with WRAL-TV emboldened him.

In 1960 A. J. Fletcher convinced Helms to join WRAL-TV. Already committed to the conservative movement, he began touting Senator Barry M. Goldwater as a presidential candidate in December 1960. A few months later he praised the Young Americans for Freedom and cautiously defended the John Birch Society. The conservative periodical *Human Events* published Helms's writing throughout his career. Its publisher, James Wick, became a personal friend who recruited the young North Carolinian for a permanent position at the magazine. Helms corresponded with Buckley and donated money to *National Review*.[12] But these were only the most visible signs of the conservative movement. Helms was a key figure in the South advocating the new conservatism.

The 1960s and Pious Incitement

Television gave Helms a large audience. Delivering twenty editorials a month and reading his mail as a poll, he found the issues that resonated with voters. Fletcher gave Helms more freedom to get involved in politics than had the Bankers Association. He wanted Helms to deliver conservative editorials, report news from a conservative perspective, and help elect conservatives to office. They particularly sought to undermine the commitment of eastern North Carolina whites to the Democratic Party and liberal economic policy, and they understood that race was the means. Drawing on traditional southern roots but departing from them in significant ways, Helms added ideological rigor, a sophisticated grasp of modern media, and Republican Party connections to southern conservatism. Media politics—the savvy deployment of television as a form of political communication and the critique of the mainstream news media for its alleged bias—would play a crucial role in the transformation of southern conservatism and the emergence of a national New Right. Helms stood at the center of this process.

Helms expected movement conservatism with its unbridled pro-business slant to be a hard sell in eastern North Carolina. Democrats had assembled a bottom-up coalition, combining most low-income voters and enough affluent voters for a majority. This liberal coalition included union members, Catholic ethnics, urban African Americans, and southern whites. Democrats held the coalition together with policies that spread the benefits of government widely through "give-away programs" that Helms derided. Rural whites in the eastern half of the state benefited from these policies. Recognizing that race made the liberal coalition vulnerable, Helms allied movement economic elitism with populist racial and cultural politics to build a white cross-class alliance. All along he remained convinced that his state and nation would wake up to the dangers that liberalism presented.

As the 1960s unfolded, Helms's despair and euphoria fed off each other. The southern social system was challenged but intact in 1960; by 1972 it was shattered. Yet the civil rights movement was only the first in a series of egalitarian social movements that transformed the nation. Helms deciphered it all for eastern North Carolina's voters. Ammunition for his ideological warfare came from numerous sources: protesting minorities and students; riots; Supreme Court rulings on school-led prayer, "smut," and busing; new rights and new entitlements; liberal impotence in the Cold War, especially Vietnam; rising taxes and inflation; a counterculture challenging traditional values; and the growing welfare state. The developments that caused Helms the most anxiety gave him the most hope for a conservative future. He believed the eventful decade would drive voters into conservatives' arms, if conservatives would use the issues the decade gave them. On WRAL's evening news, viewers saw the civil rights demonstrators, the antiwar protesters, and the urban riots; then Helms came on the air to express his anger and theirs. He laced his wrath with ridicule and sarcasm. He entertained and proselytized. He claimed cultural and political authority for movement conservatism. Helms labeled illegitimate the changes later summed up as "the sixties." The events of the decade fueled the conservative movement.

On WRAL, Helms engaged in what the *Raleigh News and Observer* labeled "pious incitement."[13] Pious incitement was an outrage-driven, symbolic politics that offered moral indignation to build conservatism. It relied on sensation and exaggeration. It involved expressing righteous anger to gain attention, deny legitimacy to others, and claim victimhood. It was grounded in a populist religious and racial politics. With pious incitement, Helms accused adversaries of disloyalty and proclaimed the moral superiority of conservatives. He created a rhetorical moral community of conservatives and denied entry to liberals and moderates, including most Democrats and African Americans.

Pious incitement was rooted in southern racial politics. Helms added moral and religious incitement to the racial incitement and red-baiting of southern demagogues. His addition of religious moralizing to racial politics made the racial incitement seem respectable. It also appealed to southern fundamentalist and evangelical Christians and helped draw them into politics. The developments of the 1960s—from the Supreme Court rulings on prayer to the emergence of a counterculture challenging traditional values—gave Helms's pious incitement more traction. He began pious incitement during the 1950s in response to the civil rights movement, but its resonance depended on the numerous challenges to tradition in the 1960s. Helms's pious incitement was part of conservatives' broad cultural opposition to the social and cultural changes unleashed in the decade. The cultural politics of President Richard Nixon and Vice President Agnew were a major factor in Helms's finally registering as a Republican. He often disagreed with the Nixon administration's policies on school desegregation, the economy, and foreign policy, especially China. But Nixon and Agnew's attacks on the media, on civil rights, black power, antiwar protesters, and the counterculture won his admiration. Helms's pious incitement was further to the right than the Nixon administration's and was rooted in southern religious and racial views. His pious incitement landed some of the first blows in the culture war. And Helms's pious incitement was also media politics.

Helms developed pious incitement at the North Carolina Bankers Association during the 1950s. He first attracted public attention with a

Tarheel Banker commentary advocating private schools to avoid "forced integration." The criticism of Helms's advocacy from the state's major newspapers publicized his plan beyond the limited reach of the *Banker*. His experience confirmed a lesson he had learned in Washington: sensationalism boosted conservatism. Intentionally raising an uproar, pious incitement built up giants for Helms to slay. His favorite foils were liberal and moderate Democrats, the media, the University of North Carolina, mainline Protestant churches and ministers, protesters, and the civil rights movement.

Helms resented civil rights activists' moral and religious argument against segregation. He believed the deeply religious white South was morally superior to African Americans and really to most people outside the South. He repeatedly held up southern segregated communities as models for the rest of the nation and expressed distaste for big cities and African Americans—never mind the religious faith of African Americans and northern liberals. Helms not only dismissed the civil rights movement's religious arguments against segregation but also attacked the National Council of Churches as an extremist organization for its liberalism and especially for its support for civil rights. Instead of Christianity, the civil rights movement and the National Council of Churches were motivated by left-wing sympathies, he claimed. Pious incitement, then, allowed Helms to associate liberals and civil rights activists with immorality, communism, and lawlessness and to question their moral and religious convictions. "Martin Luther King's so called Southern Christian Leadership Conference . . . is heavily laden at the top with leaders of proven records of communism, socialism and sex perversion," he wrote. The "15 New England clergymen" who participated in civil rights protest in eastern North Carolina "came to break laws . . . and promote bitterness, not to advocate brotherhood."[14]

Pious incitement also allowed Helms to use southern racial politics and red-baiting to undermine the Democratic Party and promote movement conservatism. In 1962, with Congress debating literacy tests, Helms told a story of a taxicab ride across Harlem. Filled with Helms's and white southern voters' anxieties regarding big cities and black voters, his tale was a parable illustrating why the dangerous combination of liberals and black voters made literacy tests important. "Nodding towards the dirty, steamy, crowded sidewalks," the cab driver observed, "Mister, this is a jungle. You can get your throat cut out there." Helms underlined the cabby's point. Elsewhere in Harlem, "young hoodlums" murdered "a policeman and a storekeeper" during a robbery. The cab driver insisted that African American Democratic congressman Adam Clayton Powell "gets money for public housing, sticks these people in it, puts them on relief. They don't have to work. All they have to do is vote right. A lot of 'em can't even read." The driver lamented, "I have to work myself to death to pay taxes to support these people."[15]

The religious moralizing of Helms's pious incitement was often intertwined with race-baiting. The cab driver and WRAL's white audience were morally superior to the black voters in Helms's story. The cabby, Helms believed, knows "what is causing the crime rate and the irresponsibility" because he witnessed what happens to people "who have learned that if they do not work to support themselves and their families, the government will step in and take care of them."[16] The story of the cab ride used pious incitement to build support for elitist economic conservatism. According to Helms, the viewer similarly paid taxes to the federal government so that liberal Democrats could keep the votes of undeserving poor minorities. Recognizing that it had become unacceptable to express a belief in white supremacy, Helms instead claimed moral supremacy. He cast Democrats and African American voters along with the national media out of the moral community.

On the face of it, the perspective of Helms and other movement conservatives contained contradictions: it embraced both free enterprise and traditionalism, elitism and populism, authority and freedom, individualism and duty, order and rapid economic growth. But as David Farber explains, "American conservatism is a disciplinary order generated by hostility to market restraints and fueled by religious faith, devotion to social order, and an individualized conception of political liberty." Liberals wanted to discipline the market, while conservatives wanted to discipline the individual.[17] The heroes and victims in the story Helms's cabby tells were the hardworking taxpayers who lived by the discipline of the market. The villains were the immoral, illiterate Harlem residents who were freeloaders and criminals because of welfare and public housing. But as much as Helms relied on racial politics, he did not just mean African American welfare recipients when he criticized government aid. The entirety of the New Deal was suspect. Helms described farmers as going to Washington for "handouts" and Social Security as a "disguised welfare program." Liberalism was a danger because it threatened to make the rest of the country like "Harlem." Democrats' borrowing and spending had "affected our sense of morality." "Ours is a cake-eating, cake-having generation; high spending and high borrowing."[18]

Pious incitement was most effective when Helms connected Democrats to African Americans, civil rights protesters, and cultural elites. Attacks on the television networks and the state's major newspapers were central. "The news of the 'civil rights struggle,' as it is called, has been so distorted, so exaggerated, so magnified out of proportion that the people have learned to expect one-sided, contrived, and often manufactured reports having scarcely any resemblance to the truth." But the most important development was Democrats' reluctant support for the civil rights movement. The WRAL news department, with Helms in the lead, bombarded "liberals" and civil rights activists with every rumor or accusation Helms and his reporters could unearth. The "recent Negro 'March on Washington' included 'literally scores' of fake ministers" in "rented" vestments. Because of his connections to prominent Democrats and the praise of the mainstream media for his leadership, no public figure was more important to pious incitement than Dr. Martin Luther King Jr. Most significant for the conservative movement, Helms entangled Democrats in his allegations directed at King. "Dr. King can incite his followers to riot and President Kennedy hails it as a great adventure of freedom."[19]

Helms honed pious incitement into a powerful tool during his eleven years on WRAL. His questioning of the "liberal" media made viewers distrust mainstream media and justified establishing a conservative alternative. Helms tapped into viewers' anger and frustration over the civil rights movement, taxes, Supreme Court rulings, and liberal elites everywhere. He claimed Christianity for conservatism and offered moral indignation as a distraction from public debate of issues that favored liberals. He associated Democrats, the federal government, and elites in universities, print, and broadcast media with everything viewers found unsettling. Making government action ridiculous or threatening undermined the means of reform. Helms's pious incitement and WRAL news transformed the Democrats from the party of the "solid South" into the black party and remade the Republican Party into defenders of a Christian republic.

With Fletcher's backing, Helms intended to use WRAL's influence to elect conservatives. In 1950 he worked on the Senate campaign of conservative Democrat Willis Smith while covering it at WRAL radio. Many times in his career he repeated this dual role in an election by participating in a conservative political campaign or cause while his news department provided coverage and his commentaries' endorsement. He disguised his involvement whenever desirable. Conservative textile executive Charles Reynolds of Spindale Mills tried to persuade Helms to become co-chair of a committee opposed to income taxes. Helms declined: "I can be of more value to you as an 'objective observer.'"[20]

Helms believed that Senator Goldwater's vote against the 1964 Civil Rights Act would lead white Democrats to vote Republican. His commentaries and WRAL's news explained why North Carolinians should support the Arizona senator. Although Goldwater lost North Carolina in 1964, his campaign left an impression on the state. Two years later, Republican James Gardner defeated longtime congressman Harold Cooley with decisive support from the station. WRAL's conservative advocacy led to two Federal Communication Commission (FCC) investigations for violations of the Fairness Doctrine and the Equal Time Rule. Daring the FCC to enforce it, Helms found ways to use the Fairness Doctrine against his opponents.

Night after night, Helms spelled out the real and imagined connections between African Americans and Democrats. In the midst of social transformation and a failing war effort, his conservatism sounded like common sense to many white Democrats. He gradually convinced them that the Democratic Party and liberalism no longer represented their interest. These eastern North Carolina southern Democrats supported Willis Smith over Frank Porter Graham in 1950, but they also voted for Adlai Stevenson over Dwight Eisenhower. Many voted for John Kennedy and Lyndon Johnson in 1960 and 1964, for George Wallace in 1968, and for Republicans Jesse Helms and Richard Nixon in 1972. Helms spent the 1960s moving white North Carolinians to the right as they sat and watched television in their homes. His commentaries on WRAL-TV were critical to the transformation of these formerly reliable Democrats into Republicans.

1

"There Is Another Way"

Free Enterprise, the Mainstream Media,
and Southern Realignment in the 1950s

Helms was born in 1921 and grew up going to a Baptist church in Monroe, North Carolina. Monroe was a southern piedmont town of three thousand where segregation and cultural conservatism were taken for granted. Helms's father served as police chief.[1] Given this background, Helms's conservatism would not be surprising, except that he was not a typical southern conservative. By the 1950s, he opposed the New Deal and advocated realignment of the state with the Republican Party. That marks him as something other than a regular southern Democrat no matter how conservative.

Before his thirty-second birthday, Helms had become an award-winning newspaper reporter, city editor of the *Raleigh Times*, news director for radio station WRAL, administrative assistant to Senator Willis Smith, and media adviser to Senator Richard B. Russell Jr.'s run for the 1952 Democratic presidential nomination. After his stint as Smith's assistant, Helms left Washington for Raleigh and a position as executive director of the North Carolina Bankers Association in the fall of 1953. The Bankers Association hired Helms for his public relations skills. Helms's main responsibilities were promoting banking and the Bankers Association, but his position also afforded him an opportunity to advance conservatism. As editor of the *Tarheel Banker*, he wrote commentaries that promoted free enterprise—a mix of anti-tax, pro-business policies with a healthy dose of anti-statism. Rarely using the words "liberal" or "conservative," he identified liberal economic policy with socialism and conservatism with free enterprise.

Helms's decision to join the Bankers Association came a few months after Willis Smith's unexpected death. His resignation caught Smith's appointed replacement, Alton Lennon, off guard. Helms denied rumors that Lennon's support for Adlai Stephenson precipitated his departure. He "had had enough of Washington," Helms declared. Still, Helms returned to North Carolina and cautiously defended the Eisenhower administration.[2]

Helms arrived back in North Carolina convinced that realignment of the political parties was the best way to advance conservatism and protect the South's interests. Yet he found Eisenhower's modern Republicanism and the influence of moderate Republicans frustrating. During most of his tenure at the Bankers Association, Helms was guarded in his political commentaries unless it directly involved bankers' interests. His preference for Eisenhower over Democratic nominee Adlai Stevenson was expressed mildly, as was his advocacy for realignment and pleas for bankers to run for office. Even this limited political advocacy sometimes made bankers uncomfortable, and occasionally he held nothing back.

As editor of the *Tarheel Banker* and then as a city councilman, Helms began reconfiguring southern racial politics in support of conservatism rather than the racial status quo. His ultimate aim was undermining white southerners' support for liberal economic policies. In the *Banker* he castigated the mainstream media, including *Time* magazine and the state's large-circulation papers, particularly the *Raleigh News and Observer*. Religion, too, became central, particularly in his rejection of the civil rights movement's claim of moral and religious authority. Helms's pious incitement, which blended populist racial and cultural politics with free-enterprise economic policy, became a powerful weapon against liberalism.

Helms's intention at the Bankers Association was realignment of the white South with a conservative Republican Party. His hopes centered on Vice President Richard Nixon. Helms's praise for Nixon after the 1956 presidential election made the state's other Democrats howl: "I have been told," Helms wrote Nixon, "that I am a liar, a dupe and a disloyal Democrat." He had taken "a calculated risk" when he decided "to defend you in my magazine." A few weeks after his commentary, Helms invited Nixon to address "about 1000 of the top people in North Carolina of both parties" at the Bankers Association's annual convention. Helms was frank about his political intentions: "Mr. Vice President, I hope and pray that you will be elected President in 1960—and with North Carolina's electoral votes in your column."[3]

Helms's political ambitions for himself and conservatism were expansive. His main audience at the *Tarheel Banker* consisted of bankers and their employees. While they were certainly influential, he longed for a broader audience. Pious incitement sometimes garnered mainstream media attention. And in 1957, he won election to the Raleigh City Council. Often outnumbered six to one on the council, he found his voice in opposition to annexation, taxes, and fluoridation. Late in the decade, Helms tentatively began delivering Sunday-afternoon editorials on A. J. Fletcher's WRAL-TV. Television suited his purposes: direct advocacy of conservatism to an audience that would never read the *Banker*.

Republican Sympathizer

In 1964 Helms replied to a critical Duke University student, "A quarter century ago when I was a college student, I held many convictions—and held them strongly—that I now reflect upon with some chagrin." During the Great Depression, Helms had benefited directly from the New Deal. A National Youth Administration job had allowed him to attend college in the late 1930s—exactly the kind of liberal program he later opposed.[4] What changed Helms's perspective between 1939 and 1953? This is a difficult question to answer, because the documentary record begins in 1953, after his views were formed. The decisive factor appears to be the time he spent in Washington, D.C. His two years as assistant to Willis Smith took him far from Monroe and exposed him to conservatives from other regions.

Helms left Monroe in 1939 to attend Wake Forest College near Raleigh. While a student, he landed a job as proofreader for the *News and Observer*, the state's most influential newspaper and a prominent voice of white southern moderation. He left Wake Forest early to work as a freelance reporter and eventually as sports and then city reporter for the *News and Observer*. There he met his future wife, Dorothy Coble, a journalism graduate of the University of North Carolina and editor of the women's section. The *Raleigh Times*, the *News and Observer*'s afternoon competition, made Helms assistant city editor in 1941. His reporting won a North Carolina Press Association award in 1942.[5]

Helms served as a naval recruiter during World War II. Stationed in Columbus, Georgia, he recruited by day and spent nights as sports and city editor for the *Columbus Enquirer*. Helms always did the work of two or three people. Once the war ended, he resumed his newspaper career in his home state, becoming city editor of the *Raleigh Times*. Helms, like most southern Democrats, opposed President Harry Truman's support for African American civil rights and his New Deal–like social welfare program—the Fair Deal. His friend Alvin Wingfield Jr. introduced Helms to conservative economist Ludwig von Mises's *Human Action*.[6]

In 1948, Helms left the *Raleigh Times* for a job in radio. He began his relationship with Alfred J. Fletcher, a wealthy conservative and founder of WRAL radio, the Tobacco Radio Network, and later WRAL-TV. Fletcher, an ideologically driven conservative, became a "second father" to Helms. As a WRAL reporter and news director, Helms "locked horns" with Governor Kerr Scott, a moderate Democrat.[7]

Helms's first significant political experience came in the bitter 1950 contest for a U.S. Senate seat. The election pitted the conservative lawyer Willis Smith against the former president of the University of North Carolina, Frank Porter Graham, the South's most visible liberal. Graham asked Helms to serve as publicity director. But Helms supported Smith. Unlike most elections in the one-party South, the candidates embodied competing ideologies. Graham expressed dissatisfaction with segregation and backed federal aid to education and collective bargaining. Casting Graham as an out-of-touch extremist, Smith's supporters charged that Graham favored the "mingling of the races" and blindly worked for communist front organizations.[8]

Helms advised the Smith campaign while he covered the race for WRAL radio. He later downplayed his role in Smith's election, but his friend and fellow campaign worker Pou Bailey spoke frankly about the young reporter's involvement: Helms "had no official position, but I don't think there was any substantive publicity that he didn't see and advise on. He was deeply involved." Graham won 48 percent of the vote in a four-way race. But on June 6 the Supreme Court issued three decisions that chipped away at segregation.[9]

The fear surrounding these cases offered an opening for Smith, but he appeared ready to accept defeat. With Fletcher's backing, Helms broadcast a message calling for voters to gather at Smith's house. It ran every ten to fifteen minutes from 6:00 to 9:00 p.m. on WRAL. Several hundred people rallied in the candidate's yard. Helms and others spoke to the crowd between chants of "We want Willis." Years later, Helms acknowledged "the importance of our little spontaneous rally at Willis Smith's home." The candidate "said he would not have run had it not been for the folks who came out that evening."[10]

The Smith campaign won the runoff by pounding the racial themes. The biggest shifts came in the rural Black Belt counties of the east. In the June runoff, Smith won seventeen of the twenty-seven eastern counties that Graham had won in May. Graham's racial views outweighed other issues.[11] Helms learned a key lesson from the geography of Smith's victory: white voters in eastern North Carolina were supportive of Democrats' economic policies, but conservatives could win eastern North Carolina with racial politics.

Smith's victory was part of a conservative turn in southern politics. The failure of union organizing, the Democratic Party's support for African American civil rights, and an emerging white middle class all strengthened southern conservatism.[12] The 1950 campaign was Helms's first taste of victory. Helms and other conservatives defeated a formidable liberal candidate backed by the most influential Democrats in the state. He formed friendships and political alliances with Hoover Adams, Pou Bailey, and Tom Ellis. All three became close friends to Helms and political allies. Adams founded the *Daily Record* in Dunn, North Carolina. Bailey, a successful and politically connected lawyer, served as the Bankers Association's legal counsel. Ellis, also a lawyer, became Helms's campaign manager and head of the National Congressional Club. Smith, a former speaker of the North Carolina House and president of the American Bar Association, was another conservative influence on Helms.

In 1951 Helms joined Smith's Senate staff. This Washington experience gave him a national perspective on conservatism. Smith served on the Senate Internal Security Subcommittee chaired by conservative Democrat Pat McCarran of Nevada. McCarran was one of the few Democrats who had opposed the New Deal. Helms's role as an assistant to Smith, "a prominent member" of the committee, was a formative experience. He cited insider information from his years in a "rather sensitive position" when defending his commentaries. He "first learned," for example, from the committee of the communist plan "to make a 'Black Republic' out of the entire South." Helms shared Smith's Senate ties to conservatives in both parties—not only southern Democrats such as Richard Russell of Georgia and James Eastland of Mississippi but also Republicans Robert Taft of Ohio, Joseph McCarthy of Wisconsin, and Richard Nixon of California. Helms had lunch with Senator Taft and listened to him criticize

President Eisenhower. Taft thought the president had been "misled" by liberals. Helms admired Taft and other conservatives from outside the South. He saw McCarthy's attacks on the Truman administration and found them impressive. "Senator McCarthy had a way of creating resentment," Helms would concede in 1965, "but he was not far from right about the state department."[13]

When Helms left Washington in 1953 after Smith's unexpected death, he was less a partisan southern Democrat than an ideologically driven conservative. He had breathed in the conspiracy-laden atmosphere of conservative Washington, and it became central to his thinking and his politics. He used his Washington contacts to gather ammunition for commentaries. Deeply skeptical of the New Deal, even Social Security and farm programs, Helms viewed the GOP favorably years before the Republican Party nominated Senator Barry Goldwater for president. Washington transformed the southern Democrat into a Republican sympathizer.

A Free-Enterprise Booster and Traditionalist

Helms's background in radio and newspapers, coupled with his political experience in the 1950 election, Smith's Senate office, and Russell's 1952 presidential bid, made him a formidable advocate of free enterprise. But the Bankers Association's hiring of him caused a stir. Many found his perspective and methods distasteful. Hard feelings within the North Carolina Democratic Party lingered from the 1950 election, and newspaper editors reminded their readers of Helms's involvement. The *Hereford County Herald* accused Helms of being a hatchet man who turned out the "scurrilous, degrading, and slime pit type of stuff" in the Smith-Graham election. Norman McCulloch, editor of the *Bladen Journal*, pressed his readers to "realize the threat that people like Helms and McCarthy present to our way of life." Newspaper editors expected him to be an advocate for the right: he did not disappoint.[14]

"Banking has been the whipping boy of politicians for generations," Helms complained. And from newspapers, bankers and businessmen expected regular scolding. "We're accused of being glass-eyed, scoundrels, tight-fisted reactionaries, Republicans, ultra conservatives," and "tools" of the Eisenhower administration. Helms believed bankers and other businessmen were partly to blame for their unpopularity because they shied away from politics. Americans "believe in free enterprise," Helms declared, but "when business vacates the field and lets the socialists dispense their sugar-coated pills, you can't blame the average fellow for being misled." American "capitalists have a proud story to tell," but it must be conveyed in an engaging fashion. Moreover, "bankers cannot afford to be aloof from politics. They should participate actively."[15]

Helms advocated a vision of business as progressive and modern to counter the negative image of bankers. In his first few months at the Bankers Association, he launched a public relations campaign trumpeting "The Big Change," the monumental shifts in the state since the turn of the century. As part of the campaign, the association sponsored an oratorical contest for high school students that associated bankers with growth and modernization. Helms expected the contest to mold the "thinking and attitudes of the young people" and counter "the vicious propaganda" about the state's backwardness. He sent "promotion material" to every North Carolina bank for its executives to distribute to local newspapers and radio stations. Bankers spoke at hundreds of high schools to celebrate their role in modernization. The "Big Change" campaign generated positive coverage of bankers and their influence in their communities. "If you read the paper even a little bit or listen to the radio at all," observed the *Belmont Banner*, "you know something about 'The Big Change.' . . . Most of those changes have been brought about by men like John Stedman of Lumberton, president of the N.C. Bankers Association." The *Banner* also noted that the Bankers Association had "a speaker, a writer, and a cracking good public relations man" in Helms. After reading an issue of the *Tarheel Banker*, Helms's friend and ally Hoover Adams remarked, "As usual you did a magnificent job. You really make heroes out of those guys. They ought to love you—and double your salary."[16]

Because he was working for bankers who were politically cautious, Helms was circumspect in his political commentaries even when primarily advocating free enterprise. This was especially true in the early 1950s. Still, partisan neutrality in a southern state like North Carolina was significant, and particularly so when it leaned Republican like Helms's. In a 1954 commentary he observed mildly that he had not "always agreed with" Adlai Stevenson. Eisenhower, certainly not an ideologue, was still the first conservative and the first Republican elected president since Herbert Hoover. Helms especially supported Eisenhower's secretary of agriculture, Ezra Taft Benson, who had tried to shift federal agricultural policy toward a market-based approach. The *Tarheel Banker* published an annual farm edition in February that coincided with the Farm Credit Conference co-sponsored by the Bankers Association. Helms's commentaries defended Benson and pushed bankers to embrace a role in guiding farm policy away from subsidies. "Why, you could shoot Mr. Benson" and "the situation would not be one whit better." Benson had merely tried to restore farming to "its one time rugged individualism" and stand up to those willing to make farmers "virtual wards of the government" in securing their "bloc" vote. He published an article by Benson in 1955 and persuaded Assistant Secretary of Agriculture Earl Butz to speak at the 1956 Farm Credit Conference. A. J. Fletcher's Tobacco Radio Network carried the speech. Butz became one of Helms's most important Republican friends.[17]

But the Eisenhower administration had limited success in changing farm programs. Helms acknowledged that agribusiness was the major barrier: "The era of the small family farm, whether we like it or not, is a thing of the past. Meanwhile, big farm corporations are getting the lion's share of the federal funds." Helms hated farm subsidies' departure from "supply and demand," but resistance to Benson made him recognize the depth of opposition. By 1956 he had concluded, "The farm problem will give the Republicans a lot of trouble this year" because it "is too complex for a politician to try to explain honestly to the farmer." In the Senate, Helms would be the foremost defender of federal tobacco programs, but he remained an occasional critic until his first Senate campaign in 1972.[18]

Many of Helms's most politically pointed commentaries in the *Tarheel Banker* defended bankers and their interests. And the origins of his assault on the mainstream media lay in countering what he regarded as newspapers' "vicious, and sometimes absurd, editorials about banking." When the *News and Observer* accused bankers of using the state's banking commission to impede competition in the spring of 1955, Helms wished "that the *News and Observer* would, for once, try to be fair when it digs into a matter involving banks." The *Greensboro Daily News*' criticism of the Bankers Association's recommendation for amending the state's taxes also elicited a sharp rebuttal: "We happen to believe that from a long range viewpoint, our tax structure is North Carolina's biggest obstacle to progress and prosperity." The *Daily News* clearly doubted that companies were avoiding the state because of taxes. "Perhaps *The Greensboro Daily News* should read our statement again, and more closely."[19]

The issue of the decade for bankers, however, was the withdrawal in 1956 of $71 million in state funds from banks. The withdrawal "meant a financial loss" for many banks and "pinched" the state's economy. The state attorney general recommended that the state invest its surplus funds in federal securities rather than banks, and Governor Luther Hodges and other state officials went along. Newspapers backed the shift of funds and labeled legislation to reverse it the "bankers' bill." The *News and Observer* threatened the bill's supporters in the general assembly with defeat, while the Bankers Association lobbied for its passage. Helms criticized Hodges because the governor's primary concern appeared to be how supporting banks would look in his next campaign. But Helms reserved his strongest words for the *News and Observer*: "Bankers have learned never to expect fair play from *The News and Observer*." The paper's unfairness was not limited to banks: "Any business or any individual who speaks up for free enterprise can usually expect the same treatment." After the bill's passage, Helms gloated that "certain newspapers" were quiet, since banks were paying the state more than "Uncle Sugar's treasury bills."[20]

Helms's *Tarheel Banker* commentaries sought to counter the distrust of bankers and other businessmen lingering from the Great Depression. The *Banker* included two pages, the first usually focused on business, politics, and association news, while the second relied on gossipy, humorous anecdotes. The first page advanced an ideologically tinged pro-business agenda. The second rambled in a conversational tone—with amusing stories about prominent bankers and politicians that made bankers and their conservative allies seem like regular Joes rather than an untrustworthy elite.

One story concerned his friend Hoover Adams, Willis Smith's publicity director in 1950 and founder of the *Dunn Daily Record*. Adams had an adversarial relationship with bankers. The would-be publisher, Helms explained, had to "borrow the shoestring" that he pulled himself up with. Adams was confident of his success, but his "zeal and self-confidence were at times incompatible with the bankers' objectivity." Adams had always considered "damyankee" to be one word, and during the early years of his paper he made "dambanker" one word, too. Helms reported that the *Daily Record* was out of financial danger and that Adams now "admits that banker is one word."[21] Helms's story acknowledged the animosity directed at bankers while suggesting that the bankers had Adams's best interest at heart.

Although it rarely showed up in the *Tarheel Banker*, Helms's conservatism was rooted in traditionalism. Helms sought to preserve the face-to-face community and values of the small-town South, including conservative Christianity and segregation. Limits on Washington's power not only gave business a free hand but also allowed local tradition to prevail on social and cultural matters. A visit to his hometown two decades after he left inspired a bout of nostalgia in a commentary titled "Monroe? Why That's a Place Called Home!" Monroe and the rest of the South were idyllic places. "I shall always remember the shady streets, the quiet Sundays, the cotton wagons, the Fourth of July parades, and the New Year's Eve firecrackers. I shall never forget the stream of school kids marching uptown to place flowers on the Courthouse Square monument on Confederate Memorial Day." But the stress Helms placed on small-town values was more than just nostalgia. His understanding of race, religion, and the South originated in Monroe. He and others raised there had "a lot of character and fortitude and patience and wisdom to live up to."[22]

Tradition and religion constrained individuals, and Helms believed it was the duty of elites to maintain these constraints. He was active in charities, his church, and civic organizations. He served on the boards of the Wake County Tuberculosis Association and the Raleigh United Fund. A deacon in the First Baptist Church of Raleigh, he served in various church offices, including chairman of the budget committee. Helms was also an active member of the Raleigh Rotary Club, eventually as president of the organization. In demand as a public speaker, he made the rounds of the state's civic organizations, graduating classes, and business associations.[23] His vigorous activity beyond the Bankers Association and his family fulfilled his sense of community responsibility, but he never hesitated to put conservatism forward.

In 1959 Helms served on a pulpit committee, conducting a national search for pastor of Raleigh's First Baptist Church. After the committee interviewed Dr. Claude Broach of St. John's Baptist Church in Charlotte, Helms felt it necessary to explain his aggressive questioning to Broach: "Too many clergymen have made the mistake of plunging into controversial issues without too much consideration for both sides of the question." Rev. Bill Finlator of Raleigh's Pullen Park Baptist Church, he complained, had "insulted many men who possess Christian motives as well as American ideals." Finlator supported the civil rights movement from his pulpit, and Helms apparently feared that Broach would, too. Divisions on the pulpit committee ran deep. Within a few years, Helms and his family moved to Hayes Barton Baptist Church.[24]

Despite his traditionalism, Helms recognized that economic expansion meant change. He praised "the ever-increasing number" of women working in banks for "doing a splendid job." Rising employment among married women was a national trend, despite the emphasis on domesticity during the 1950s. His comfort with working women depended on the control of businessmen. No legislative, judicial, or presidential mandates were involved, and no political activism was required. Helms expected working women to bring few changes beyond their "swishing skirts." "I have a secret to tell you," a memo from Helms's secretary, Alice, intimated: "I'll give you three guesses, but I don't believe you'll need but one." Alice was pregnant. Neither she nor her boss considered any option besides resignation.[25] Helms, like most observers, failed to anticipate that women clustered in low-paying jobs during the 1950s would generate political pressure for increased opportunity.

Desegregation and a Populist at the Bankers Association

In September 1955, Helms burst into the spotlight with a *Tarheel Banker* commentary on segregation. "There Is Another Way" criticized the state's leaders for their response to the *Brown* decisions. The "private enterprise way," he asserted, provides "the same wide horizon for enlightenment" as public schools and would allow the state to maintain segregation. North Carolina governor Luther Hodges pressured "Negroes to accept voluntary segregation" to avoid closing public schools. Moderate Democrats backed him. Helms chided the governor and his allies for agreeing with the NAACP "that the *public* schools must be maintained at any cost." The "only choice," Helms asserted, "is between integrated public schools and free-choice private schools." Those "hell-bent on forced integration" pushed the state's citizens into an unnecessary quandary. "It is this minority which will decide whether our public schools shall be preserved."[26]

During the 1950s, the primary difference on segregation between conservative and moderate Democrats in North Carolina was the best method of defending it. Assistant Attorney General I. Beverly Lake proposed a massive resistance plan that would appropriate state funds for segregated private schools. Helms and other conservatives favored Lake's approach. Helms's "Another Way" commentary advocated it. The approach of the governor and his moderate allies substituted various surrogates for race to forestall compliance with the *Brown* decision. They delayed meaningful integration in the state for over a decade. The state's major newspapers defended the governor and public education while chastising the North Carolina Bankers Association. The *News and Observer* denounced Helms's commentary as the "silliest suggestion yet." The *Charlotte Observer* called it "overreaching extremism." The *Ashville Citizen* supposed "red-hot tar" clung to the Bankers Association's "heels" after Helms's commentary. National publications such as *Time* contrasted North Carolina and Hodges favorably with neighboring states and governors.[27]

Helms's advocacy of private schools and his sensational connection of the governor to the NAACP generated controversy. But the controversy gave him space to advocate conservatism and tear into the papers for their support of moderation. If "private enterprise was the keystone of education," education's costs would decrease and "political sociologists" would be unable "to dictate" policy. Even though they were critical, the newspapers quoted from his editorial and gave his ideas a larger audience than ever read the *Tarheel Banker*. A widely published Associated Press story quoted "Another Way" extensively, alongside Helms's statement that his editorials were not the official position of bankers.[28]

The month after "Another Way," Helms supposed the "virtual windsquall of reaction" surrounding his framing of school desegregation was intended to "make us run for cover." The newspapers reacted as though he had proposed to "lynch grandma." Helms rebuked the state's papers and public officials: "What is important is that the people be told the truth." And the editors and other leaders were "not telling the whole truth" because "*public* schools mean *eventual* integrated schools."[29]

Helms's controversial statements were a spontaneous part of his personality. "I have never hesitated to give my opinion on anything," he confessed. "That's why I've been able to corner the market on hot water, in which I constantly stay." Such outbursts occurred in his private life when no political benefit could accrue. In 1956, Helms offered to resign as an usher at Raleigh's First Baptist Church because he refused to seat African Americans. He insisted, "If Negroes sincerely wished to come to our church for the purpose of worship, I would be delighted to sit with them."[30]

During the 1950s, jumping into hot water grew into a political strategy for Helms, who admitted in his next editorial that he had "expected" the papers' reaction. Banks were the last place Americans looked for attacks on other elites. The *News and Observer* recommended a skeptical attitude regarding a bankers' magazine that advocated "unrestricted private enterprise" when banks needed government to guarantee financial stability. Helms's previous attacks on the media had responded to newspapers' populist criticism of bankers and other corporate elites, but "Another Way" and the follow-up commentary, "Let's Face the Issue," marked a reversal in roles for the first time. On segregation, Helms claimed the populist ground and painted moderate southern Democrats in the media and public office as untrustworthy elites. "Another Way" accomplished something that Helms did repeatedly over the next five decades: capturing the media spotlight with a sensational statement to advance conservatism.[31]

"Another Way" also said nothing directly about race-mixing. Helms's framing of segregationist arguments in the language of free enterprise gave them a respectable veneer. He assured readers he supported education for all children "regardless of race, creed or color." Allen Chappell congratulated him on his editorial "so well expressed that it deserves far more attention than it will probably receive." Chappell, like Helms, headed a professional organization—the Carolina Farm Dealers' Association. The dean of a small college, Price Gwynn, expressed relief that someone had finally called out the governor and the papers for their "wishful thinking." But "Another Way" did not just resonate with elites. Mason Yeager, a man of modest background, learned of Helms's commentary from the *Charlotte Observer*. Yeager, like Helms, supported public schools, "BUT NOT AT ANY COST OF PRINCIPLES."[32]

Many bankers expressed their support, too. A Wachovia Bank and Trust executive, George Geoghegan, called the commentary "intelligent, interesting, and constructive" and suggested the association send it to every paper in the state. But not all bankers were happy—particularly given the criticism, which was leveled at bankers along with Helms. John Stedman, president of the Scottish Bank in Lumberton, expressed his and others' displeasure over Helms's "There Is Another Way," writing that the *Tarheel Banker*'s "editorials and articles should be confined to banking." Stedman, who was president of the Bankers Association when Helms was hired, was immensely influential. Certain that his editorializing had powerful backers, Helms responded to Stedman by defending his right to "maintain a two-fisted attitude about what I consider to be right."[33] Helms's penchant for inflammatory statements and his realization that the media's reaction would often redound to his favor evolved into pious incitement. But Stedman's displeasure probably had a chilling effect. Helms's commentaries continued over the next few years to discuss race and politics, but they became more subdued. And the next time he drew media attention with incendiary words, it would be as a city councilman.

Helms echoed the perspective of southern elites on racial issues in the *Tarheel Banker*. The region's problems were "prompted by outsiders." White southerners could always find deferential blacks, who would affirm white views. Helms said he had discussed race "with my Negro friends" and reported that "most of them have said that they wish the Supreme Court had not handed down that 1954 decision." Helms shared with a black elevator operator a letter from "an Arkansas farmer" to the Supreme Court: "I am sorry to report that my white coon dog won't hunt birds with my black bird dog. Could I get an injunction to make them hunt together?" He "enjoyed it more than I did." Helms concluded, "The Negroes aren't taking this thing nearly so seriously as the Supreme Court thinks they are."[34] Helms's "Negro friend" occupied a position of service to white men in downtown Raleigh, so deference to them would be a prerequisite for the job, perhaps even the main qualification.

Privately, Helms acknowledged the legitimacy of African Americans' discontent. In the late 1950s, Rudy Scott, an old friend from the Tobacco Radio Network and fellow free-enterprise promoter, asked Helms for information regarding a full-page NAACP ad in the *New York Times*. Scott, who was president of America's Future, Incorporated, assumed it was "grossly exaggerated." The ad pictured an African American girl asleep on a school bus in North Carolina while she endured an eighty-mile, eleven-hour round-trip to and from school. Helms regretted to relay the ad's accuracy. "Frankly," he admitted, "I don't blame the parents of the 28 children for being bitter." The county should "get busy on a school for the Negro kids." Helms added, "I don't like integration, but right is right and truth is truth."[35]

In his private correspondence of the 1950s, Helms was calm regarding the prospect of desegregation. After his endorsement of private schools, he wrote *Charlotte Observer* editor Pete McKnight that school integration was "inevitable" and that "I am not one of those who forecast doom for the land" when it happens. A few months later, he doubted that school integration "standing alone" was "of any particular consequence." Yet "Another Way" was the beginning of decades of advancing conservatism with assaults on "forced integration." Once desegregation of public schools was under way in North Carolina, he became one of the loudest voices predicting doom. The contrast between Helms's private observations and his public outrage suggests the latter was in part strategic. But his efforts to advance conservatism were never far removed from his fears over liberal influence. What troubled Helms was school desegregation "as a part of the whole scheme of things," particularly black voting. The "Negro race is not yet ready for leadership," but "outside forces would use the Negro as a balance of power at the polls."[36] Helms feared that an increase in the number of African American voters would make a conservative party unattainable.

Realignment: "The sheep on one side, the goats on the other"

During his years in Washington, Helms had become acutely aware of the ideological jumble of American political parties. Southern Democrats often allied with Republicans against liberal Democrats. Republican presidential nominees were invariably more conservative than the Democrats. Although he had never voted for a Democratic presidential nominee, Helms remained a registered Democrat until 1970.[37] He stayed with the party for practical reasons. Most other North Carolina conservatives were Democrats. Conservatives waged a fierce battle for party control, and the Democratic primary decided North Carolina elections.

During the 1950s, Helms's call for realignment and his overtures to Richard Nixon demonstrated his desire to make the GOP a vehicle for southern conservatism. Helms believed the Republican Party could be competitive in North Carolina. Eisenhower-Nixon won the state west of Raleigh in 1952 and 1956 but lost statewide because the Black Belt counties in the east went overwhelmingly for Adlai Stevenson. These eastern counties had the largest African American population, widespread voting-rights violations, and a strong attachment to the Democratic Party. Eastern North Carolina Democrats favored New Deal economic policies and Jim Crow. In 1952 Eisenhower's coattails allowed Republican Charles

Jonas to win election in a district stretching from Charlotte west into the mountains. Helms remembered Jonas's initial meeting with the state's congressional delegation as the first Republican elected since the Great Depression. "I have been on your team ever since," wrote Helms. Jonas was a fiscal conservative and the state's first Republican reelected to Congress in the twentieth century.[38] Jonas's victories and the close presidential races gave Helms's reasons for optimism in the 1950s. But Republicans did not win a statewide race until Helms and Nixon culminated two decades of gains in 1972.

During the 1950s, Helms worked for conservative North Carolina Democrats, offering his aid behind the scenes with fund-raising and strategy. He dispensed advice, edited conservatives' speeches, and hid his hand whenever desirable. "The reports that I constantly hear about your running for Governor in 1956 are very pleasing," Helms wrote Lieutenant Governor Luther Hodges, a former textile executive. "While I don't have much to offer in the way of political strength, it will be a pleasure to have the opportunity of supporting and assisting you in any way." In 1955 Helms offered his support to Edwin Pate, a past president of the Bankers Association, who was considering a run for lieutenant governor: "I just wanted to say, for the record, that you have a volunteer publicity man, campaigner and worker-at-large in case you decide to run." President of Commercial State Bank in Laurel Hill, North Carolina, and a former state legislator, Pate was exactly the kind of conservative executive Helms had in mind when he encouraged bankers to enter politics. After the death of Senator Kerr Scott, Helms lobbied Governor Hodges to appoint Pate to the Senate.[39]

In 1958 Helms's close friend and future campaign manager Tom Ellis ran for state senate. Helms helped put together a mailing list and arranged for Ellis's campaign to use bank executive Robert Holding's "automatic typewriter" to print a letter. The letter promised development without "additional tax burdens."[40]

Shortly after Helms left Washington, C. Aubrey Gasque, a conservative member of the Democratic National Committee, expressed his worry that the Bankers Association had "taken from us the makings of a great congressman from North Carolina." Relaying hope for a "reconstruction of our Party along the lines we have known it in the South," Gasque assured Helms that a plan was under way "to regain" control of the Democratic Party. He suggested that Helms rely on him to make "your views" known to "the right people." Helms willingly collaborated with other conservative North Carolina Democrats to resist the left-wingers.[41] Helms, however, had already concluded that conservatives could not regain significant influence in the national Democratic Party, and he had his doubts about the state party as well.

One sign of Helms's distrust of Democrats was his adversarial relationship with his old employer the *News and Observer*. The paper had been aligned with the Democratic Party since Josephus Daniels bought it in the 1890s. As a Democrat and an editor, Daniels helped establish the southern racial order in North Carolina and then in Washington while serving President Woodrow Wilson. By the 1950s, Josephus's son Jonathan was editor. "The prestige of the paper," Helms complained, "died with Josephus Daniels." Jonathan, like his father, served Democratic administrations, most notably as Roosevelt's last press secretary and Truman's first. But the party had changed. Roosevelt made the Democratic Party dominant by assembling a majority coalition supporting liberalism, which included farmers, unions, white ethnics, white southerners, and urban African Americans. These groups expected the federal government to help them realize the American dream. After World War II, President Harry Truman tentatively committed the Democratic Party to civil rights, including the desegregation of the military, and proposed his Fair Deal, which included national health insurance and increased social welfare spending.[42]

In the 1950s, many of the state's Democrats and large-circulation newspapers supported the policies begun under Roosevelt and Truman—some more selectively than others. Helms rejected them whole cloth. And he routinely expressed disdain for other North Carolina Democrats and the state's papers. Jonathan Daniels had a "bleary-eyed and haggard" look, Helms observed in a commentary, but if "I ran a newspaper like Jonathan's, I wouldn't sleep well either." In his private correspondence he was contemptuous: the *Charlotte Observer*'s Pete McKnight "just ain't honest," and Helms's congressman Harold Cooley was "a faker." In 1955, Ed McMahan, a conservative North Carolina Democrat and Helms's friend, was passed over for an appointment to the Interstate Commerce Commission. Helms considered McMahan's non-appointment emblematic of conservatives' exclusion from power. He blamed the "ultra liberal faction" among the state's Democrats, especially Senator Kerr Scott and Jonathan Daniels. Daniels had ties to "the radical elements" in the national party. Scott's failure to support McMahan should weigh on his conscience. "Trouble is, they tell me that jackasses don't have consciences." Helms appealed to Vice President Nixon to intervene and assured him that none of Mc-Mahan's opponents were allies of the Eisenhower administration or any conservative.[43]

Although Helms labeled them left-wingers, radicals, and ultra-liberals, the North Carolina Democrats he most despised were moderates in a national context. Helms was often dissatisfied with the conservatives too. Governor Hodges was exactly the kind of individual Helms wanted in politics, but Hodges disappointed him. Not only was the governor willing to work with moderates, but being elected governor did not satisfy his ambition. Before the 1956 election, Hodges moved to the right on school desegregation and accused the newspapers of writing "slanted stories" in their coverage of the issue. Helms was delighted. He praised Hodges in the October *Tarheel Banker* just before the 1956 election. But by 1958, after Hodges supported the withdrawal of state funds from banks, Helms had soured on him again. "Hodges stock has picked up some," he wrote. "He might now get 10 per cent if he ran for something."[44]

All in all, Helms deserted the party of the Solid South reluctantly. He felt a special connection to Georgia senator Richard Russell, a southern Democrat and a conservative with national aspirations, whose style Helms emulated. He served as Russell's media representative during his "ill-fated bid" for the 1952 presidential nomination. In 1955 Helms offered to form a "Russell for President" organization in North Carolina, but the senator declined. Helms tried again in 1958, but Russell left no possibility of another presidential campaign.[45] The party's rejection of Russell and McMahan, along with other signs of the national party's rejection of conservatism, fed his desire for realignment.

Helms's political commentaries during the 1956 presidential election year were restrained compared to "Another Way," but he made his views clear. In April, Helms shared with *Tarheel Banker* readers an important lesson learned from Russell's failed effort: "I still think that Dick Russell is the best qualified man in the Democratic Party for the presidency," but the "Northern big-city bosses" enforced "an unwritten rule against Southerners being nominated." Then he turned his attention to President Eisenhower: "Remember all of those Democratic suggestions back in the late forties that he run for President—on the Democratic ticket? Now that he's a *Republican* President, Democrats can't think of a good thing to say about him." Congressman Cooley, chair of the agriculture committee and the administration's main opponent on farm policy, "called the Democrats who voted for Ike in 1952 rats." The truth is, "Democrats wish to gosh that they had Ike in the White House."[46]

A few months later, Helms laid out his hopes for the future. A typically "right sensible" guy claims "that the voter who doesn't support his political party from top to bottom is asking for dictatorship in America" and "that the so-called 'independent voter' is unstable." The troubles of the American political system were not caused by the independents, who decide "our elections," but instead by the parties abandoning their purpose. People sharing "the same ideas and philosophies of government" formed the original parties. Today "our party leaders" insist that everyone should have the same philosophy, just because they are in the same party. "The people of the Democratic South, fundamentally a conservative people, will never be able to reconcile their views with such people as Senator [Hubert H.] Humphrey, Senator [Herbert H.] Lehman, and—to a lesser degree—even Adlai Stevenson." All three were northern Democrats. "What is needed, of course, is a complete realignment of the two parties—the sheep on one side, the goats on the other."[47]

Helms admitted that the regulars in both parties would probably continue to cooperate—at least during elections—and that the South would have limited influence. Southerners, "believing as they do in states' rights and basic conservatism, have no place to go." Helms protested that "on most of the issues which seem important, both parties may be observed going thataway." The two parties competed vigorously for African American votes—key swing voters in many states outside the South. Most Democrats and many Republicans agreed that an activist federal government held responsibility for maintaining American prosperity. To the dissatisfaction of Helms and other conservatives, the Eisenhower administration embraced this vision. Helms later dismissed Eisenhower as a "lukewarm 'conservative.'"[48]

The Eisenhower-Nixon ticket came within a few thousand votes of winning North Carolina in 1956. Helms's limited enthusiasm for Eisenhower showed in a post-election commentary: the president had "at least *talked* of a return to a free economy, of states' rights, of individual freedom." Helms, however, had high hopes for Nixon, who, he believed, was the best hope for drawing the South into the Republican Party and in the process moving the GOP to the right. In his first commentary after the election, Helms defended Nixon against Democratic attacks: "I like to think I've been a pretty good Democrat (Southern variety that is)," but "I'm not a strong enough Democrat, to hate Nixon." Helms claimed first-hand knowledge from his Washington experience. Working in adjacent Senate offices, Nixon and Willis Smith got along well. Both were Duke Law School graduates. "My observation of Nixon and my knowledge of the kind of fellow he impressed me as being, have made me a bit resentful of some of the epithets bordering on slander that have been thrown at him."[49]

In the 1950s, many of Helms's efforts to promote conservatism and re-alignment led nowhere. Nixon did not visit North Carolina in 1957, nor did he win the state in 1960. Ellis lost a humble beginning for the team that would create the National Congressional Club. Pate remained in private life, and Governor Luther Hodges became John F. Kennedy's commerce secretary. And in September 1957, a crisis in Little Rock, Arkansas, and the passage of the first civil rights bill since Reconstruction stoked Helms's deep fears about African American voting.

Competition for African American votes between northern Democrats and Republicans made civil rights central to the 1956 campaign. After the election, the Eisenhower administration introduced a civil rights bill aimed at voting-rights violations in the South. The bill threatened to tear the Democratic Party apart. The Democrats' Solid South depended on African American disenfranchisement. The bill passed, but only after Senator Russell and Majority Leader Lyndon Johnson weakened the legislation with the support of northern Democrats like Senator John Kennedy.[50] Eisenhower signed the 1957 Civil Rights Act in September, a few days after Governor Orval Faubus defied a federal court order to integrate Central High School in Little Rock. Eisenhower sent army troops to enforce the Court's decision. National media coverage supported the president and cast Faubus as a demagogue.

The Little Rock crisis created a dilemma for a conservative who hoped for southern realignment. Helms refused to question Eisenhower's "integrity" and declared his neutrality on Faubus's actions. Instead he turned his attention to black voting and news coverage: "We do resent the nauseating violations of journalistic integrity by such publications as Time and Life and the claptrap that is spewed forth by the radio and television experts." He condemned anyone who campaigned for black votes. "The pious politicians in both parties who grab for what they believe is the silk purse of minority votes will, one day soon, realize that they have grabbed merely the sow's ear of dissension and strife." Helms's assaults on mainstream media and both political parties had a better chance of uniting conservatives nationally than a defense of segregation. He avoided singling out Republicans and discussion of race-mixing while pleasing segregationists' with old-fashioned red-baiting. "Perhaps, as some contend, integration is inevitable." But it was a "phony issue" benefiting America's enemies. "What is happening in America is exactly in tune with the forecast of Karl Marx. . . . The cackles you hear have a Russian accent."[51]

Pious Incitement: A Conservative City Councilman

"America sorely needs a businesslike government," Helms contended during the 1956 election. "By avoiding politics," businessmen had "reaped pretty much what they've sown." A few months later he announced his candidacy for the Raleigh City Council. He outlined concern for the "over-burdened taxpayer" and opposition to fluoridation. His expectations were low: "[I] will undoubtedly be defeated." And after his victory, he was almost apologetic about his conservatism: "I know, of course, that my so-called conservative views will not win any popularity awards for me." His assessment was accurate in a sense. His conservatism led to bitter fights over the financing of a new city hall, taxes, and annexation. But his oppositional stance built a devoted following, and he easily won re-election in 1959.[52] The city council gave Helms a platform from which to advocate conservatism. His actions were news. In his two terms, Helms learned how a conservative minority could build support, even when losing most legislative battles.

In the 1950s, Raleigh experienced rapid growth. The city needed a new city hall, new personnel, and expanded services. Mayor Bill Enloe and a majority of the council believed that increasing taxes was necessary. Their immediate concern was getting a new city hall. Helms concurred with the consensus that Raleigh had outgrown its old one. Plans for the new building, however, sharply divided the council, because the project's supporters proposed issuing bonds without a referendum. Helms led the opposition. He objected to the bonds "without permitting the people to vote" and thought the council was ignoring alternative construction sites that would cost taxpayers less. The council decided four to three to issue bonds anyway. "The whole City Hall matter," Helms wrote months after the vote, left "a great deal of bitterness," and "the new location of City Hall will be a long-time monument to hasty judgment." His opposition drew strong support. One voter wrote, "I greatly admire your stand on bond matters." Helms opposed the new tax proposal as well.[53]

Helms had developed a reputation for opposition even before the fight over city hall. He was the single no vote on an urban renewal project. Civic groups and the city's leaders wanted to redevelop Smokey Hollow— a rough working-class neighborhood. Helms voted against the condemning of private property for redevelopment, despite the certainty of losing. "The folks who worship an all-powerful government will try to confuse the issue," but "urban redevelopment has the distinct odor of tyranny."[54]

When Helms was first elected in 1957, Raleigh had just decided in two referenda to fluoridate its water. The incumbent fluoridation opponent lost his reelection bid. Voters, the mayor, and the other city council members considered the matter settled. Helms managed to win the support of fluoride's opponents without alienating others. With fluoridation opponents, Helms faced a dilemma common for postwar conservatives: what to do with the extremists? Raleigh's anti-fluoride voters saw a communist conspiracy in what most understood as a public health issue. They embraced Helms. He presented his opposition to "forced fluoridation" as a principled stand for freedom similar to his views on taxes. When opponents appeared before the council, he agreed that fluoridation was unconstitutional and extended their allotted time to speak. Yet Helms acknowledged fluoride's value. "I feel that fluoridation of water probably would be beneficial for my family, particularly my children." Acknowledging that fluoride benefited public health satisfied mainstream voters.[55]

Helms grew adept at speaking to the fringe without alienating mainstream conservatives. On the city council he also gained experience reaching voters on race, an issue with much greater political potential than fluoridation.

Although his *Tarheel Banker* commentaries allowed Helms to address readers without mediation by other news outlets, the regular audience for his editorials consisted mainly of bankers. More people learned about his advocacy of private education through critical newspaper coverage than through "Another Way." His actions as a city councilman were also filtered through the papers. Conservatives in every region of the nation faced this problem. How could they communicate conservative ideas to voters through a skeptical media? Although Helms was often infuriated by newspaper coverage, his experience in the 1950s made him confident that he reached voters despite the papers. In January 1958 Helms manipulated the state's major papers into covering his actions, which were calculated to incite racial hostility and fear of liberalism.

As a city councilman, Helms wrote a letter to the Raleigh city manager, W. H. Carper, concerning threats directed at speakers scheduled to appear at the Institute of Religion. The speakers included Martin Luther King Jr., Senator Hubert Humphrey, and labor leader Victor Reuther, brother of United Auto Workers president Walter Reuther. These three men—a civil rights activist, a northern Democrat supportive of civil rights, and a union leader—embodied his fears regarding American politics. The United Church of Raleigh, the Raleigh Woman's Club, the Parent Teacher Association, and the League of Women Voters sponsored the Institute of Religion. News of Helms's letter was leaked to the *News and Observer*. The paper covered the letter in an article and then an editorial accusing Helms of "Pious Incitement."[56]

The article quoted extensively from Helms's letter. The city councilman wrote that he was "concerned" about "the number of expressions of resentment I have heard regarding the series of speakers." He recommended that Carper prepare for trouble: "I write this letter to suggest that you consult with our chief of police." Helms's letter prompted the city manager to make fearful statements about political unrest. "Mob violence will not be tolerated in Raleigh," he declared. The city would commit the whole police force, if necessary.[57]

While the *News and Observer*'s article publicized Helms's perspective, the next day an editorial in the paper accused Helms of "Pious Incitement." "The concern of City Councilman Jesse Helms," the editorial began, "who helped put on the race-baiting campaign against Dr. Frank Graham, for protection of public speakers at the Institute of Religion, may seem a sign of civic enlightenment. Actually, the Councilman's letter was obviously an effort to stir up trouble." The institute's speakers "need the protection of Jesse Helms like they need holes in their heads."[58]

Just as his advocacy of private schools created a media reaction that publicized his perspective, the *News and Observer*'s coverage of his letter opened opportunities. Helms complained in the *Tarheel Banker*, "My little chums at *The News and Observer* . . . wrote an editorial which was so absurd that even the folks who agree generally with the paper's editorial policy were calling me and expressing their contempt for *The News and*

Observer." The "entire thing was a falsehood." In contrast to the news-paper, Helms did not explain any of his opponent's perspective, but he boasted that the events increased his confidence. "*The News and Observer* isn't fooling people any more. . . . I have received hundreds of telephone calls, letters, postal cards, telegrams and personal visits. Only two of these were unfavorable—one anonymous, profane telephone call, and one letter from Chapel Hill."[59]

An editorial in the *Raleigh Times*, which the Daniels family had ac-quired in 1955, was equally dismissive. Helms wrote the *Times'* editor, Herbert O'Keefe, "I did not release the letter to the press, nor did I autho-rize its release." He defended his actions as a straightforward concern for public safety: "I felt it my duty to report to the City Manager the nature of several expressions I had heard so that we can be properly prepared."[60]

Helms's attacks on the speakers and the papers delighted conservatives. Even when writing his allies, Helms initially maintained an image of con-cerned public servant. "I take the position that if there was, indeed, any incitement, *The News and Observer* did the inciting." But a year and a half later, Helms revealed his political intentions to a conservative minister, James Dees. "As I had expected and perhaps hoped the memorandum fell into the hands of *The News and Observer.*" His righteous anger over its publication was just a performance. Helms resented "the attempt to lend respectability to the so-called 'Institute of Religion'" and their speak-ers. The police presence "would remind those in attendance the speakers were not operating from a portfolio of sweetness and love." His anxieties centered on race. The United Church of Raleigh, a sponsor of the speaker series, "is a strange assembly of citizens with left-wing leanings. It is also an integrated church." Protest callers especially objected to King's ap-pearance, which was scheduled for "the white school auditorium." They threatened to throw "rotten eggs."[61]

Helms's pious incitement demonstrated not only a willingness to ma-nipulate the Raleigh papers but also a sophisticated grasp of how modern media functioned. Readers did not simply read the news and an edito-rial and reach the same conclusion as the editor. The "ultra-liberals" had targeted him "in senseless neglect" of the fact "that everything they said" focused attention on "the ridiculous slate of speakers."[62] Helms's leaked letter created news. The vague concern for "physical demonstrations" in his letter led the city manager to assert that the police were ready for "mob violence," even though the callers only threatened to throw rotten eggs.

Helms created the impression that the Institute of Religion and its speakers posed a threat. Through it all, he successfully painted himself as the victim.

Helms's pious incitement not only satisfied segregationists but also led moderates to question the *News and Observer*. Pious incitement denied legitimacy to opinions different from his and expressed outrage to drown out other voices. It claimed moral superiority for conservatism and discredited liberalism with fear, while undermining the basic processes of public discourse critical for democracy. Voters bought into his posture of fearful moral indignation. Pious incitement also succeeded in slipping exaggeration and distortion into mainstream media's political coverage.

In the midst of the incident, Helms boasted of his political theater's success to Jack Spain, Senator Sam Ervin's administrative assistant: "The reaction here—I believe—has been heavily in my favor except with the Negroes and the liberals whose votes I would never get." Helms won re-election in May 1959. He also believed his actions had pressured the Institution of Religion into moderating its choices. The 1959 speakers, he wrote, were "not so insulting as Humphrey, Reuther and King."[63]

The key issues before the city council during Helms's second term were annexation and taxes. When the general assembly passed a bill that allowed North Carolina cities to annex territory against residents' wishes, Raleigh moved to add five areas. Helms vigorously opposed annexation. During the 1950s, annexation emerged as an issue in cities throughout the nation. The American dream for the postwar middle class featured a suburban home, but suburbanization reduced cities' population density and tax bases. The vanishing urban middle class made the "forced annexation" that Helms opposed essential for maintaining the quality of life in growing cities. Those American cities that successfully annexed a significant portion of their suburbs maintained their tax base and their quality of life. Because of the permissive state annexation law, Raleigh expanded by 550 percent between 1950 and 1990. Over the coming decades, municipalities with expansive boundaries like Raleigh avoided extreme income disparities between central city and suburb.[64]

On taxation and local government, Helms's *Tarheel Banker* editorials and city council proposals did not offer unwavering opposition in the 1950s. "Big government on the State level unquestionably is with us to stay. It seems painfully obvious that we cannot hope to reduce our total tax requirements."[65] In January 1960 Helms wrote an article for *State* magazine, edited by his friend Bill Sharpe, in which he offered a local income tax as an alternative to annexation. Helms recognized that, as engines of growth, cities had a claim on the suburbs that their economies nourished. "We find it hard to muster sympathy for the citizen who . . . makes his living *in* the city while living just *outside* its legal boundaries." The suburban resident was "willing to mooch" off the urban taxpayer. "He makes his living *because* there is a city, but he does not want to bear his share of the cost." But Helms insisted that this was only half the story. When a city annexes new territory, the city invariably expects the citizen who already paid for a well and septic tank to help pay for the city's expanding water and sewer system. Thus "forced annexation" strains property owners' finances. To solve this dilemma, Helms advocated "a city income tax, or sales tax or both," which would spread the burden of taxation among the city's beneficiaries.[66]

His own tax proposal was "obnoxious," as Helms acknowledged, and received little attention, while his opposition to the existing tax structure and annexation drew considerable support. At a city council meeting, Helms declared that "our present tax rate can and should be maintained and that no serious infirmity will result insofar as the city's services are concerned." A tight budget, he admitted, would require painful cuts from city departments, including the inability to add needed personnel. Since "thousands of citizens" were "brought into the city against their will," the city council must avoid adding new taxes. "The tax burdens of the American people are nearing the intolerable point."[67]

Voters expressed their gratitude for Helms's opposition to taxes. A husband and wife were "glad to know there is one financially responsible councilman." A voter wrote, "You are the only member of the council that should be reelected. . . . [I]f something is not done to cut the tax burden instead of increasing it—no one will want to come to Raleigh."[68]

Those annexed against their will also turned to Helms. "I simply do not see any justification for inclusion of my FARM in the city limits," wrote Frank Parker. Parker, age seventy-five, and his wife were retired. "We do all of our work. Even produce most of our food." City services were useless to them. Parker disposed of his garbage, had well water "far better than city water," and even maintained his roads with a tractor. He asked Helms for help.[69]

Helms was a lone voice against annexation. From a practical point of view he could do little to stop annexation or taxes, but Helms relished defending the Frank Parkers of the world. His local income-tax proposal would have shifted the burdens of an expanding city to those who benefited from it the most and away from retired property owners such as the Parkers. The tax proposal also raised the possibility of shifting power from federal to local government. Helms recognized, though, that opposition to all taxes worked best as an issue. His reelection and the supportive letters confirmed his nascent sense of how conservatives could win. First, he had successfully meshed populist stances on segregation and the media with economic conservatism. Second, the media echoed his perspective, even when critical. Finally, he could also strike a populist note against taxes and big government while defending business interests.

A few months after his election to the city council, the Little Rock crisis provided Helms with a reason to raise the temperature of his rhetoric. His commentary on Little Rock was more strident and ideological than he had previously dared in the *Tarheel Banker*. The sensationalism, fear, and outrage of pious incitement infused Helms's commentaries through the 1960 election. During the 1958 recession, he accused the "prophets of gloom and doom" of advocating "more socialism." "They have never believed in free enterprise and they never will." His commentaries more and more claimed that liberalism would lead to communism. Soviets believed that communism would triumph after socialism replaced capitalism. Do you think "if the world abandons capitalism" that "it would work?" "If not, then how about the socialism all around you?" Businessmen, including bankers, were a part of the problem. "Even now, with a big, all-powerful government mushrooming all around us, it is not unusual to see bankers leading the parade in various 'progressive' something-for-nothing gimmicks of the federal government." The growing salience of civil rights only confirmed his accusations. Our "faint-hearted" leaders say "the South 'may be able to *compromise*.'" Compromises were the problem. "If freedom is right and tyranny is wrong, why should those who believe in freedom treat it as if it were a roll of bologna to be bartered a slice at a time?"[70]

In a 1959 commentary, sounding an alarm at Senator Hubert Humphrey's influence, Helms named liberalism as the villain for the first time. Humphrey's "so-called civil rights program has been thrust, almost entirely, upon the South. The liberals are in the saddle everywhere and complete socialism is just around the corner." The senator has no inclination toward "free enterprise" or "fundamental Constitutional government."[71] Previously, Helms's private correspondence had labeled Democrats ultra-liberals, radicals, and leftists. His commentaries made vague criticisms of New Deal–style economic liberalism as socialist. But he had never used the term "liberal" with a negative connotation in the *Tarheel Banker*, nor had he attacked any politician so harshly. He also had not tied Democrats directly to civil rights. This new formula became a regular feature of his commentaries on WRAL-TV.

A combination of factors lay behind his increased stridency. In part Little Rock meant he could be confident that most bankers were with him. While he was editor, the *Tarheel Banker*'s subscriptions had tripled, and advertising had grown proportionally.[72] Pious incitement and Helms's other successes as a city councilman led to growing confidence. The Humphrey commentary suggested an awareness of the conservative movement and the direct attack on liberalism by national figures like William F. Buckley. The movement assured him that conservatives from other regions saw socialism everywhere, too. He was disappointed with the Eisenhower administration and Governor Hodges. The civil rights movement and black voters had a growing influence in American politics. Eisenhower's reaction to Little Rock and the passage of the 1957 Civil Rights Act made that clear. Although African Americans sometimes supported conservative Republicans like Eisenhower or Congressman Jonas, black voters' influence tended to push the nation leftward. And in the summer of 1958, Helms began delivering editorials on Sunday afternoons for WRAL-TV.

WRAL-TV and the 1960 Presidential Election

Helms's attack on the Institute of Religion, calculated to gain mainstream media attention, demonstrated his hunger for a larger audience than the *Tarheel Banker* afforded. An opportunity opened in December 1956 when his old boss at WRAL radio, A. J. Fletcher, added a television station to his Capitol Broadcasting Company. With years of experience in radio and a substantial fortune, Fletcher launched WRAL-TV as a "loud and strong" advocate of "free enterprise." Capitol Broadcasting's Tobacco Radio Network provided extensive news coverage, which translated smoothly to television. In 1957 Fletcher tried to lure Helms back. Confident that Helms could use race to separate voters from the Democratic Party and the *News and Observer*, Fletcher wanted his political commentary on the evening news. He was angered by a *News and Observer* headline for the

1957 Civil Rights Act, "Senate Votes to Take Up Ike's Civil Rights Bill." Fletcher doubted Eisenhower was a strong backer of the civil rights bill and believed Jonathan Daniels was. The station owner inferred that the Democratic editor presented it as Republican legislation because the bill was unpopular with white southern voters. "I wish we had someone of sufficient stature," Fletcher declared, "to stand up on Channel 5 [WRAL-TV] and tell the people the honest truth."[73]

Fletcher was bullish on the influence of television in countering newspapers: "If there are as many TV homes as there are newspaper homes after only a few years of TV operation, then what may we expect say in ten or fifteen years." Helms found the offer from WRAL-TV "most flattering" but was worried about how leaving the Bankers Association would affect his family. By the 1950s Helms had made it, with a home in Raleigh—near good schools for his daughters—and a vacation home on the coast, but this prosperity depended on his salary. After careful consideration, Helms declined. Fletcher offered him a Sunday editorialist spot instead. Helms's videotaped editorials began broadcasting in July 1958 on Sundays at 3:45 p.m.[74]

Helms's WRAL commentaries began six months after the *News and Observer*'s "Pious Incitement" editorial. His attacks on the paper left many viewers with a sense of relief. One supporter wrote, "I agree with you 100% in your views in regard [to] the *Raleigh News and Observer*. They have made their vast fortune off the white people of N.C. and I do think that the least that they could have done would have been to support our Governor and our Legislature in their attempt to maintain our race purity." Another of Helms's commentaries praised eastern North Carolina congressman Graham Barden. As chair of the Education and Labor Committee, Barden blocked a labor bill co-sponsored by Senator Kennedy.[75]

Helms was a significant presence at the station even before joining its staff part-time. He and Pou Bailey moderated a WRAL-TV program that covered the state general assembly beginning in 1957. Fletcher also consulted him on WRAL's coverage of the Institute of Religion's speakers. WRAL planned to emphasize the institute's "overtones of Socialism," identifying the speakers' philosophy with that of the *News and Observer* and stressing King's appearance as "a very disturbing factor in race relations."[76]

Helms had high hopes for conservatism in the 1960 elections. With support from "a substantial number of people," he considered running for a seat in the state senate but decided against it.[77] Helms remained actively involved in politics particularly with the gubernatorial race. But 1960 also brought considerable anxiety. Civil rights and African American voters remained central to both parties' election plans. African American students escalated civil rights protests throughout the South, and a second civil rights bill passed.

In April 1960, Helms recommended as an "unlikely source" of entertainment "last month's civil rights debate" in the *Congressional Record.* Russell's filibuster had "tied his colleagues in knots." The Georgia senator's ability to paralyze Congress embodied Helms's understanding of a conservative's role. Under Russell's leadership, southern Democrats managed to weaken another voting-rights bill before it passed. But this was the second civil rights act in three years.[78]

In February 1960, four students from historically black North Carolina Agricultural and Technical College began a sit-in at a Woolworth's lunch counter in Greensboro, North Carolina. The protests spread to other cities, including Raleigh. Helms criticized "young Negro college students" in March for demonstrations that closed downtown lunch counters. "A city which yesterday could have been considered 'enlightened' is on the verge of a racial crisis," he wrote. "And for what?" He conceded that the college students believed they were "fighting for their rights" but dismissed their concerns as "pious semantics." He also targeted the media coverage: "Permit us to thumb a nose at the press and television which have fanned the flames by an undue amount of publicity." Although disparaging the protests, his editorial was mild. Helms even recommended "other ways" for the students to protest, such as an "economic boycott." He seemed to think them unimportant. But after the election of a Democratic president who reluctantly supported the civil rights movement, Helms would miss no opportunity to connect the Kennedy administration to protesters. And in a little over a year, seventy thousand African Americans had engaged in direct-action protests and even more in boycotts. Their potential political impact was unmistakable.[79]

Despite his limited editorial reaction, the protests in Raleigh led to a significant political shift for Helms and provide insight into the origins of privatization of public space. As a city councilman, Helms had supported expansion of the city's parks. During the summer of 1960, Africans American efforts to integrate the Pullen Park swimming pool persuaded Helms to oppose further park expansion. Helms wrote to a voter upset at the protests, "It is not mandatory that we have public swimming pools or tennis courts or parks. Private enterprise . . . will provide these facilities" with no cost to the taxpayer and "a profit to the investor."[80]

For governor, conservative North Carolina Democrats, including Helms, supported I. Beverly Lake, a former Wake Forest College professor and assistant attorney general. Helms endorsed Lake's proposal for segregated private schools. Lake ran a massive resistance campaign. He was a fiscal conservative, but his primary appeal was racial. His main opponent was Terry Sanford, a skilled, better-funded politician with a strong statewide organization. Sanford identified himself with John Kennedy and progress in industry, education, and race relations. He advocated moderation on segregation and increased spending on schools and roads. Lake promised "'a climate of opposition' to all forms of integration." Sanford countered that Lake's "foot-stomping appeal to blind prejudice" would prompt the federal courts to intervene in the state.[81]

Duplicating his dual role in the 1950 race for the Senate between Willis Smith and Frank Porter Graham, Helms served as a key Lake adviser and a controversial reporter covering the election for WRAL. Lake finished second behind Sanford in the May Democratic primary, and supporters hoped for a Smith-like upset in a runoff. George Myrover of the *Fayetteville Observer* accused Helms of making "the first speech" for Lake's runoff campaign as a reporter covering the race from Lake headquarters. Helms "really plugged for the professor, on television, while at the same time he slapped at newspapers which opposed Lake." The president of the Bankers Association fielded questions about whether the organization had endorsed Lake. WRAL-TV also received complaints. Helms answered his critics in the *Tarheel Banker*: "Maybe the television boys also have some advice about neutrality in gubernatorial elections. I'm here to tell you that neutrality *doesn't* pay."[82]

Sanford won the runoff, 56 to 44 percent. The North Carolina Republican Party with Robert Gavin as its nominee was in a position to capitalize on Sanford's relatively liberal stance and identification with Kennedy. Gavin declared after the runoff that he was "far to the right of Terry Sanford." For the 1960 election, the Republican Party began "Operation Dixie" to recruit candidates including Gavin and compete for white votes in the South. Conservative Republicans hoped Operation Dixie would allow them to gain control of the party.[83]

In the September and October 1960 issues of the *Tarheel Banker*, Helms was hopeful for Republican victories. In September he wrote, "In a solidly

Democratic state—which North Carolina unquestionably is—speculation about who will be the next governor never comes up after the Democratic primary. Yet, this year the question is a very real one." A Raleigh reporter who was "a dyed-in-the-wool Democrat" believed that Nixon would defeat Kennedy and that Sanford could lose.[84]

Nixon and his campaign reasoned that conservatives had no alternative. He gave Republican moderates, particularly New York governor Nelson Rockefeller, what they wanted in the party's platform.[85] Darkly apprehensive of the liberalism he perceived in both parties, Helms protested the lack of "choice of philosophies and principles." The only differences between Republicans and Democrats were "semantical." Helms's sense that liberalism was a pathway to communism led to apocalyptic conclusions. "America's peril lies within, not without," he warned. "Perhaps it is unpatriotic to say so, but we rather imagine the principal beneficiaries of this legacy—the fellows in the Kremlin—must be in a state of restrained jubilation." In the next issue of the *Tarheel Banker*, Helms clarified whom he believed to be the most dangerous candidate. Anxiety over John Kennedy's Catholic faith was merely a distraction. Voters should "wonder about Senator Kennedy's relationship with Walter Reuther," Helms protested, "the Americans for Democratic Action, and others whose philosophies bear only a faint resemblance to the fundamentals of America."[86]

Helms's election-eve commentaries were his last at the *Tarheel Banker*. He also promised not to run for reelection for city council. In the fall of 1960, Helms joined Capitol Broadcasting as vice president for programming, news, and public affairs. Abandoning his lonely Sunday-afternoon time slot, Helms editorialized five days a week during the evening news, reaching not only the Raleigh-Durham area but also most of eastern North Carolina. He left the Bankers Association, a position of "absolute security," reluctantly. Two factors overcame his worries about leaving: money and his desire to promote conservatism. Fletcher made the position irresistible with "a stock consideration" and a salary guaranteed in a "long-term" contract. This lucrative offer freed Helms to follow his heart's desire.[87]

At the Bankers Association, Helms's main responsibilities were promoting banking and protecting bankers' interests. His opportunities to advance conservatism were secondary. But at WRAL, promoting conservatism, realignment, and electing conservatives were top priorities. "My duties primarily will be to establish policy, political and otherwise, for the television and radio stations," Helms wrote a disappointed banker. "The compelling factor in my decision was the opportunity to provide 'another' voice for this area. At present, our people are being brainwashed by a press monopoly which constantly slants down the left-wing line." Fletcher wanted Helms's pious incitement on WRAL. The criticism over Helms's coverage of Lake had not shaken his desire. Fletcher sent a memo to everyone at WRAL revealing his intentions: "I want to thank all of you most sincerely for such effort as you may have put forth in behalf of Dr. Lake."[88]

Before he joined the station, Helms made Fletcher's political intentions and desire for realignment clear in a letter to Vice President Nixon's assistant Robert King: "As I have mentioned to you before, Eisenhower and Nixon carried North Carolina from the west to Raleigh, but lost it because of the very liberal east which almost block-voted for Stevenson." The *News and Observer* "dominates eastern North Carolina." It has "hit all-time lows in its condemnation of Mr. Nixon." The paper's editor is "a former Truman waterboy named Jonathan Daniels." Fletcher, Helms explained, wanted WRAL "to present the *other* side of the story insofar as government and politics are concerned." WRAL, Helms implied, could help Republicans win votes in eastern North Carolina, maybe even allowing Nixon to carry the state.[89]

Not only did Sanford win the governor's office in 1960, but his endorsement also helped Kennedy win North Carolina. Still, Kennedy and Sanford won the state by fewer votes than Democrats usually did. Nixon and Gavin ran strong in the mountains and piedmont. Eastern North Carolina—the most conservative region on race—kept the state Democratic.[90] Helms's position at WRAL would allow him to reach those voters. They supported the liberal economic policies of Democratic presidential nominees and moderate state leaders like Sanford, but they were virulently opposed to racial change.

Helms joined WRAL more confident than ever in his ability to advance conservatism. He had gained valuable insights at the Bankers Association and on the city council. Opposition even in the face of certain defeat advanced conservatism. Voters often resented government as much as they appreciated its benefits. Sensationalism helped conservatives reach voters through the mainstream media. Populist racial and cultural politics drew support even when allied with economic elitism. But the GOP's competition for black votes jeopardized the chances of forming a conservative alliance.

Six months before joining WRAL as vice president, Helms protested the firing of a conservative commentator at WNCT in Greenville. He asked the station's general manager, "Does a powerful medium like a television station—or a newspaper—really serve the people by avoiding controversy?" Television was "an educational medium." Controversy pushed viewers to think.[91] To shift the attitude of eastern North Carolina Democrats toward their party, Helms welcomed controversy. At WRAL-TV he would hone pious incitement into a powerful tool for tapping into viewers' anger and frustration over the civil rights movement, taxes, Supreme Court rulings, mainstream media, and liberal elites everywhere.

2

"The Voice of Free Enterprise"

A Conservative Commentator and News Director

Aired twice a day five days a week on WRAL-TV, Jesse Helms's commentaries were rebroadcast on radio and appeared in a number of small-town newspapers. Helms claimed that WRAL was nonpartisan, but this was true only in the sense that the station supported conservatives from both parties. "We don't care which party balances the budget" and "calls a halt to the myriad of give-away programs—just so one of them does," Helms fumed in his second week. "We don't care which party honestly sets about a program of tax reduction" and "wakes up to the undeniable fact that a great nation must be built and maintained by hard work, imagination, and initiative—just so one of them does." "We don't care which party first decides to quit playing politics with minority groups . . . just so one of them does." The station hoped to cause "people to think for themselves," since "neither party will do any of these things" until voters "demand them."[1]

The station's tagline, "The Voice of Free Enterprise," declared WRAL's conservatism. Biased media, Helms asserted, compelled a conservative alternative. The station expressed opinions and aired news "not reported elsewhere" to counter network television and the state's major papers. WRAL initially produced *Viewpoint*, he explained, to counter *The Today Show*. The networks' evening newscasts also figured prominently in the station's calculations. The Daniels family owned the city's papers, both of which, Helms thought, possessed a liberal slant. The state's other large-circulation papers were the same. "So, simply said, we felt that the people of our area were entitled to both sides of the news, views and opinion."[2]

With A. J. Fletcher's backing, Helms's purpose was twofold. First, he wanted WRAL to win converts to conservatism, and that meant tearing down liberalism and the Democratic Party. Second, he wanted to elect conservatives. This, Helms expected, meant realignment of eastern North Carolina and the rest of the white South with the GOP. He believed the key to both was winning over the voters of eastern North Carolina and voters like them throughout the South.

Editorializing on WRAL's daily newscasts afforded Helms something the Bankers Association could not—a broad audience in eastern North Carolina. *Viewpoint* made Helms the "Voice of Free Enterprise." The station's viewing area included the Sun Belt cities of Raleigh, Durham, and Chapel Hill and their suburbs as well as the rural communities of eastern North Carolina. The area was majority white and overwhelmingly Protestant. African Americans made up a little less than a third of the population. Eastern North Carolina was committed to the Democratic Party, while the western half of the state, including Charlotte, was already open to Republicans. These eastern North Carolinians voted for Democrats because New Deal programs and policies benefited them. In the early 1960s the voters were disproportionately white because of restrictions on black voting, especially in rural counties. These rural white voters supported Democrats' economic policies, but they were fiercely committed to segregation and deeply religious.

On *Viewpoint* Helms enlarged the strident cultural and racial politics of pious incitement he had begun at the Bankers Association. He did every day on WRAL what he had rarely dared in the *Tarheel Banker*: calling out presidents and other politicians by name, directly condemning liberalism and liberals, and backing the conservative movement. Pious incitement's exaggeration, embellishment, and outrage made good television. Helms blamed Democrats for the civil rights movement, politicized the decisions of the Supreme Court, and made voters fear their government. His commentaries blurred class lines and began to convince white voters that the Democrats in control of the federal government failed to represent their interests. Even more fundamentally, Helms's anti-statist broadsides targeted government to delegitimize liberals' means of reform. So before President Lyndon Johnson's Great Society, Helms's pious incitement developed into a potent mix of racial and religious politics, populist opposition to taxes and deficits, and anti-elitism aimed at liberalism in the courts, universities, and the media. All of this gained attention for him and conservatism.

WRAL's news and public affairs programming reinforced *Viewpoint*'s conservative message. Helms pushed his reporters to present the civil rights movement in a negative light, question the National Council of Churches, criticize moderate Democrats like Governor Terry Sanford, and give positive coverage to movement conservatives like Barry Goldwater and William F. Buckley. With Fletcher's backing, Helms intended to use WRAL's news and editorials to elect conservatives and especially to promote Senator Goldwater.

Writing for television was different from writing for print. Helms strove to make his delivery on *Viewpoint* as conversational as possible. "You would be surprised," he explained, "at how much time I spend rewriting, polishing, reading aloud." *Viewpoint* was broadcast at 6:20 during the evening news program, *Stateline*, and again the next morning at 7:25 during the *Today* show. Early in the decade, more than four hundred people in twenty states subscribed to a *Viewpoint* newsletter. Several newspapers and more than twenty-five radio stations also carried it. Most of those stations were part of Capitol Broadcasting's Tobacco Radio Network, but Helms's commentaries were available to any station or newspaper free of charge.[3]

The Conservative Movement and WRAL

On WRAL, Helms was free to advocate the conservative movement's personalities and organizations. Shortly after the 1960 election, he lauded Senator Barry Goldwater. Goldwater was the most visible movement figure nationally, and Helms was an enthusiastic supporter. The conservative movement challenged the liberal consensus in the early 1960s. Helms discerned the beginning of these developments and was hopeful because "people in all walks of life, and at all economic levels" were questioning liberalism. Helms chastised "the news out of Washington and from Raleigh" for minimizing the movement. "Even the rise of conservatism, which is apparent all around us, is most often dismissed with explanations that it is exaggerated, or nonexistent."[4]

Conservatives pressed for Goldwater's nomination as president and then vice president at the 1960 Republican convention. They soon began organizing for his nomination in 1964. Helms praised Senator Goldwater from his twelfth *Viewpoint* through the election. Goldwater's *The*

Conscience of a Conservative "has been ridiculed by liberals, but they have not been able to laugh it off of the best-seller list." Goldwater did and said "what he thinks is right" rather than calculate how to win a higher office. Yet "those who jeer at him the loudest are those who nervously know best that he is getting through to the people."[5]

Goldwater's popularity was one sign of a conservative revival. Helms detected others. Pointing to organizing efforts among college students and in the suburbs, Helms argued that conservatism was building momentum. In a 1961 debate, William F. Buckley and Gore Vidal identified a "trend among young people to reject liberalism in favor of conservatism." Buckley believed that "many students have awakened to the great nothingness of liberalism," while Vidal charged that conservatives were "un-American." Helms found Vidal's comments indicative of "the most difficult problem faced by conservatives." Liberals allege that everyone who rejects them "is un-American, or greedy, or unenlightened, or unprogressive." Conservatives had not had a "fair hearing" in decades, but now things were changing.[6]

Praising Young Americans for Freedom (YAF), a national organization for conservative college students, in March 1961, Helms declared that "today's young people—to a greater degree than ever before—are beginning to think for themselves. They have discovered that there is something fundamentally American about the difference between 'opportunity' and 'security.'" A YAF "rally of young conservatives" in New York City filled Manhattan Center to capacity and left many standing outside. Helms found in college students' affinity for YAF hope for a conservative future. "They can, if they will, demand a return to economic sanity, a restoration of faith in the freedom of the individual, a renewed recognition of the honor and dignity of the profit motive."[7]

The same week Helms celebrated the Young Americans for Freedom, he cautiously defended a chapter of the John Birch Society (JBS) in Kinston, North Carolina. The *Raleigh News and Observer* worried that the local JBS chapter was a "secret, conspiratorial organization." The front-page story "added darkly" that their antagonism "was aimed at churches and textbooks." The JBS, Helms countered, is a "nationally known study group" that was no more secretive "than the average church circle." The group disagreed with "many things which *The News and Observer* advocates— but, then, so do many other sensible people who never heard of the John Birch Society." Some textbooks supported questionable "philosophies," and some ministers endorsed "communist-front organizations," just as the JBS alleged. Helms concluded that Dr. J. C. Peele, the group's leader, "and his associates are doing something on the local level at Kinston that needs doing throughout America." A few months later in the summer of 1961, WRAL interviewed JBS founder Robert Welch.[8]

This defense of the JBS led Peele to contact Helms. "Our thoughts," Peele observed, "run along similar channels." Peele, a physician, wrote an endless stream of letters to local and national political and media figures. He asked Secretary of Defense Robert McNamara, "Do you think it is possible that you could leave our nation a few sling shots and pop guns to fight with?" He praised Alcoa and Ford Motor Company for their sponsorship of ABC's *The F.B.I.* "I think you are rendering our nation a valuable service in bringing the work of this great organization and its outstanding Director, J. Edgar Hoover, to your TV viewers." Rather than distancing himself, Helms encouraged Peele, "I wish we had thousands more writing similar ones." Peele was a grassroots leader Helms relied on. He asked Peele to send JBS literature to a "young man" interested in the United Nations: "I try to encourage these youngsters all I can." When Peele loaned WRAL a JBS film, Helms was enthusiastic even before he saw it: "Your appraisal of its contents is endorsement aplenty."[9]

In 1963, Helms challenged Robert Welch's critics on *Viewpoint*. He recounted Welch's biography and praised his intelligence. Helms then criticized California congressman Ronald Cameron and the state's "'liberal' Republican" senator, Thomas Kuchel, for labeling "practically everybody" who disagreed with them a "'hate monger' and a 'John Bircher.'" The "list of citizens" they implicated read like a selection from *Who's Who*. If the list was accurate, Helms goaded, the JBS had more influence than he thought.[10]

The YAF and the JBS played a central role in the conservative takeover of the GOP in the early 1960s. They organized grassroots conservatives when everything seemed hopeless. Peele, Helms knew, not only formed part of the conservative movement, but he and others like him built its bulwarks and manned its ramparts. But the JBS and its founder remained controversial because of Welch's proclivity for spinning wild conspiracy theories. Even Helms privately wished "there were fewer kooks in the JBS." As the conservative movement sought to gain mainstream support and win elections, the extremists in their ranks posed problems. Instrumental in organizing the YAF, Buckley also led many conservatives in repudiating

Welch. But conservatives who rejected extremists lost support. When Buckley ran for mayor of New York City in 1965, some conservatives refused to donate money to his campaign because he had debunked Welch's conspiracies. The media still tied his campaign to the radical right.[11]

Helms was less willing than Buckley to criticize the fringe. The South had a long history of respectable extremism. The Ku Klux Klan and other white supremacist groups had influenced southern politics for a century. Helms possessed an affinity for conspiracy theories and relished being labeled an extremist: "We are most often called an 'idiot.' We are accused of being a 'John Bircher' and a 'Ku Kluxer' and a 'right-wing extremist.'" He wondered of liberals, "Is *this* the best they can do when their views are challenged?" So Helms welcomed the support of the JBS and even the Klan. On *Viewpoint* he treated the Klan as the civil rights movement's moral equivalent. Klan supporters were delighted.[12]

A Conservative Commentator: Free Enterprise, Religion, and the Civil Rights Movement

Helms's driving ambition was his desire for a conservative party capable of winning a majority. The conservative movement suggested this was within reach. The 1960 Republican presidential nominee, Richard Nixon, Helms believed, ran as only slightly less liberal than Democrat John Kennedy. Analyzing Nixon's mistakes in December 1960, Helms speculated on what the outcome would have been if Nixon had run as a conservative. Maybe Nixon would have lost anyway. "On the other hand, it may be that America is looking for a man who would rather be right and lose, than be wrong and win. It is conceivable that a man could be right—and win."[13] Despite his disappointment in Nixon, Helms knew the GOP was the party most likely to move to the right. His first *Viewpoint* complained that Kennedy won the presidency with "the most liberal campaign in the history of this nation." Helms had not felt at home in the party of John Kennedy, Hubert Humphrey, and Terry Sanford for a long time. "The trouble with me," he wrote a childhood friend, "is that I cannot acknowledge that the present leadership of the Democratic Party are Democrats. Our party has been taken from us."[14]

In twenty commentaries a month, Helms advocated conservatism to a wide television audience. He depended on pious incitement. He aimed his free-enterprise advocacy at average viewers. He made deficit spending and taxes key issues. He attacked the mainstream media and the state and federal governments, and he undermined the Democratic Party. He even tentatively questioned Social Security and farm programs. Conservatives, though, needed drama to get people to change their voting behavior. The unexpected Supreme Court rulings on prayer and surge in civil rights protests in the early 1960s provided it.

With a liberal Democrat in the White House and a governor from the moderate wing of the state's Democratic Party, Helms used pious incitement to undermine the party, the governor, and the president. Shortly after Kennedy took office, he seized on Arthur M. Schlesinger Jr.'s statement that the "welfare state is the best defense against Communism" to depict the new administration as hostile to "the profit motive" and "free enterprise." Helms thundered, "This borders on an endorsement of Communism." Schlesinger was a Pulitzer Prize–winning Harvard historian and presidential adviser. Helms portrayed him and, by association, President Kennedy as ideologically suspect and hostile to business, when really the professor was praising American economic productivity and claiming that liberal policy had a role in it. Deliberately provocative and sensational, Helms distorted Schlesinger's words to express outrage at them.[15]

One of the first *Viewpoints* declared that Helms wanted viewers to know that "the free enterprise system is the one thing, above all others, that has made this country great." But selling free enterprise with its pro-business perspective to WRAL's broad audience in eastern North Carolina was quite different from advocating it to bankers. Helms defended free enterprise in a way that unified white voters across class. He targeted taxes and cast government as threatening and foolish. "The federal government today has more than 50,000 people on the payroll just to collect taxes from you." Typically, rather than defending big business and the wealthy, he discussed free enterprise as opposition to Democrats' economic policies. Federal aid "confiscates private property from the productive to give to the unproductive," he said. Government unemployment figures were inflated because they included "thousands who could get work if they didn't prefer welfare payments." The "red haze" that astronaut Gordon Cooper saw while in orbit was "no doubt" the federal budget "going into the red on the highest scale in history."[16]

In March 1961, Helms thanked Governor Sanford, a "liberal," for making the conservative case against taxes easy. Sanford advocated repeal of the state sales tax exemption for food. Helms believed the governor revealed the truth that taxes always "end up the little man's burden." Now a "housewife" buying groceries would know just how much public schools cost.[17]

Inviting viewers to play "Seek the Silly," Helms ridiculed liberals and the federal government. "Anybody can play," but only conservatives would enjoy it. "Liberals who are caught participating are required to turn in their New Frontier coloring books." Players searched out apparently absurd federal expenditures. Helms highlighted a series of animal studies: "$1,600,000 spent to find out how much baby monkeys love their mothers," $64,500 to study "the wondering albatross," $16,500 for earthworms, $2,100 for "the social behavior of the 'barren-ground Caribou,'" and $20,600 for "the communications signals of birds." And the United States was spending $15,200 "to study the society of a country that no longer exists," ancient Babylon. Helms created the impression that federal spending was wildly irresponsible. "If you have any rats around the house that are drinking too much, well, cheer up. Your government is spending $18,000 of your money to study the modification of alcohol preference in rats."[18]

Helms's slippery ideological definitions on display in his attack on Schlesinger were central to pious incitement. Most of his criticism of Democrats and Democratic economic policy avoided mention of specific programs. He tarred leaders and programs he opposed with the brush of communism and socialism. "Liberal" was just "a polite way of saying socialistic." Kennedy's Medicare proposal was "a foot in the door for socialized medicine." In a vague ideological assault, Helms associated liberal policies, including the New Deal, with the Soviet Union: "Socialism at home, sugar-coated and bearing a fancy name, is exactly the same thing as socialism under any dictatorship around the world. . . . [W]e are simply copying the Russians." And everybody should know that "the Russian government is socialistic, not communistic." In his imprecise ideological rambling, he questioned Democrats' loyalty for creating the very policies voters valued most.[19]

In 1967, before a small audience in Miami, Helms expressed his fundamental contempt for Social Security. The "so-called Social Security program . . . forevermore will steal from the young in order to buy the votes of the older." He would never say anything so radical in front of a television camera. But his commentaries sought to undermine support for Social Security and similar policies. When Helms directly criticized liberal programs on *Viewpoint* like Social Security and farm subsidies, he relied on pious incitement's sensationalism. He charged, "Today's workers are being taxed to provide monthly payments for persons no longer in the nation's workforce—people who paid *into* the Social Security system only a fraction of what the law says they shall *receive* in the form of Social Security checks. The program is laying nothing aside to take care of you in *your* latter years." Social Security, he concluded, was "just another disguised welfare program operated with a compulsory tax and a political dole."[20]

The government, Helms said, "does not launch a large, costly program without at one time or another, assuming a large role in control of the program." This was true of federal support for public housing, mortgages, welfare, schools, and colleges and universities. It was also true of farming. "And any farmer who pleads for and votes for such programs might as well go shout at the moon" if he dislikes government's "drastic controls." Complaints about "the ever-deepening intrusion by government into our daily lives" come from "the very ones who still go, hat-in-hand, to Washington for handouts."[21]

Helms was a reluctant critic of these popular but expensive programs, and his criticism was rare. The two developments of the early 1960s that caused him the most anxiety—the Supreme Court rulings prohibiting state-required prayers in public schools and the Democrats' hesitant support for the civil rights movement—also afforded him his best opportunities to make his case for conservatism. In June 1962 and June 1963, the Supreme Court issued two landmark rulings on the separation of church and state. The first, *Engel v. Vitale,* ruled that a state-required prayer in public schools amounted to establishment of religion and violated the First Amendment. The Court invalidated a "carefully non-sectarian" prayer composed by Catholic, Protestant, and Jewish clergy. The Court, Helms seethed, destroyed "the very keystones of our American heritage." Politicians across the spectrum and from both parties condemned the ruling. Catholic leaders strongly opposed the decision, too. But many Protestant leaders, including conservative fundamentalists and evangelicals, accepted the Court's decision. Helms's own Southern Baptist denomination supported it. Fundamentalists and evangelicals such as the Baptists rejected nonsectarian prayers and were more worried about Catholic influence—particularly under President Kennedy—than about the Supreme Court. They interpreted the ruling as having a narrow application.[22]

Helms anticipated that the ruling's implication concerned not just a state-composed prayer but applied generally to religious observance in public schools. He envisioned the United States as a Christian republic, and in December 1962 he expressed concern that the Court threatened this vision: "When we see them protesting prayers, or readings from the Bible, or observance of Christmas, we wonder when they last saw the sparkle in a child's eyes . . . as he heard the story of the shepherds and the guiding star. This is where belief and faith begin, where they really count, where they serve as a foundation upon which decent, God-fearing lives can be built." Helms was both ecumenical and a deeply religious conservative. He did not share Protestant leaders' concern about Catholics; in fact, he saw Catholics as likely allies. Catholic leaders warned that the Court's decision weakened America in the Cold War, and Helms agreed. He held in high esteem the most prominent Catholic politician of the 1950s, Senator Joseph McCarthy. Many leaders of the conservative movement, including William F. Buckley, were Catholic, and a conservative party defending a Christian America would need Catholic voters.[23]

Helms immediately realized the potential political advantage for conservatives. The Supreme Court's decision in *Engel v. Vitale* was "a blessing in disguise," because Americans from all sections of the nation would recognize the Court's radicalism. Helms seized on the discontent over the decision to advance the conservative movement. He hoped the rulings on prayer would energize apolitical evangelicals and fundamentalists and draw socially conservative Democrats into the Republican Party. President Kennedy's inadequate response to the prayer rulings was "that all of us should pray more at home."[24]

In June 1963 the Court prohibited Bible readings in public schools in *Abington Township School District v. Schempp*. Helms's commentary had an I-told-you-so tone to it: "Let the fact be faced: the Supreme Court is gradually but steadily barring God from the public life of the American people." Some conservative Protestants, including the National Evangelical Association (NEA), reversed their prior acceptance of the ruling on school prayer. The NEA and other conservative Christians proposed an amendment to reverse the Supreme Court. Democrats, including some liberals, opposed the rulings, and some Democrats supported the amendment. But it was Republicans who seized on the issue. The GOP added support for a prayer amendment to their platform in 1964. The Democrats did not. Helms expected the Court's decisions to benefit Goldwater.[25]

The prayer issue also gave Helms an opportunity to question Christian support for activist government and social change. Helms scorned the

National Council of Churches (NCC) when "a spokesman" declared after *Engel v. Vitale* "that 'many Christians will welcome this decision.' Well, we wish he would name them, one by one. This is not the first time that the National Council of Churches has presumed to speak for a large segment of our Christian society." The NCC included mainline Protestant, African American, and Orthodox denominations. It supported the civil rights movement with funding for protesters and backed a range of other liberal policies. Helms repeatedly criticized the NCC, particularly on issues of race, claiming that it advocated "ideas and ideals that tear at the fabric of America" and "has been in the forefront of the racial disorder that has fanned out across the United States."[26]

Religion provided Helms with a powerful political weapon for advancing conservatism. Race, however, was the most promising of all. But Helms rejected an explicitly racist defense of a never-ending segregation as a losing strategy. A year after I. Beverly Lake's defeat in the 1960 gubernatorial primary, Helms speculated on whom conservative North Carolinians should back for governor. The candidate should not be "burdened with the 'race issue' thing, as was Beverly Lake last year," he reasoned. "Beverly lost a lot of conservative support because they thought he was too strong on the race thing." If this was true in a southern primary, the "race thing" would, Helms expected, be an even larger barrier in a national contest. To win elections in the South and the nation, however, a conservative party—especially one as conservative as Helms wanted—needed Lake's segregationist voters.[27]

On *Viewpoint*, Helms developed an alternative racial politics that appealed to segregationists without alienating others. His commentaries tapped into white unease over racial change and marshaled an updated, sanitized white supremacy to defend tradition, build support for conservatives, and divide the liberal coalition. Helms amplified some aspects of southern racial politics—allegations of communism, immorality, and criminality—and dropped or minimized others. Pious incitement substituted a moralistic discourse for an explicitly racist language and a moral community for a racial one, but the segregated white community of the South and Helms's moral community looked awfully similar. He kept out white liberals—politicians, preachers, and editors—while allowing at least the possibility of including African Americans. However, their inclusion depended on "learning that equality must be equated with personal decency and personal responsibility."[28]

Helms even employed anti-racist liberal rhetoric when he could bend it to his purposes. In opposing Robert Weaver as Kennedy's choice to head the Housing and Home Finance Corporation, Helms asserted that "while a qualified Negro should not be rejected because of his race, neither should an unqualified Negro be accepted because of his race." Weaver lacked appropriate credentials because of communist associations and his failed efforts at integration in New York. Helms left the specter of race-mixing up to segregationists' imagination. The emphasis on qualifications reassured the conservative who embraced a color-blind vision of American rights.[29] On *Viewpoint* Helms formulated the racial politics that Ronald Reagan and others would follow in creating a media-genic conservative politics grounded in the white South but without the taint of explicit racism.

The surge in civil rights protests of the early 1960s and the success of activists at keeping civil rights in the news infuriated Helms. He developed his racial politics in response. In his second week on the air, Helms took a swipe at Martin Luther King Jr., the most visible civil rights leader. "King apparently believes he has the right to pick and choose which laws he wanted to obey."[30] Hoping to break eastern North Carolina's attachment to Democrats, Helms never missed a chance to associate first the Kennedys and later Lyndon Johnson with civil rights.

Kennedy won the 1960 election by carefully balancing appeals to African Americans and white southerners. In May 1961 the Congress of Racial Equality (CORE) organized a biracial group of bus riders to pressure the Kennedy administration to enforce a 1960 Supreme Court decision desegregating interstate travel. The Freedom Riders faced violence from mobs and law enforcement all along their route, including a firebomb in Anniston, Alabama. Helms condemned the mobs and the Freedom Riders because they were "both seeking trouble." In Alabama, he raged, both "received the cracked skulls they asked for and deserved." The incidents would not only "be grist for the anti-American propaganda mills around the world" but also advance the integrationist cause. His second Freedom Riders commentary accused Dave Garroway (host of NBC's *The Today Show*) and most media outlets of ignoring the prevalence of "atheism, communism, and deceit" among the protesters. Helms's commentaries in some ways resembled his response to coverage of the Little Rock crisis, but this time he could entangle Democrats. Like Helms, the Kennedy administration worried about America's reputation in the Cold War. More than anything, though, the Kennedys wanted to avoid the political costs of intervening in the South. Helms intended to make them pay with votes whether they intervened or not. He charged Bobby Kennedy and the Justice Department with "cheering" the riders on and supposed that "one word from Mr. Kennedy would have served the purpose of turning the bus bearing the freedom riders around."[31]

In 1962 civil rights organizations focused on Albany, Georgia, but Albany would not build on past successes. The city's leaders, especially Police Chief Laurie Pritchett, managed to avoid violence in front of cameras. The national media counted it as a defeat for King. The Kennedy White House and Georgia Democrats agreed that authorities' successful evasion of media attention meant no federal involvement. Helms rejoiced over the outcome in Albany and recognized that official restraint had drained Albany of spectacle. "Newspaper and television newsmen have done their best to keep the story alive," he judged, "but, without violence, the story lacks the sordid appeal that makes grist for the news mill." Helms seized on the stalemate in Albany to portray African Americans as threatening. "Negro leaders—Martin Luther King, for example," had failed "to urge Negroes to seek and to grasp personal responsibility." This failure was a costly one. White people in the nation's capital, Helms explained, were angry at "the conduct of the ever-increasing Negro population" because "it has become unsafe for a white woman to venture out of doors."[32]

Helms's *Viewpoints* on the Freedom Riders and Albany established a pattern for pious incitement in his civil rights commentaries. They were a sensational and inflammatory mix of his religious and media politics with old-fashioned white supremacist campaigning and red-baiting. He portrayed black men as dangerous. In place of the "Black Republican Party," he made Democrats the party of African Americans and blamed the protesters for the violence of vigilantes and southern law enforcement. He cast civil rights activists and their Democratic allies out of the moral community with allegations of atheism and communism. He denigrated the mainstream media coverage. And finally, he offered another crisis as a distraction that the press, black leaders, and the nation should give priority. The alternative was variously the Cold War, crime, immorality, communist infiltration, or integration efforts Helms termed failures. Helms's civil rights commentaries ostensibly made nonracial allegations. Conservatives turned off by Lake's insistence on segregation's preservation accepted Helms, even admired him. Segregationists loved him.

Helms opposed the majority of federal spending. He was reluctant to name popular programs, however, because convincing voters to oppose them seemed implausible. Building a conservative party required something other than a frontal assault on the New Deal. Pious incitement's focus on taxes and deficits (and apparently ridiculous budget items), its insistence that liberalism was socialism, its religious and racial provocation, and its ominous warnings about government intrusion obscured the way activist government, including most federal spending, benefited taxpayers. Helms's commentaries operated on a symbolic level. His cultural politics of race, morality, and religion possessed an emotional impact that exaggerated his topics' actual economic, political, or cultural effect. *Viewpoint* made Helms a TV personality. He claimed a cultural authority on par with the elites he challenged—King, Sanford, and the Kennedys. Viewers laughed, and then felt fear and rage: the same emotional rollercoaster as a Hollywood blockbuster. TV news, Helms understood, had to entertain just as surely as *Peyton Place*.

From the very beginning, Helms excited intense passions. "You are, sir, a political Neanderthal," a viewer wrote. "You represent everything that is distasteful and repugnant in the South. Your moronic comments on world conditions are unbelievable." Helms just scribbled "WOW!" in the margin. Most dissenting opinion was not so harsh. An accountant explained that he opposed Helms's tax proposals because "the relative burden is greatest on the least prosperous." Lincoln Faulk, the station manager and editorialist at WCKB radio in Dunn, North Carolina, was a regular critic of Helms. "Please line out for us," Faulk demanded, "instance after instance, where our precious freedoms have been denied by big government."[33]

Helms's and WRAL's mail, however, ran "about 90 to one in favor." The station "most often hear[d] from the so-called 'little' man—and from housewives, and a very great deal from young people, both college and high school." Business owner Joe Norman believed the networks should be envious of WRAL and sent CBS's Walter Cronkite copies of *Viewpoint*. He observed, "Your *Viewpoints* improve with time, even though it would seem impossible." A schoolteacher, Charles Miller, wrote, "You are doing a great service to the community." A Salisbury radio station manager, Harry Welch, thanked Helms "for trying to save this country." Viewer letters allowed Helms to assess which issues and opinions moved viewers. Miller praised Helms's opposition to school bonds. Welch was primarily concerned with race. Helms thought his mail constituted "a pretty good public opinion poll."[34]

WRAL News: A Conservative Alternative

Helms built a conservative news organization at WRAL. He was frank about his intentions regarding the station's news and public affairs programming. "We're spending in the neighborhood of $50,000 a year in producing and presenting programming to help the conservative movement," he wrote Buckley in 1963. The news, he believed, should focus viewers' attention on what government cost them, including taxes, deficits, and regulations. It should paint the civil rights movement in a bad light and question liberals' motives. It should tell the story of American faith and freedom. And most of all, it should give conservatives and conservative ideas positive coverage.[35]

Helms expanded the news department's personnel and gave them a conservative mission. In the early 1960s, WRAL's evening news, *Stateline*, ran from 6:00 to 6:45, with *Viewpoint* at 6:20. NBC's *Huntley-Brinkley Report* rounded out the hour.[36] Helms hired the staff necessary to cover national, state, and local government. The news department grew from three to sixteen with cameramen and reporters throughout eastern North Carolina. He also kept a correspondent in Washington, D.C. The station had half a dozen additional reporters for sports, agriculture, and home-making. Helms's reporters were not just talking heads. The anchors and reporters used "very little" of the Associated Press's copy because of its bias. "We want to give our viewers news that they cannot get anywhere else," Helms explained. "All of our news is written by the reporters who deliver it on the air." The farm reporters won national awards, but it was the stories with a conservative take on American public life that drew attention. "I frankly want our men to be hell-raisers," Helms declared. "If they find corruption in a poverty program, I want them to talk about it on the air. If a candidate tries to engage in double-talk, I want our people to point it out. If somebody is playing hanky-panky with the public's money, I want the public told about it."[37]

A year after arriving at WRAL, Helms pushed journalists at an Associated Press convention to report stories from a conservative angle. His recommendations indicate how he operated WRAL's news department.

The AP, he suggested, should frame the Kennedy administration's Medicare proposal in a way that made it possible for conservatives to debate the president's plan. The reporting had covered only the president's insistence that "old people ought to have medical care." No opening for conservatives there. Helms advocated focusing on "the financing of Mr. Kennedy's proposal" because it was "debatable." Helms affected amazement at the AP's lack of "curiosity" over two African students' judgment that the South was prejudiced. He believed the students' visit was a staged media event and wanted the AP to report it as such. Who "conducted the tour" and "who paid the expenses?" Reporters have "the responsibility of portraying people and their actions in their entirety," he admonished.[38]

Helms followed his own recommendations at WRAL. The station's reporters framed the news from a conservative perspective. WRAL, for example, ran critical stories on the local impact of the 1964 Civil Rights Act. *Stateline* covered the integration of mental health facilities, focusing attention on the transfer of white patients. The news stories often reinforced Helms's commentaries. On *Viewpoint* he repeatedly attacked the National Council of Churches and called for conservative Christians to question their churches' affiliation with the organization. When an Enfield, North Carolina, church severed its ties to the NCC, WRAL-TV covered the story on *Stateline*. The reporter interviewed church members and highlighted their criticism of the NCC.[39]

Like *Viewpoint*, *Stateline* questioned the civil rights movement. "Our people leave out an immense amount of material that the Negro militants would like for us to use," Helms explained, "and much of what we do use makes them unhappy." When a conservative Baptist minister agreed to go on the record with criticism of King, Helms sent a news crew. "Bravo!" he wrote. "The people need to know that all ministers have not been taken in by Martin Luther King."[40]

The Cold War also received extensive coverage in the station's public affairs programming. In 1961 WRAL ran two documentaries, *Operation Abolition* and *Hollywood's Answer to Communism*, that raised fears of an internal communist threat. *Operation Abolition* covered student protests over House Committee on Un-American Activities (HUAC) hearings in the San Francisco Bay area during May 1960. HUAC arranged for the making of *Operation Abolition*. Helms ran the film twice because it revealed "the communist-inspired riots against the House Un-American Activities Committee." Locally, he arranged for retired FBI agents to discuss the threats the film raised. *Hollywood's Answer to Communism* covered similar ground. It "described in unmistakably clear fashion how Communists operate, and how easily innocent people can be used to advance the cause of Communism." The following year WRAL produced the documentary *Cold War Seminar,* which featured speakers from the National War College explaining the communist threat.[41]

WRAL's news and public affairs programming supplied conservatives with airtime unavailable elsewhere. Whether it was local conservatives or nationally prominent figures such as Welch and Buckley, Helms wanted them on the air. He pressured Buckley to notify WRAL-TV next time he was nearby. "Our news department has had to catch you on the wing on your last two visits." In 1963 WRAL broadcast a Goldwater speech. I. Beverly Lake discussed the potential impact of Fair Employment Practices legislation. Tom Ellis joined *Legislative Report,* a regular program covering the state legislature. When Thurman Sensing, executive vice president of the Southern States Industrial Council and conservative columnist of *Sensing the News,* spoke at North Carolina State, Helms finagled a "one-minute" interview for *Stateline* to promote the speech.[42]

In the summer of 1961, cost-cutting measures at the conservative radio program *The Manion Forum* led to the show's cancellation on Raleigh's WPTF radio, WRAL-FM's local competition. *The Manion Forum* was the main platform of Clarence Manion, a former dean of Notre Dame's law school, a critic of Eisenhower's modern Republicanism, and an early Goldwater supporter. His program combined commentaries with interviews of prominent conservatives such as Thurman Sensing, South Carolina senator Strom Thurmond, and Nebraska senator Carl Curtis. Helms, who deemed Manion's perspective "too vital" to allow financial concerns to interrupt it, contacted Manion and offered to carry *The Manion Forum* on WRAL-FM and the Tobacco Radio Network for free. Manion and Helms became mutual admirers. "I always enjoy your interesting and completely distinctive *Viewpoint,*" Manion observed, "and then proceed to plagiarize you scandalously." In 1963 Helms arranged for Manion to give a speech in Raleigh and taped it for broadcast. Helms also "wished" for a televised *Manion Forum.* When a TV show became available, WRAL ran it on Sundays. *The Manion Forum,* he crowed, makes "the lib'ruls howl."[43]

Helms also orchestrated an address by Dr. Edward Annis before the Raleigh Chamber of Commerce in 1964. Annis was president of the American Medical Association and a conservative opponent of Democrats' proposals for Medicare. Helms went all out to promote Annis, inviting every physician within a hundred miles to attend through the state and county medical societies. WRAL videotaped Annis's speech for broadcast on television, and the Tobacco Radio Network carried it live. Annis subscribed to *Viewpoint* and promised to "steal your ideas time and time again."[44]

Helms promised a "substantial amount of coverage" to the four conservative congressmen whose districts fell within WRAL's broadcast area: Democrats Alton Lennon, L. H. Fountain, and Paul Kitchin and Republican Charles Jonas. Much of the coverage was unfiltered promotion. Helms assured Fountain that the station would only edit his recorded comments for "effectiveness and time," since "Our people 'consider you good copy.'" WRAL covered Lennon's appearances at tobacco markets, repeatedly praised Jonas's fiscal conservatism, and applauded Fountain's attempt to "hogtie" federal school desegregation efforts. Helms hoped WRAL's support would enable runs for statewide office, especially for Jonas. Before 1962, WRAL did not reach any of Jonas's district, but Helms offered the station's help in case Jonas was headed "for bigger things." Helms coupled the positive news coverage with praise on *Viewpoint*. Jonas "has pleaded" for reductions in the "tax burdens" of the voters, but Democrats rejected him.[45]

Conservative Democratic senator Sam Ervin received similarly positive coverage on the news and *Viewpoint*, while the station grew increasingly critical of the state's moderate (by comparison) junior senator, Everett Jordan. Ervin voted against Medicare because it was fiscally unsound, but Jordan "threw principle to the winds and yielded to the pressures from the White House." WRAL also regularly targeted moderate Democrat Harold Cooley, whose district included Raleigh. In 1963, for example, the station singled Cooley out as the only member of the North Carolina congressional delegation to oppose cuts to foreign aid. The conservatives recognized WRAL's importance. Fountain believed the station's criticism of federal school desegregation coupled with his legislative attacks would weaken the Department of Health, Education, and Welfare's effort to desegregate North Carolina schools. Jonas expressed "deep appreciation" for Helms's service to "the conservative cause."[46]

In 1962 North Carolina lost one congressional seat to redistricting. The Democratic legislature considered a variety of plans. Since an incumbent had to go, Helms hoped they would pit Kitchin against Cooley, a clear ideological choice. Helms promised Kitchin that WRAL would help introduce him to Wake County. But instead, Kitchin had to face Jonas. Jonas had an advantage because he had represented Charlotte, the new district's largest population center, for a decade. Because of his hopes for Jonas and the GOP in the state, Helms leaned more toward Jonas than a strictly ideological perspective would warrant. The eastern half of the new district fell into WRAL's viewing area. At the campaign's outset, WRAL lauded Jonas's opposition to extension of the debt ceiling. Kitchin's hometown newspaper accused Democrats in the general assembly of sacrificing the state's most conservative Democratic congressman. For Helms it was one more reason to feel disconnected from the party. Just after the election, he wrote an aide to Senator Jordan that he was the "same kind of Democrat I always was" but felt "like an illegitimate child at a family reunion." The redistricting was a double loss for Democrats. Jonas defeated Kitchin, and adding the Republican-leaning western half of Jonas's old district to Democrat Hugh Alexander's district allowed Republican James Broyhill to beat Alexander. Helms was soon praising Broyhill and Jonas for voting against another debt ceiling increase.[47]

Perhaps the most important contribution of WRAL's news department to the conservative movement was its undermining of the North Carolina Democratic Party. In addition to Cooley and Jordan, Helms and his reporters routinely condemned Governor Sanford's administration, contending that the Sanford administration awarded state contracts to pay political debts. Sanford initially appealed to Helms in private through their mutual friend Hargrove "Skipper" Bowles. "All state purchase contracts are by law awarded to the low bidder in publicly advertised bids," the governor insisted. Helms and his reporters ignored Sanford's denials. In the summer of 1962, WRAL-TV reported on another "virtually private road paved at the public expense." The reports alleged that the Sanford administration, especially close Sanford ally and Highway Commissioner Cliff Benson, paved roads for private real estate developers out of tax funds. Helms explained, "It is still against the rules to use public funds for paving residential subdivision roads." Benson, a real estate developer and construction materials supplier, had a financial interest in the Waco Heights development, one of the projects that WRAL questioned. WRAL's allegations eventually forced Sanford to address the charges publicly. The governor insisted that the station had the "facts wrong." But on *Viewpoint* Helms replied that he was "amused by Governor Sanford's outburst at his news conference" and expressed "a measure of pride" at WRAL reporter Bill Armstrong's efforts "to keep the Governor on the subject."[48]

This was the kind of controversy that Helms insisted a TV station should welcome. He relished the opportunity to slug it out with Sanford and his political allies. The process weakened the governor and helped to raise the reputation of WRAL and its commentator. The pressure of WRAL's reporting made the governor's news conference necessary, and Helms used Sanford's defensive statements to undermine him further. He accused the governor of rudely interrupting "Mr. Armstrong in mid-sentence." Sanford's behavior may work "for a lawyer who is defending a weak position, but it is hardly an impressive way for a Governor to conduct himself."[49]

Cuba, Communism, and a Longing for MacArthur

Helms politicized foreign policy in much the same way that he did prayer, taxes, and federal spending. He claimed an intimate connection between internal and external threats and demanded an uncompromising response to both. Fighting Soviet influence around the world was the same as resisting "government intrusion," the National Council of Churches, and the civil rights movement at home. He rejected the liberal view of the Cold War as primarily a political, ideological battle and insisted on a military response. American moral superiority as a Christian nation would guarantee victory. General Douglas MacArthur personified the inflexible approach Helms favored. His admiration for the general embodied his distaste for liberal responses to communism: containment, limited war, and the welfare state. A "babble of inconsequential arguments," Helms avowed, obscured the reasons for MacArthur's defiance of Truman: "To compromise with the communists, he said, was to surrender to them."[50]

On the evening of October 22, 1962, President Kennedy announced the presence of nuclear missile bases in Cuba and a quarantine of the island. The president demanded the Soviets remove the bases. Helms applauded Kennedy's response as "a return to sanity." War, he believed, would follow. "The die has been cast and the showdown is ahead." Helms's confidence in America's triumph stemmed from his understanding of the nation as a Christian republican. "The question is whether truth and morality and faith in God will endure. They will endure." Kennedy feared that a war with the Soviet Union would be the "final human failure." Helms recognized no limits on American power.[51]

Notwithstanding the grave international crisis, Helms pressed what he perceived as a conservative advantage. Republicans had warned since August of a Soviet arms buildup in Cuba and insinuated that the Kennedy administration suppressed information because of the midterm elections. Helms echoed the GOP's charges: "Much as we admire the President's message on Monday, only the naïve will accept the explanation that the United States Navy, not to mention our intelligence forces, did not know what was going on in the middle of our backyard." Even though it was an "election year," Helms insisted, "the American people deserve to be told the truth."[52]

After a few tense days, Kennedy and Soviet premier Nikita Khrushchev negotiated a solution. Helms's limited support for Kennedy ended with the crisis' resolution. The president, Helms sniped, should "not entertain the notion" that the United States can "negotiate with Mr. Khrushchev at any time on any subject." The Soviets were cowards, Helms advised. "The Russians have never yet failed to retreat when challenged. Their campaign to conquer the world has been based on bluff and bluster." He thought peace required war. "Sooner or later, if peace is to prevail in our hemisphere, Cuba will have to be invaded."[53]

Birmingham, the Universities, and the Communist Speaker Ban

On *Viewpoint*, Helms made the state universities a regular foil for pious incitement. Helms and WRAL covered a recommendation for an investigation into communist influence at the University of North Carolina by the Chapel Hill American Legion Post and then advocated a ban on communist speakers in 1963. Civil rights protests in North Carolina were central to Helms's and the American Legion's concerns. In assaulting the university, Helms conflated liberalism with socialism and communism and connected Democrats to civil rights. He made outrageous allegations about the presence of communists, though even he admitted there was a good chance there were none in Chapel Hill. Helms cared little whether his allegations were true, or even if they made sense, as long as they advanced conservatism.

WRAL's questioning of the universities was not limited to UNC. In December 1961 Helms assailed North Carolina State College for an address to the Raleigh Lions Club by Dr. Abraham Holtzman, a professor of history and political science at the college. Holtzman demonstrated "little admiration for the South and its traditions" while criticizing southern congressmen for voting against federal aid. Washington "can *give* nothing it does not first take from the people," Helms warned. "The bigger the government, the smaller the people." He challenged college administrators to assure taxpayers that their faculties included conservatives to balance liberals like Holtzman.[54] Much like his attacks on the mainstream media, questioning the universities narrowed the range of legitimate opinion and drew conservatives into a cross-class alliance.

Helms orchestrated his attack on the state universities with Colonel Henry Royall of the Chapel Hill American Legion Post. In the fall of 1962, the legionnaires adopted a resolution recommending that the general assembly "investigate the University of North Carolina to determine to what extent if any Marxism has permeated the University." When Chancellor William Aycock assured the public that the investigation was unnecessary, Helms retorted on *Viewpoint*, "The Legionnaires obviously think otherwise." In January 1963, Royall mailed copies of the resolution and two of Helms's *Viewpoints* supporting it to every member of the general assembly.[55]

In the *Viewpoints*, Helms singled out a UNC student group, the New Left Club, and its sponsorship of appearances by Milton Rosen and folk-singer Pete Seeger. "Seeger has been clearly identified as a known communist," Helms claimed. And the day before Seeger's appearance, "Rosen delivered a rousing speech against America." Helms derided the "academic freedom set" for tolerating Seeger, Rosen, and the New Left Club.[56]

Helms's commentary castigating Chancellor Aycock, however, emphasized not the small campus left but liberalism: "There is much concern among the people of North Carolina that their University has become a center of wall-to-wall political liberalism." A few days later, Helms acknowledged the limited radical presence at UNC. "It may well be true that all of the known, card-carrying Communists in Chapel Hill could meet comfortably in a broom closet." And, "There may not even be any." Helms's intent was to restrict debate in the state and build support for conservatism.[57] In the summer of 1963, Helms's and Royall's assault on the state universities received an unexpected boost from the civil rights movement.

The failure in Albany led civil rights leaders to reach a conclusion similar to Helms's. Activists needed the sustained media coverage that only confrontations brought. King and the Southern Christian Leadership Conference chose Birmingham, Alabama, to challenge segregation in April 1963. Police Commissioner Eugene Connor, King believed, lacked Chief Pritchett's restraint. Connor held King in solitary confinement, which prompted President Kennedy to intervene.[58]

Helms charged that in Birmingham "the Negro race is being used as a pawn in the greatest political power play in the history of our nation." Who moved these pawns? Helms pointed to the president. According to a White House "press release," Kennedy had "'made arrangements' for King to call his wife." The president's intervention, Helms insisted, was a political ploy. He intended to make Democrats pay with votes. "No election, the political career of no man, is worth the discord being created by efforts to weld together the votes of Negro Americans into a solid bloc."[59]

As protests escalated, Connor ordered the police to attack marchers, including women and children, with dogs and nightsticks. "We are persuaded that the demonstrations have hurt the Negro's cause," Helms insisted. The Kennedy administration's involvement demonstrated the opposite. Television coverage of Connor's unrestrained police action turned ambivalent viewers against segregation. Watching the evening news, President Kennedy said the police assaults made him "sick." The administration began preparing civil rights legislation.[60]

The events in Birmingham led to demonstrations in two hundred cities, including Raleigh. There, students from historically black Shaw University and St. Augustine's College made up the majority of the protesters, but a small number of white students and faculty from North Carolina State University and the University of North Carolina at Chapel Hill also participated. "Regardless of what Mr. Robert Kennedy or anyone else may say," Helms snapped, "the demonstrations here have been anything but 'peaceful.' A mob is a mob, whether in Birmingham or Raleigh, and whether it consists of Ku Kluxers or Negro College students." The spread of protests struck fear in the Kennedy administration. On national television in June, the president advocated passage of a civil rights bill that would guarantee equal accommodations and voting rights.[61]

Nothing could further southern realignment more than Democrats' support for black civil rights. "Adam Clayton Powell the Negro Congressman from Harlem," Helms told viewers, "described President Kennedy's civil rights proposal as 'the greatest . . . statement since the Emancipation Proclamation.'" Helms asked, "And what made it great? Congressman Powell said that he wrote half of it for the President." Helms also ensnared Governor Sanford in Kennedy's proposals. "As the head of a sovereign state, how does the Governor feel about Mr. Kennedy's proposal to shut off federal funds to any state not complying with the federal government's exact wishes in matters of race relationships?"[62]

Civil rights protests intensified in Raleigh and other North Carolina cities during June 1963. Helms's commentaries created the impression of a seamless alliance between liberals, radicals, and civil rights activists and depicted the universities as the source of civil rights demonstrations. Helms explained to viewers that a conservative UNC professor listed faculty who participated in the protests. These professors supported the "'Ban the Bomb' movement," "the release of the convicted Communist, Junius Scales," and the abolishment of HUAC. Helms repeatedly used Scales to paint North Carolina Democrats as fellow travelers. Scales had joined the Communist Party while a UNC student in the midst of the Depression and served fifteen months in prison for his party membership. Kennedy commuted his sentence in 1962. Helms linked Democrats to supposed communists no matter how tenuous the ties. A professor at State College "is an announced leader and promoter of racial demonstrations downtown. During his student days at Chapel Hill, he is remembered as having been a close friend of Junius Scales. He is also a close friend of one of Governor Sanford's top assistants."[63]

A week after his commentary on UNC and Junius Scales, Helms praised Ohio legislators for voting "to forbid Communists and Communist-fronters from speaking at any state-supported college." He thought Ohio's action provided a model for those "who have been too timid, or just too disinterested, or both, to take a stand." Four days later, the North Carolina General Assembly passed a communist speaker ban with language similar to the Ohio bill's. Helms's advocacy of a ban just before it passed was more than a coincidence. He later observed of the ban's passage, "We mousetrapped them at the last minute!" The speaker ban was a triumph. Notice "what happens," Helms boasted, "when so-called 'liberalism' receives a setback." The ban bedeviled the state's universities and their supporters until a federal court declared it unconstitutional five years later. Helms had made an obscure resolution by an American Legion post news and entangled the state's Democratic leadership. His assault on the universities magnified nascent anti-liberalism to build conservatism.[64]

Clear-cut Choices: Civil Rights and the 1964 Election

As the civil rights movement gained momentum, Helms worried that liberals would increase their black vote without losing white votes. A Democratic president supporting civil rights legislation, however, made realignment a real possibility: "No realistic political observer will deny the political implications, nor the political timing, of the racial unrest in America. But it is an ill wind that blows no good." The 1964 election would test the conservative movement and Helms's and Fletcher's experiment in conservative television. Could the "Voice of Free Enterprise" deliver eastern North Carolina to a conservative Republican and tip the balance statewide? Helms believed developments since 1960 favored conservatives: Supreme Court rulings on religious observance in public schools, the surge in civil rights protests, the Cuban missile crisis, and the slowly evolving war in Vietnam. Successful realignment, however, depended on Republicans nominating Senator Goldwater, a movement conservative and, most significantly, an opponent of civil rights legislation. If the Republican Party offered voters "a clear-cut choice" between a conservative and a liberal, Helms believed, Kennedy would be defeated.[65]

On *Viewpoint*, Helms examined a 1963 *Newsweek* poll of the GOP presidential hopefuls which showed African Americans opposed to all Republicans. He liked what he saw. The poll had Goldwater capturing 2 percent of the black vote, while moderate Nelson Rockefeller totaled an insignificantly higher 3 percent. "This is a political reality," Helms calculated, "that may turn to the Republicans' advantage." Yearning for an all-white Republican Party, Helms pressed Republicans to use race as a lever. "Racial unrest is no longer sectional and confined to the South. Most Americans want to do what is right for Negro citizens, but there are millions who are disturbed at the possibility of surrender to pressure politics and fear. These millions cast votes also." In the fall of 1963, Helms highlighted racial backlash in the North. Louise Day Hicks's election to the Boston School Board filled him with hope. She won, Helms judged, because she opposed "shuttling both Negro and white children all across town."[66]

Helms drew two lessons from Hicks's success. The first was that "the people of Boston are getting out of sympathy with Negro demands." What was "true in Boston" was probably "true in Philadelphia, Chicago and other heavy voting centers." The second lesson displayed Helms's adroit racial and religious politics and his aversion to African Americans. The key to "Negro advancement lies in the direction of hard work, self-reliance and moral behavior," he insisted. "The Negro race now needs to get to work to prove the equality that its leaders have for so long proclaimed." The limits African Americans faced, Helms implied, derived from their moral failings—not discrimination. His "prove your equality" challenge appealed to segregationists, while his focus on self-reliance and hard work gratified advocates of color-blind rights. His audience was deeply religious, and his moralizing invoked a religiously grounded sense of moral superiority. In correspondence with a minister, Helms clarified his views on religion and the racial "equality matter": "As for equality under the law and in the sight of God, there can be no debate," but equality in "character and morality" was a different matter.[67]

After the Kennedy assassination, Lyndon Johnson made civil rights a priority. His legislative skills and Kennedy's martyrdom got the bill moving. It was, Helms charged, "Mr. Johnson's bill" and "violate[d] the Constitution in a dozen different ways." The furthest-reaching sections would desegregate public accommodations—hotels, restaurants, public transit, parks, pools, beaches, and other public spaces—and prohibit job discrimination based on race, ethnicity, religion, or sex. The bill easily passed the House. Most observers expected it to stall in the Senate. In hundreds of efforts, the Senate had failed to overcome a filibuster on civil rights.[68]

When the Senate took up the bill, Helms made a typically inflammatory statement: "This civil rights bill is the single most dangerous piece of legislation ever." On a personal level, the bill's implications mortified him. During a trip to New York City, Helms and his wife had glimpsed what the legislation might mean. "Dot and I spent the weekend in New York. She was shocked: Somebody had told her that there was no danger of social mixing of the races." They, as Helms explained to a friend, counted interracial couples. "We saw at least 25 Negroes with white partners—in restaurants, shows, even the hotel."[69]

As southern senators filibustered, Helms charged that "something akin to a conspiracy" was affecting coverage of the legislation. "The arguments of Senators opposed to the so-called 'civil rights bill' now before Congress will not, of course, be reported by the press, radio and television." And the media would imply "that a 'filibuster'" was somehow "evil and undemocratic." Helms denied legitimacy not only to civil rights protesters but also African Americans voters who supported the Democrats and Republicans behind the legislation. Helms focused attention on the politics of legislating to obscure the substance. Senators knew the bill was poor legislation, he alleged, but "Congress is now legislating by mob rule." The bill's "true purpose" was surrendering "to the federal government absolute control of the lives of the American people."[70]

On *Viewpoint* Helms insisted that politics motivated support for civil rights, but privately he expressed confidence that political advantage lay in opposition to civil rights. Governor George Wallace's 1964 primary challenge to President Johnson garnered significant support outside the South. Helms thought Wallace's success demonstrated the white working class, including union members, was moving to the right except on issues of "immediate self-interest." He discussed northern voters with Wallace when the governor campaigned in Raleigh, and Wallace corroborated his sense of growing working-class conservatism outside the South "certainly on the race issue."[71]

While Congress and the president maneuvered over civil rights legislation, North Carolina held its Republican and Democratic primaries. Helms played a role in both parties in the run-up to the 1964 election. Most of all, he wanted to defeat whomever moderate Democrats nominated as Sanford's successor. Secondarily, he hoped to build a viable Republican Party in the state. Although many considered Lake the favorite, Helms was ambivalent about Lake running for governor again. In May 1963 he met with Congressman Jonas in Washington, D.C., to persuade him to run. A popular Republican in western North Carolina, Jonas would need WRAL's support to win Democrats in the east. The prospect of Jonas for governor and Goldwater for president thrilled Helms. The two candidates had the potential to make a decade of talk about a two-party system in the state a reality. With Goldwater's backing, the GOP had expended considerable resources on Operation Dixie. All Jonas needed to do was announce, and the Republican nomination was his. Jonas's defeat of Kitchin in 1962 indicated he could run strong statewide. But Jonas was unwilling to give up a secure seat in Congress for an uncertain gubernatorial run.[72]

The Democrats' primary was a three-way contest with race at its center: two conservatives—Lake and corporate lawyer Dan K. Moore, a former superior court judge—faced moderate federal judge Richardson Preyer. All three opposed civil rights legislation, but Preyer's moderation attracted African American support. Preyer had the backing of Governor Sanford's organization. Although he had not encouraged Lake to run, Helms supported him once he was in the race. Helms was worried that Lake and Moore would split the conservative vote and allow Preyer to win. Helms served on a committee charged with choosing Lake's publicity director. He recommended someone who would "soft-pedal segregation." Moore received endorsements from executives in the state's leading industries and Senator Sam Ervin. He claimed a position of moderation between the diehard segregationist and the "liberal" federal judge. Although Preyer finished first in the primary, with Moore second and Lake third, he failed to win enough votes to avoid a runoff. WRAL's campaign-night coverage emphasized that Preyer won 98 percent of the "Negro vote." When demanding a runoff, Moore followed WRAL's lead and criticized Preyer for winning "the bloc Negro vote."[73]

Four days passed without Lake endorsing Moore. While Lake and his campaign made demands, Moore insisted on his independence and believed Lake's supporters had nowhere else to go. Helms intervened because he wanted conservative Democrats unified. He invited Lake and Moore to a meeting at his house. They reached an agreement, and Lake endorsed Moore the next day. Moore easily won the runoff.[74]

Robert Gavin secured the Republican nomination for the second time. He had hoped for a Preyer victory to go along with a Goldwater nomination. Running against the conservative Democrat Moore made 1964 a much more difficult contest than 1960.[75]

Helms worried that Moore would move to the center for the general election, and on *Viewpoint* he pressured the nominee to maintain his conservatism. With a "clear-cut choice" in the primary election, the "conservative majority of North Carolina's people" chose Moore. The nominee needed Democrats unified, but he must not "embrace the curious philosophies of those who fought him." Throughout the fall, Helms had regular access to campaign manager Joe Hunt. "I am constantly assured by Joe" that Moore "has no intention of changing his course." Gavin's conservatism and the threat of a Goldwater victory in the state kept Moore to the right.[76]

The 1964 Republican presidential primary featured a battle between the party's conservative supporters of Goldwater and the moderates who backed New York governor Nelson Rockefeller. The June 2 California primary was decisive. Helms charged the network commentators with trying "to influence the outcome of the California vote." He singled out the national broadcast on "our own station." ABC's Howard K. Smith "told the nation that Governor Rockefeller had the support of all 'respectable' Republicans while Goldwater was merely the candidate of California 'Birchites.'" Helms charged that the networks' post-election analysis showed bias, too. Goldwater's victory, which sealed his nomination, left the broadcasters "visibly shaken." NBC's Chet Huntley asserted that "all the educated people voted for Rockefeller," while CBS's Eric Sevareid reported that Goldwater won support in southern California because "Los Angeles is full of elderly people and Southerners."[77]

Throughout the campaign, Helms gave North Carolinians reasons to vote for Goldwater. "Goldwater dared to vote right on the civil rights bill." The Supreme Court banned "prayer and Bible reading" in public schools, and Helms asked, "Who is more likely to support the court's position— Lyndon Johnson or Senator Goldwater?" If a conservative president replaced two liberals with two conservatives, this "long series of incredible decisions" would end. The federal debt, inflation, foreign aid, "moral collapse," "respect for law and order," and the possibility of "less government," Helms thought, favored Goldwater. "And then there is the war in South Vietnam which we pretend is not a war."[78]

Goldwater had a strong base of support among conservatives, but he would have difficulty widening his appeal. His statements suggested that he would make Social Security voluntary and eliminate the graduated income tax. The senator wanted victory in the Cold War. If that meant nuclear war, he was ready. At the July Republican convention in San Francisco, Goldwater's speech veered to the right. It confirmed many voters' doubts. The nomination of Goldwater delighted Democrats as much as it had conservatives. LBJ led him in the polls two to one. The "opinion polls," Helms joked, "offer the puzzling information that Mr. Goldwater's popularity is so low that he hardly can count on Mrs. Goldwater's vote." Johnson's political ads highlighted his opponent's reputation as an extremist, and the press coverage reflected the Democrat's theme.[79]

Helms especially found coverage of the Cold War prejudiced. Goldwater was cast as "a trigger-happy warmonger," while Johnson was depicted as the guarantor of peace and security. "Why is it necessary to misrepresent and distort Goldwater's words about nuclear weapons?" he asked.

"Is there, or is there not, a communist stronghold in Cuba, 90 miles off our shores?" Vietnam, Helms insisted, was the worst. Johnson adroitly avoided discussing it. Former North Carolina governor Luther Hodges suggested that Goldwater's election "would endanger the peace." Helms thundered, "What peace?"[80]

WRAL's news department undermined Johnson and advanced Goldwater. When the president made an election-year stop in North Carolina to highlight his war on poverty, WRAL's coverage made an issue of the theater of presidential politics. Reporter Carl Goerch dismissed the event as a "publicity stunt" and reported on its staging. The president's staff had searched for "a tenant farmer who lived in an unpainted, deteriorating house with no plumbing and with a large number of children." They settled on the Marlow family and even installed telephones for reporters. "For a few brief minutes, the Marlow world was a stage and all of the people were actors. The President came and went, and Rocky Mount became a national poverty dateline." Another WRAL reporter, Pete Young, asked Mrs. Marlow why her family was chosen for a presidential visit. "'We represented,' she said, 'everything the President was pushing.'"[81]

Goldwater's North Carolina campaign stop prompted a celebratory mood: "We do not propose at the moment to measure or evaluate the ovations given Senator Goldwater during his nearly 12 hours in Raleigh," Helms enthused. "There is nothing, really, with which to compare them." The station produced a panel discussion with Goldwater that ran on WRAL's *In My Opinion*. In addition to local reporters, two prominent southern conservative editors participated: Jack Kilpatrick, conservative columnist and editor of the *Richmond News Leader*, and Tom Waring, editor of the *Charlestown News and Courier*. Nine stations in three states ran it. The national press covering Goldwater could only watch. Their reaction to the friendly questioning was generally dim. "What is this," CBS reporter Roger Mudd asked, "a paid political broadcast?"[82]

In the early fall, Helms expressed cautious optimism regarding Goldwater's chances in the state. The senator had "brought to life in North Carolina a heretofore slumbering and virtually motionless two party system." Goldwater, he reminded voters, had to overcome "the massive bloc vote," but he could win "the support of Democrats whose craws are full with disappointment and disillusionment." But the Arizona senator never overcame his extremist image and suffered the largest popular-vote rejection in U.S. history. Deeply frustrated, Helms blamed the voters for rejecting

Goldwater. "We certainly took a licking, didn't we?" Helms wrote conservative ally Andrew Beck. "Still, I am delighted to know the precise number of Americans who are willing to stand up for very clear and undisguised principles."[83]

Lyndon Johnson and Dan Moore, a liberal and a conservative Democrat, both won North Carolina. Gavin failed to do as well in 1964 as he had in the previous election. A conservative opponent with a southern president—no matter how liberal—at the top of the ticket was unbeatable. To Helms's frustration, the North Carolina Democratic Party's ideological diversity was the key to its dominance. *The Robesonian*, a newspaper in Lumberton, spelled it out: Moore "is conservative enough to suit almost anybody," and the party's nominee for lieutenant governor, Robert Scott, "is liberal enough to suit almost anybody." The only reason to vote for Gavin is "just to be voting Republican."[84]

Conservatives in both parties appreciated Helms's and WRAL's "bipartisan" efforts. Joe Hunt, Moore's campaign manager, wrote, "For all you did in the interest of Dan's campaign I am grateful." Herman Saxon, chairman of the North Carolina Republican Party, thanked Helms for "the all out efforts you and your entire staff put forth on the Barry Goldwater interview." Helms just hoped Goldwater's candidacy would leave an impression on the Republican Party. He wrote Gavin, "I confess an obsession in my hope that the Republican Party in its hour of disappointment will stand fast for the right."[85]

Earl Butz, the former assistant secretary of agriculture, had long urged Helms to switch parties. He thought that the Republican Party's nomination of Goldwater was reason enough. Helms assured him, "I am still thinking about switching my party registration." But Helms blamed his hesitation on moderate Republicans such as Nelson Rockefeller and New York senator Jacob Javits. "I am waiting to do so until I see whether the GOP is going to be taken over by Rockefeller, Javitts [*sic*], et al. If so, I might as well stay put with LBJ and Hubert."[86]

Helms was already a Republican in all but registration. Switching his registration would mean giving up his power in the Democratic Party. He could still support Republicans. But no Republican could negotiate an agreement between two Democrats like Lake and Moore as Helms did in the 1964 primary. Helms's commentaries and his private correspondence kept Moore to the right. He was confident that Moore's campaign heard his pleas. But did Helms vote for Moore? It was unlikely. After he registered as a Republican in 1970, Helms explained his switch to Congressman Fountain: "I had even reached the point that I found GOP nominees for Governor and other offices preferable to the nominees of what was my own party."[87] Helms certainly voted for Gavin over Sanford in 1960. He probably voted for him again in 1964.

As the prospect of Goldwater's election slipped away, Helms expressed doubts about the value of WRAL's conservative alternative. "We are, as you say, continuing our editorials. Every day it seems to be less worth the effort. We pull the mail like crazy—but, then, we pulled it in the weeks prior to last November. And look what happened!" Despite the frustrations of the presidential election, Helms saw in the 1964 Democratic primary evidence that WRAL's political effort was succeeding. "Lake carried Wake because the state employees were fed up with Sanford and wanted to demonstrate it." Helms reflected that "WRAL may have had a lot to do with the attitude around here simply because we kept pounding Sanford with the truth for four straight years." Wake County was WRAL's home base and Lake the station's candidate. Lake's local victory also indicated to Helms that WRAL was winning the media battle. "I think there is general disgust with the *News and Observer*. This sounds immodest but I don't think there's any comparison between the influence of WRAL and The N&O."[88]

Realignment was not happening fast enough for Helms. Certain that pious incitement was a winning formula, there was zero chance Helms would cancel *Viewpoint*. A month after Goldwater's defeat, Helms avowed, "All of a sudden, sin isn't sin anymore." Those of us "who cling to the old principles" were "bigots of the most old-fashioned variety." News stories regarding sex and college students prompted his comments, including one on the University of South Carolina student newspaper. The female editor denied that the key question regarding sex was "moral." She asked instead whether sex was "personally healthy" and "meaningful." Who was responsible for the new student attitude toward sex? A National Council of Churches pamphlet approving premarital sex had circulated on college campuses since 1961. Helms reminded viewers that "one of the candidates for President repeatedly expressed concern about the moral breakdown in America." He had been defeated.[89]

Helms's cultural and religious provocation would grow in importance over the next few years. He also remained committed to the proposition that Republican candidates in national and statewide campaigns had to play the race card to win, convinced that this was the only path to realignment and conservative unity. Democrats, the media, the universities, and the civil rights movement—particularly King—served as foils. But pious incitement had a political cost. The station's support for conservative candidates and attacks on the civil rights movement would lead to Federal Communication Commission investigations of bias on WRAL.

3

"An Uncommon Number of Moral Degenerates"

The Conservative Alternative and the Fairness Doctrine

The Federal Communication Commission required broadcast stations, radio and TV, to renew their licenses every three years. Renewals were routine before Helms arrived at WRAL, but his editorials and changes at the FCC meant scrutiny of the station's political activity. Eisenhower's FCC maintained a hands-off approach as television grew rapidly. A couple months after Helms joined WRAL-TV, President Kennedy named Newton Minow FCC chairman. Minow, a young enthusiastic New Frontiersman, came to the FCC as an outsider. He believed stations should carry editorials, but he also made it clear that license renewals would be a serious process. The Fairness Doctrine along with the Equal Time Rule held TV and radio stations accountable to the public.[1]

In July 1963 the FCC issued a public notice reminder regarding the Fairness Doctrine. It focused on civil rights issues. The Fairness Doctrine meant stations "had an affirmative obligation" to seek out opposing opinions on "any controversial issue" the station covered. If a station deals with "an issue of current importance such as racial segregation, integration, or discrimination," it must offer "similar opportunities" for the other side, especially "the views of the leaders of the Negro and other community groups." In the event of a "personal attack" on an individual or organization, the station should send a transcript of the remarks and notify the target of his or her chance to respond. "In determining compliance with the fairness doctrine the commission looks to substance." Unsurprisingly, Helms held a dim view of the Fairness Doctrine. "The government is deciding what is 'fair,'" he contended, "and this in its practical application amounts to censorship."[2]

Helms's political intentions at WRAL meant that he pushed what the station could get away with to the limit, and A. J. Fletcher backed him. In *Viewpoint*'s second week, Helms affirmed the station's willingness to defy the FCC. "It may be that we are running some risk, since radio and television are controlled by the government, but it is a risk that we are willing to take."[3] His use of WRAL to advance the conservative movement would lead to challenges to license renewals in 1963 and 1966. North Carolina's moderate Democrats recognized Helms's and Fletcher's intentions. The party's moderates had objected to Helms's pious incitement in the *Tarheel Banker*; television was a much more powerful medium than a magazine for bankers. Democrats pushed the station to follow the Fairness Doctrine and the FCC to enforce it. The FCC investigated the station and issued warnings. WRAL adopted new policies, but little changed. Helms chose whose dissent to air and shaped what they could say. In many cases he managed to use the opposition to conservatism's advantage.

The FCC and Free-Enterprise Broadcasting

Helms and A. J. Fletcher never intended to follow the Fairness Doctrine. Shortly after Helms joined Capitol Broadcasting in 1960, Helms, A. J. Fletcher, Fred Fletcher, the other stockholders, and the station's lawyer, Frank Fletcher, met to discuss the "perils" of editorializing under the Fairness Doctrine. Fred and Frank Fletcher were A. J.'s sons. Frank had worked for the FCC after earning his law degree. He advised his father on getting his first radio license in 1939 and securing his television station in 1956. Frank became a partner in a Washington, D.C., law firm specializing in communication law.[4]

"As a business proposition," Frank cautioned, "you will be buying trouble if you begin to air conservative editorials. You know the prevailing philosophy in Washington."

A. J. responded, "We'll buy trouble."

Frank went further. "Well, let me say it like it is: You may lose your license."

A. J. cut off the discussion. "Well, by God, if we lose it, then we lose it."[5]

WRAL faced its first license renewal under Helms in December 1963. In September the station had learned that it faced an FCC investigation concerning complaints about the station's news coverage and *Viewpoint*.

The investigation centered on WRAL's 1964 Democratic primary coverage and the civil rights movement. The state's moderate Democrats lodged many of the complaints against WRAL. They hoped the Fairness Doctrine would allow them to blunt pious incitement. Helms's *Viewpoints* on the civil rights movement also created problems for the station, particularly his criticism of Bayard Rustin and Jack O'Dell.

Two investigators arrived in Raleigh in early December and spent over a week going through WRAL's files, including Helms's personal files. For another week, they traveled through the region soliciting comment and interviewing the station's critics. The investigators returned to Washington to consider the evidence. The FCC, through Secretary Ben Waple, periodically required a response from WRAL to the complaints. This process continued until the summer of 1964. "The FCC has made no charge," Helms grumbled. "It has simply 'investigated' us to the point of frustration." This was accurate only in the narrow, legalistic sense of "charge." Waple explained to the station that WRAL faced an investigation because viewers complained of unfairness in WRAL's "treatment of controversial issues," especially on *Viewpoint*. Helms spent the months from December 1963 until July 1964 organizing the station's defense.[6]

WRAL initially asserted that its conservative perspective balanced "the national and sectional expressions coming by network from New York" and "an unduly biased and frequently unfair view presented by the morning and afternoon newspapers in Raleigh." Helms maintained throughout his tenure at WRAL that *Viewpoint* balanced the *Raleigh News and Observer*. For example, he had offered Governor George Wallace of Alabama a chance to respond to his local critics in September 1963. "The newspapers hereabouts have been critical of you on numerous instances. . . . If you have material running in the neighborhood of four minutes, we would be glad to use it in response to such criticism."[7]

The FCC explained that "seeking to balance" the local newspapers "by broadcasting matter over your stations which favors one viewpoint" did not satisfy the Fairness Doctrine. The newspapers did not count. WRAL could only maintain that a local television show or editorial balanced other local programming or network shows carried on WRAL. The FCC required a "detailed statement" listing programs "which in your opinion favored one side of a controversial public issue . . . and why you believe the program one-sided." Additionally, the FCC required a list of any personal attacks the station had aired and evidence that the station had made an effort to allow a response. The FCC protected the identity of some individuals who made complaints, so Helms and his news crew had to try to figure out who might have had reason to register a grievance and show they offered equal time.[8]

The complaints leveled against WRAL involved numerous objections to Helms's commentaries and allegations of bias in the station's news coverage, including personal attacks on civil rights activists Bayard Rustin and Jack O'Dell; unfair treatment of Ralph Campbell, president of the Raleigh NAACP chapter; the televising of Clarence Manion's speech in Raleigh; showing favoritism to I. Beverly Lake's 1960 campaign; claims of corruption in Governor Terry Sanford's administration; and bias against Richardson Preyer's ongoing campaign for governor.[9]

Helms's pious incitement regarding Rustin and O'Dell had ignored the FCC's Equal Time Rule, which required that individuals who were criticized be offered on-air response time. During August 1963, Helms had used O'Dell and Rustin to reproach King, the Kennedys, and the 1963 March on Washington. O'Dell, Helms asserted on August 1, was "a Communist, clearly identified," and "Dr. King offered not the slightest indication that he was embarrassed or concerned about his relationship with such an individual." Helms also drew the Kennedy administration into the allegations. Attorney General Robert Kennedy "should ponder" O'Dell's relationship to King. "Mr. Kennedy told Congress the other day that he had been 'unable to find' any Communists in the civil rights movement."[10]

On August 20, Helms derided an NBC executive's report to the FCC on *Viewpoint*. The executive declared that NBC's "coverage of racial news" was "absolutely impartial." WRAL carried NBC's network news—*The Huntley-Brinkley Report*. "Obviously the gentleman," Helms suggested, "has not watched his own network recently."[11]

Helms pointed to *The Huntley-Brinkley Report*'s coverage of preparations for the March on Washington for Jobs and Freedom as an example of biased coverage of racial news during August 1963. He found coverage of Rustin especially troubling. Rustin "was admiringly identified as 'Mr. March-on-Washington Himself.'" Helms faulted the network for the lack of "background data" on Rustin. "Rustin has been arrested eleven times— including once in 1953 when he was arrested in Pasadena, California, on charges of sex perversion. Rustin pleaded guilty." This was the organizer of the "'March on Washington,' in which 100,000 or more Negroes will participate." Rustin was also a former member of the Young Communist League and "served several years for draft dodging."[12]

Helms was deeply uncomfortable with homosexuality, and Rustin was a rarity in the early 1960s—an openly gay man in a public role. The gay rights movement had begun quietly in the 1950s, but it remained under the radar of most Americans and most political leaders. Gay rights developed into a major issue in the 1970s with reticent liberal support and fierce conservative opposition. As a U.S. senator, Helms became a leader in the antigay backlash, but in 1963 he was unaware of the gay movement or even the possibility of one. Rustin himself put fighting racial discrimination first.[13]

Helms primarily saw a chance to use Rustin's sexuality against King and the Kennedys. "King describes Rustin as 'a brilliant, efficient, and dedicated organizer.' But Dr. King has nothing to say about Rustin as a moral degenerate; or as a member of the Young Communist League." Helms wondered if the attorney general could "'find' Communist ties in the movement" once the march brought Rustin and O'Dell to Washington.[14] Helms's outrage over Rustin's and O'Dell's supposed communist ties and Rustin's homosexuality suggested the Kennedys and King were immoral and disloyal. The real benefit to conservatives was undermining the Democratic Party and the civil rights movement with such insinuations.

Helms and others at WRAL, including attorney Frank Fletcher, approached the FCC inquiry as a paperwork problem. WRAL's explanations satisfied the FCC on a number of issues. Helms, for example, presented Manion's speech as a reply to New York City mayor Robert Wagner, whose Raleigh speech WRAL also broadcast. Wagner was exactly the kind of big-city politician that Helms wanted to associate with liberalism and the Democratic Party. His administration hired significant numbers of Hispanics and African Americans, built large public housing projects, granted the city workers' unions the right to collective bargaining, made racial discrimination in housing illegal, and enthusiastically embraced Johnson's Great Society. No one at WRAL had conceived of Manion as balancing Wagner at the time, but as Helms wrote Manion, "We presumed, we said, that equal time meant equal time."[15]

In the case of civil rights leaders O'Dell and Rustin, the station had not offered them equal time or sent copies of the *Viewpoints* attacking them. Helms searched for a likely cover and only found one for Rustin.

He asserted that his *Viewpoint* on Rustin balanced Rustin's "lengthy appearance on NBC's *Huntley-Brinkley Report*."[16]

Helms loved the debate format and believed debates made good TV and radio. The station created a regular debate series, *In My Opinion*. Many of the debates were no doubt straightforward public affairs programming, but WRAL often used its control of the participants, the debates' structure, and the questions to favor conservatives. The FCC investigation included a complaint from local NAACP president Ralph Campbell concerning his 1962 appearance on *In My Opinion*. Campbell agreed to a debate on whether integration or segregation was preferable. Helms acknowledged to William Cheshire of the Charleston, South Carolina, *Evening Post* that WRAL intentionally put Campbell at a disadvantage. The station enlisted another African American, Archbishop Clarence C. Addison of East Orange, New Jersey, to defend segregation. Campbell "had expected a white opponent," Helms explained. "He was stunned when he learned that his adversary was to be a Negro." Putting Campbell at an even greater disadvantage, WRAL asked him at 7:00 p.m. to show up for an 8:00 p.m. taping. Helms added, "He lost the debate."[17]

In its defense, WRAL asserted that Campbell could have refused to debate on short notice, and even more important, he approved the tape afterward for broadcast. But Helms realized, "He could not gracefully back out." If Campbell declined to appear or prevented the airing of the debate, he would have lost a rare chance for a TV audience. Helms also would have made an issue of his refusal to debate. Archbishop Addison would have received the time slot alone. Harry Golden, author and *Charlotte Observer* reporter known for his criticism of segregation, was scheduled to debate proposed federal fair employment legislation with I. Beverly Lake. Golden decided against the appearance "without explanation," and WRAL allowed Lake to criticize the proposed legislation unchallenged.[18]

WRAL's evening news program *Stateline* had run a story accusing Highway Commissioner Cliff Benson of having a financial interest in a subdivision, Waco Heights, with the state improperly paving the roads. Sanford and Benson denied the charges. Benson's lawyer, Buck Harris, sent a letter by registered mail demanding a retraction and lodged a complaint with the FCC.[19]

Helms easily countered Benson's charges. Benson had publicly acknowledged that he loaned money to the Waco Heights developer and that he owned land adjacent to the subdivision. The difference of opinion between the station and Benson rested on the language used on *Stateline* and *Viewpoint*. Benson, WRAL maintained, had "a very definite financial interest in the successful development of Waco Heights," but this did not mean that he had directly invested in it. WRAL's emphasis was on the word "successful." The station implied that a "successful" project would not only raise the value of Benson's land but was also necessary for the developer to repay Benson's loans. WRAL's coverage had forced Governor Sanford to hold a press conference to defend his highway commissioner and his administration. WRAL wanted Benson on the record, too. Newscaster Bill Armstrong made numerous calls to Benson, and reporter Ben Runkle went to his office. Benson was repeatedly unavailable. The day he received the registered letter demanding a retraction, Helms ran into Benson's lawyer at lunch. Helms asked, "How about getting Cliff to go on the air and tell his side of the matter?" Harris balked. "Cliff ain't about to go on the air."[20]

After the FCC investigation began, the campaign of moderate Democrat Richardson Preyer alleged bias in WRAL's coverage of the 1964 Democratic primary. Preyer faced two conservatives, I. Beverly Lake and Dan Moore. Local political observers were well aware of Lake's close ties to Helms, Fletcher, and WRAL. In September, Lenox Baker offered Helms advice in facing the FCC probe. Baker was a Duke surgeon, past president of the North Carolina Medical Society, and a friend and conservative admirer of Helms. He was also Helms's son Charles's doctor. Baker counseled, "You will be invaluable to Mr. Dan Moore or any other candidate representing his side of the problem should Mr. Lake not be a candidate." Baker not only knew Helms would use the station to support a conservative candidate against Preyer, but he also assumed it would be Lake. Baker added that Moore needed "to contact any and all people in Washington whom he thinks may be supporting him." Baker himself went all out for WRAL. He wrote a letter on North Carolina Medical Society stationery praising WRAL to the FCC and pushed his friends to write. Along with a personal note to each, he sent copies of his FCC letter to thirteen political insiders, including Vice President Lyndon Johnson.[21]

Preyer's campaign manager, Newman Townsend, wrote a letter on January 9, 1964, to the FCC complaining of "biased news reporting" by WRAL-TV. The campaign continued to register grievances through the spring. Townsend took issue with WRAL's limited coverage of Preyer's announcement of his candidacy, which did not include any film, in contrast to the coverage given Lake. WRAL's defense was proximity. Lake's announcement occurred in Raleigh. The station declined to film Preyer's announcement in Greensboro and Moore's in Asheville because of the distance. Both were covered with stories, however. Lake practiced law in Raleigh and ran his campaign from the capital. This allowed WRAL-TV to cover him often and inexpensively. In January, for example, the station taped Lake's speech to the Raleigh Kiwanis Club for late broadcast. The Preyer campaign raised a similar issue in WRAL's coverage of Lake and Preyer rallies in Rocky Mount, North Carolina. The station carried film of both, but the Lake film and story were longer than his opponent's. Newscaster Bill Armstrong argued that the Lake story ran on a weekday 11:15 p.m. newscast, when ample time was available, whereas Preyer's ran on a Saturday at 6:00 p.m., with only three minutes allotted for the entire news program.[22]

More significant than the relative length afforded Preyer or whether his events were filmed was the tone and content of WRAL's coverage. A Preyer event in Greensboro was introduced as "the biggest, longest, gaudiest, and probably the costliest political rally ever held in North Carolina." A typical Lake story began, "I. Beverly Lake has announced his platform, pledging to carry out the duties of governor as a conservative Democrat."[23]

Townsend also charged that WRAL's broadcasts "failed to accord Candidate Preyer adequate coverage of his denials of the charges from the Lake headquarters" that Preyer "signed a clemency petition for Junius Scales." Helms's pious incitement routinely used Scales's conviction to associate North Carolina Democrats with communism. WRAL clearly documented that it had covered Preyer's denials. The station had played film of Lake's campaign manager, Allen Bailey, making the charge, and then quoted a brief statement noting the evidence against the allegation. But the station kept repeating Lake's allegations.[24]

A few weeks after the station and the Preyer campaign clashed over coverage of Preyer's denials, Helms announced on *Viewpoint* an offer to carry six hours of debates during primetime with all three candidates participating. If other radio and TV stations joined in broadcasting the debates, he hoped the candidates would discuss the issues before the "largest television and radio audience in the history of the state." But Helms's allegiance to Lake compromised his offer of free prime-time coverage to the candidates. First, he repeated the Lake campaign's allegation: "Preyer has volunteered an explanation of his writing a letter of endorsement to a petition calling for the release of Junius Scales, the convicted communist. Candidate Preyer insists that this was proper; Candidate Beverly Lake insists it was not." Then Helms painted Preyer as a racial liberal: "Candidate Preyer has been endorsed by the president of the North Carolina NAACP."[25]

The Lake and Moore campaigns immediately accepted the debate offer, but the Preyer campaign thought better of it. Helms's pious incitement in the same editorial as his offer to carry debates only confirmed what moderate Democrats suspected about the station. Preyer's campaign manager wrote WRAL, "I feel that the neutrality of WRAL in the current campaign is questionable and I do not believe that a confrontation sponsored by WRAL in Raleigh could possibly be fair to all candidates." He relayed Preyer's willingness to debate at "an impartial station" with arrangements "for a statewide hookup."[26]

Helms immediately exploited Preyer's rebuff. He issued a press release that included his editorial offering the debate, Lake's and Moore's acceptances, and Townsend's letter rejecting. In his next *Viewpoint*, Helms acted perplexed over the Preyer campaign's "curious conclusion" regarding "what we intended as a constructive and friendly offer." Lake used Preyer's rejection to cast his opponent in a bad light. "Since Judge Preyer is afraid to have these debates in the studios of WRAL, I will agree to having them at either of the two Charlotte stations, or at the High Point Station in Judge Preyer's home county, or even at the Greensboro station right in his own backyard."[27]

In late February, WRAL and the Preyer campaign negotiated a truce. Townsend and Preyer probably decided that mending fences was best for Preyer's election chances. They had made their complaints known to the FCC and applied public pressure on WRAL to treat Preyer fairly. Townsend called WRAL newscaster Sam Beard, whom he knew personally, and said that he hoped their "personal friendship" would survive the "unpleasantness." He added that recently WRAL's election coverage had been "fair and forthright." Townsend also promised to end the campaign's FCC complaints. Beard assured him "we had not in any way altered our manner of handling news items on either radio or television." He suggested an alternative explanation for the Preyer campaign's original dissatisfaction: the station had led with what it considered "the most important story of the day." Coverage of competing candidates "tended to even out over the course of the entire campaign."[28]

In March 1964 the state's large-circulation newspapers, the local "liberal" media Helms derided, inadvertently gave WRAL a boost in the station's troubles with the FCC. The *Charlotte Observer* broke the story of the FCC investigation, and the other papers picked it up. A. J. Fletcher held a news conference confirming the story as "essentially true" while downplaying the investigation's significance. He acknowledged viewer protests regarding *Viewpoint* and complaints of "unfair treatment" from one of the gubernatorial campaigns. The station would continue its conservative editorials, Fletcher asserted, "without fear of reprisal."[29]

Before the papers broke the story, people close to the station had written letters of support, but many average viewers were unaware of the investigation. After the newspaper coverage, supporters began calling and writing the station to register their support. As discreetly as possible, WRAL directed them to the FCC, supplying Secretary Waple's name and address. As Helms wrote one WRAL devotee, "We are trying to keep ourselves in the position of being able to say under oath that we have not promoted any support for our position. As a result, I may sound a bit silly in some of my correspondence." Some of Helms's most fervent admirers organized petition drives protesting the delay in renewing WRAL's license. Heartened by the response, Helms wrote Thurman Sensing that the FCC had received "thousands of letters of protest" regarding the delay in the license renewal. "So, you see, there is conservative sentiment hereabouts."[30]

Despite Fletcher's public stance of defiance and viewer support, Helms admitted concern. "We frankly do not know whether we are in peril or not." The waiting was nerve-racking: "We are living on a diet of fingernails."[31] WRAL and the Preyer campaign went through another round of complaints in April. This time, WRAL radio had failed to offer a Preyer press conference to other stations through FM relay, when WRAL had made a Lake press conference available the same day. WRAL insisted that the Preyer campaign had failed to give WRAL sufficient notice. Helms personally called Townsend and assured him that WRAL believed the Preyer campaign should have "equal treatment."[32]

The June primary was indecisive. Preyer came in first, with Moore second and Lake third. In the runoff, Moore attacked Preyer's "bloc Negro vote" in a conscious effort to attract Lake's supporters. WRAL's election-night coverage anticipated Moore's theme focusing on Preyer's "bloc vote" in black urban precincts.[33]

The complaints over WRAL's newscasts began before the evening ended. One viewer insisted that WRAL's coverage was "extremely biased" and declared, "The intent of your emphasis on the Negro bloc vote was quite clear." Helms professed innocence. "We think that no one will contend that the mood of the Negro voter is not news in this era of widespread racial unrest." Helms argued that African Americans had intentionally "become an important political force. Thus, in this station's judgment, Negro reaction to issues and candidates is significant news. . . . Preyer owes his success at the polls to the marvelous Negro vote which he received."[34]

In late July, WRAL-TV learned that its license would be renewed with a warning. Helms and his news department had grounds for charging Benson with inappropriate conduct, since Benson's ties to the Waco Heights subdivision were close enough to affect his decisions. But the FCC also declined to sanction the station for its treatment of Campbell and its coverage of the gubernatorial race. The FCC could not enforce good faith in a case like Campbell's. Campbell had appeared on television to speak for racial justice and had the chance to stop the debate's broadcast if he chose. His experience showed that those considering an appearance on WRAL had to remain alert to the possibility they were stepping into a trap. Sometimes the best course was to decline the station's invitation. The election coverage of Preyer presented similar difficulties. It was hard to prove biased newscasts to FCC commissioners in Washington. The thousands of letters from viewers supporting the station also made it hard to seriously punish the station. Many people adored Helms. The station under Helms's guidance carefully responded to all of the FCC complaints. In his letter to Cheshire regarding the segregation debate, Helms emphasized this process: "You cannot imagine the amount of explaining we had to do about that incident. The rest of the complaints were more or less the same sort of thing."[35]

The FCC, however, concluded "that you have not fully complied with the requirements of the fairness doctrine in certain respects." Its warning regarded the station's lack of diligence in soliciting and airing contrasting opinions on "controversial issues," coupled with personal attacks in *Viewpoint* when the individual was not given a chance to reply. After the commission refused to accept the station's general defense of balancing the liberal media, Helms and his news staff cobbled together a list of liberal programs that balanced a *Viewpoint* or other airing of "controversial issues." This only worked in some cases. Helms had often editorialized without making any effort to air an opposing opinion or offering equal time, such as his commentaries on O'Dell and Rustin. The FCC refused to accept Helms's explanation that his comments on Rustin balanced a story on *The Huntley-Brinkley Report*. The news story, Waple observed, covered Rustin's training of civil rights activists for the 1963 March on Washington, but Helms's *Viewpoint* "involved an attack on his character."[36]

In the end, it was difficult to document a station's bias, and taking away a station's license was an extreme sanction. In 1964 the FCC had never denied renewal of a TV station's license for any reason. The FCC also wanted to persuade stations to editorialize: a harsh penalty, for one of the first stations to air editorials would only discourage others. The FCC gave two reasons for renewing the station's license, despite the Fairness Doctrine violations. First, the commission declared that WRAL's failure to comply was an "honest mistake." Second, the station announced its new policies effective April 1964. WRAL followed each *Viewpoint* with a statement that offered to broadcast dissent. If Helms criticized a group or person, the station's editorial board would decide whether offering a chance to reply was necessary.[37]

Helms, however, had no intention of toning down his pious incitement or allowing a liberal perspective to balance it. He wrote Lenox Baker that "the main criticisms against us involved our failure to plead with two Negroes whom we have criticized to appear on our station to rebut us. One was Bayard Rustin, the sex pervert (self-confessed) who led the March on Washington last August. The other was Jack O'Dell, the known communist who was Martin Luther King's top man in New York. That kind of FCC criticism we can stand." On *Viewpoint*, Helms reveled in the FCC decision "that the public interest would be served by renewing the licenses of the stations which originate these editorials." He then questioned the whole process of license renewals and the FCC's Fairness Doctrine. Helms portrayed broadcast regulation as "a precedent" and warned that it could "lead to attempts to impose such controls on all media." He urged the voters and Congress to consider "the wisdom and propriety of a government agency presuming to decide what is fair and what is not in the distribution of information and opinion to the public. Fairness, like beauty, is in the eye of the beholder."[38]

Helms's comparison of television to print journalism ignored all the ways TV differed from newspapers and magazines, especially before cable. In reality, WRAL owed a great deal of its profitability to FCC regulation and Washington politics. A. J. Fletcher got his original license because he outmaneuvered the Durham Life Insurance Company, his competition, due largely to aid from his son Frank, a former FCC lawyer, and secondarily to Helms's political connections. In 1956, Durham Life Insurance Company was the favorite. A larger company, it owned Raleigh's oldest radio station. Helms said in 1967 that Fletcher won his television license because "Republicans were in control" during the 1950s.[39] For years WRAL was the state capital's only TV station because of an FCC-granted monopoly. The FCC's licensing process and the Fairness Doctrine were efforts to deal with the limited number of broadcast outlets in most TV markets. A third Fletcher son, Floyd, was part-owner of WRAL's only significant competition, WTVD in Durham. The *News and Observer* was a local newspaper monopoly, after it bought its competition in the late 1950s, but federal regulation had nothing to do with it. The *News and Observer*, like WRAL, had competition from the Durham paper. Local papers also faced national competitors such as *Time* or the *National Review*. In the 1960s, local TV stations as network affiliates broadcast the only national news. Helms might not agree with *The Huntley-Brinkley Report*, but it was the highest-rated evening news show in the early 1960s, and WRAL-TV profited from its broadcast.

On the face of it, the new Fairness Doctrine–inspired policy of soliciting dissent appears a drastic divergence from Fletcher's and Helms's purpose of creating a conservative voice, but the new policies did not mean significant change. Helms not only chose who would speak for the other side but also restricted in various ways what they said. His power allowed him to use dissent to support conservatism. His ability to shape the impact of opposition led some to decline or ignore offers of appearing on the station.

Helms flatly rejected some critics: "I would not mind using your letter if it were at all legitimate." He edited others. *Viewpoint* aired a portion of Robert Blake's letter. "The few occasions that I have found myself on your side," Blake observed, "I still could not go along because of the technique you use in fighting with words. You have been very misleading, even in getting a point across I agree with. Since I find you so far off on facts I'm acquainted with, I have my doubts about subjects I'm not up on."

When Blake wrote objecting to the editing, Helms fired back, "We deleted a charge which was demonstrably false." Even on the *Viewpoints* devoted to dissent, Helms always had the last word when he wanted it. "And by the way, Mr. Blake," Helms responded, "would you care to be specific as to when we have been misleading and infactual? Please write again." When a viewer complained about WRAL's responding to critical letters after they were read on the air, Helms answered, "I cannot agree that it is necessary that we abdicate our right to comment, when need be, on any letter we use. On the other hand, I do not think it can be suggested that we ridicule or otherwise deprecate our correspondents." Yet Helms threatened one detractor: "How do you feel about the Negro demonstrators? . . . As I say, I would not mind using your letter, but I would have to tell the true facts and that would simply make you look ridiculous."[40]

Marse Grant experienced Helms's full treatment and regretted ever having written to the station. Grant edited the *Biblical Recorder*, a weekly publication of the North Carolina Baptist State Convention. He had expressed support for the Supreme Court decisions on prayer and praised the banning of "government-regulated and prescribed prayers in the public schools." Grant, like many other Southern Baptist leaders, was more concerned with Catholic, Mormon, or Muslim influence than with the Court's decision on prayer. Helms harshly criticized Grant's position in a May 1964 *Viewpoint* shortly after the station began soliciting dissent. "We believe the *Biblical Recorder* to be precisely 100 per cent wrong. . . . [T]he publication professes to be standing up for freedom of religion when what it is really demanding is freedom from religion." Grant's dissent asked, "Who would compose these prayers? What version of the Bible would be used: Would the Koran or Douay version or the Book of Mormon be used if a majority of the local population so decreed?" Critiquing every paragraph, Helms's editorial comments were longer than Grant's letter. "I was naive enough to think," Grant explained, "that my letter would be treated like most letters to the media—aired or printed without comment. . . . The strategy was clear: A weak, effeminate voice off camera quoted from my letter as it appeared on the screen. Then Helms took it apart sentence by sentence, sarcastically ridiculing every point I was trying to make. I was made to look like a fool."[41]

On *Viewpoint* Helms said he expected the "fur to fly" when he explained the new policy soliciting dissent. He seemed genuinely surprised when the number of critical letters went down. Helms wrote Hardy Berry in the Office of Information Services at North Carolina State to ask for help. "We're getting fewer critical letters than usual, and vastly more letters of approval. I do not understand it." The lack of criticism that resulted from the FCC's failure to significantly sanction WRAL-TV added to Helms's method of dealing with dissent. In practical terms, the new policies were insignificant. Helms even went after Rustin again. The civil rights movement, he alleged, included "an uncommon number of moral degenerates leading the parade." "Bayard Rustin, who directed the 'March on Washington' in 1963, is a self-confessed homosexual who served time in jail for a sordid offense." Powerful elements in the Democratic Party had tried to rein in Helms and failed. Few had the stomach to run the gauntlet that dissenting from *Viewpoint* required.[42]

The Fairness Doctrine and Cooley v. Gardner, 1966

Helms and WRAL faced a second renewal fight in December 1966. This time, the main issue was the station's role in the 1966 Fourth District congressional election. After losing to Republican James Gardner, Democrat Harold Cooley filed an FCC complaint that centered on the station's news coverage and Helms's election-eve *Viewpoint*. Gardner, an enthusiastic Goldwater supporter, had first challenged Cooley in 1964. He almost won, despite the dismal performance of his party's presidential nominee. Echoing Helms's themes, Gardner ran again in 1966 with the political cycle favoring him. Six years' worth of *Viewpoints,* including many critical of Cooley, had laid the groundwork for the Republican victory.

In the late 1950s, while still at the Bankers Association, Helms had expressed his "zeal to unseat Cooley." Cooley was the main opponent of Secretary of Agriculture Benson's effort to move farm policy away from subsidies. Although he thought about challenging Cooley himself in the early 1960s, Helms ended up supporting Gardner in 1964 and 1966. Cooley represented Raleigh and the rest of the Fourth District in Congress. He was the powerful chair of the House Agriculture Committee and a New Deal survivor first elected in 1934. He stood for just about everything Helms disliked about southern moderates. He supported the New Deal and foreign aid and refused to sign the Southern Manifesto. Most irritating of all to Helms, however, was Cooley's ability to shepherd agriculture spending bills through Congress. This legislation included price supports for farm products like tobacco, cotton, and sugar, which Helms despised for their cost and their intervention in the market. Helms used his Washington connections, particularly Earl Butz, assistant secretary of agriculture in the Eisenhower administration, to gather information. "I do hope you will keep in touch with me, particularly in cases where we may catch Cooley off base." Helms confided to Butz, "I'm trying to build a file on him that will be of benefit to anybody who may oppose him in 1958."[43]

Cooley easily won reelection in 1958, and his power grew during the Kennedy and Johnson administrations. He supported Johnson's Great Society, including the "war on poverty" and Medicare. As chair of the agriculture committee, he helped create the food stamp program. Once at WRAL, Helms continued to gather information on Cooley mostly through Butz, who was now dean of Purdue's school of agriculture. The "intelligence" ended up in *Viewpoint*. "Cooley has presided over the committee for most of the time that this nation's so-called sugar program—indeed, the entire farm program—has snowballed into a sticky, incredibly expensive, and alarmingly dangerous hodgepodge of quotas, controls, subsidies and political manipulations." The commentary emphasized that the sugar program cost taxpayers "582 million dollars" and that imported sugar cost U.S. consumers "446 million dollars above the world market price." Helms threw in a corruption accusation. Congressman Cooley was "entitled to a presumption of innocence" in charges that he granted favors to "Dictator" Rafael Trujillo of the Dominican Republic, but "as long as he defends the present system he is merely defending the indefensible." Helms viewed the tobacco and cotton farm programs with equal disdain, but since North Carolinians did not grow any sugar, it was a safe target.[44]

Helms also assaulted the food stamp program Cooley championed. Congress, he announced, had just passed "a give away plan sponsored by Mr. Cooley." The "so-called food stamp plan . . . in effect puts the federal government in the business of distributing free food just before election time." Helms also targeted Cooley as "the only member of the North Carolina delegation" to vote for the "4 billion dollar foreign aid bill," which sent "American taxpayers' money all around the world, among friends and foes alike." When Cooley availed himself of the chance to respond to the attacks, Helms had the last word. "Still, Mr. Cooley is answering a charge that has never been made—certainly not by us."[45]

In 1964, Cooley faced his strongest opponent in years—thirty-one-year-old Republican James Gardner. Cooley had represented the Fourth District for most of Gardner's life. Gardner lost by just five thousand votes in a heavily Democratic district. Helms was instrumental in recruiting Gardner to run in 1964 and again in 1966.[46]

Helms kept the pressure on Cooley. The congressman resented the constant attacks, but he had limited options. A *Viewpoint* in July 1965 especially perturbed him. Helms described a "shaky farm bill" that was "pock-marked with compromise. Cotton farmers see disaster written for them throughout the bill." Making Cooley's position even worse, "Johnson has sent word from the White House," Helms alleged, "that farmers of the nation are to be helpless pawns if Southern Congressmen and Senators do not vote to repeal, by federal law, all of the right-to-work laws." Helms pronounced it "too late" for Cooley "to retrace his steps and to erase the trades and barters he has made in the past with those who have been so determined to impose a dictatorial control upon the people of America."[47]

Cooley wrote an angry letter to A. J. Fletcher: "Every time I go home someone asks me why Jesse is constantly criticizing me." In his *Viewpoint* on the farm bill, Helms had depicted the usual legislative process as threatening freedom. "I am certain," Cooley charged, that Helms's commentary "was maliciously inspired, factually false and prompted for one and only one purpose and that was to libel and slander me." Pointing to his vote against repealing "right-to-work laws," the congressman said, "Jesse seems to feel that he is some sort of an oracle of God." Fletcher offered Cooley a chance to appear on *Viewpoint*. Cooley decided against it. Responding to Helms's allegations might give them legitimacy, and Helms would get the last word. "I still think he is a skunk," Cooley observed, "and I do not want to get into a spraying contest with him."[48]

In 1964 Cooley benefited from Johnson's victory in the state, but by 1966 Johnson's popularity had waned. Polls revealed a backlash against the president's civil rights and Great Society programs, worries over inflation and taxes, and doubts about the administration's conduct of the war in Vietnam. Gardner echoed Helms's criticism of Cooley. He charged repeatedly that the congressman was a "rubber stamp" for Johnson's policies and argued that 70 percent of the war on poverty went for administrative salaries. Cooley had served foreign sugar interests, not the state's farmers, he said. Gardner advocated cuts in federal spending to ease inflation and taxes and doing whatever it took to win in Vietnam. Cooley emphasized his experience and his power. With voters dissatisfied, Cooley defended the status quo. His age—sixty-nine—and experience only reinforced voters' association of him with the national Democratic Party they increasingly distrusted. But Cooley had an overwhelming voter-registration advantage. Democrats outnumbered Republicans almost five to one in the district.[49]

A week before the vote, WRAL-TV and Helms became a campaign issue over the broadcast of film excerpted from a debate between the candidates at North Carolina State University. The Gardner campaign ran a newspaper ad announcing the broadcast: "Plan to see the famous N.C.S.U. confrontation between Jim Gardner & Harold Cooley tonight on Channel 5." The ad looked like a typical WRAL program announcement except for small print identifying it as a Gardner political advertisement. Although the film had run twice before, once on WRAL and once on Durham station WTVD, Cooley went to WRAL to try to stop the station from running it. Helms and Fred and A. J. Fletcher met with him. According to Cooley's account, they tried to dupe him. All three denied that WRAL had "made a tape" or had any knowledge of "the film having been edited and distorted." Cooley refused to be put off. They admitted the station had leased film of the debate to the Gardner campaign, but that was where WRAL's involvement ended. Cooley told them that broadcasting the film a second time would violate FCC regulations.[50]

Cooley's implied threat to involve the FCC must have raised alarms with the three WRAL executives. Cooley, win or lose, had powerful friends in Washington. They agreed to Cooley's request to screen the film for the three North Carolina State University professors who had participated in the debate. The professors also felt that the edited film was a "fraud and distortion" and advised against its airing. The Fairness Doctrine had a clear impact on WRAL's response. But Helms and his colleagues knew what the rules were and had a pretty good idea of what they could get away with. WRAL could not censor the paid political ad of Gardner, the executives insisted, but they did offer Cooley equal time. Cooley refused, declaring that his campaign had been "irreparably injured." He later explained, "I felt that any statement that I might make or that any member of my staff might make would be considered a partisan response to a factual situation. . . . The program in question did not present the direct editorial opinion but rather it was a distortion of an actual event which was presented in the form of news coverage." The Cooley campaign requested WRAL's film the following day. But the Cooley campaign declared the footage was a mangled mess that they could not use.[51]

Two days after the film aired, the professors—James Maddox, Abraham Holtzman, and Edward Ezell—released a statement saying that "Gardner's filmed version . . . distorts the real debate" and that the edited film "crudely" interrupted Cooley's "responses to a number of questions which were in fact answered by him." The *News and Observer* reported that the "cut film" depicted "Gardner as a smooth talking, quick thinking young politician and the veteran Cooley as bumbling and slow." Cooley attacked Gardner for making "a travesty of this forum by cropping, editing, revising and totally distorting the filmed version." His editing of the film, Cooley said, demonstrated that "my opponent . . . does not have sufficient confidence that his performance at N. C. State would stand up to the scrutiny of intelligent voters without altering the image he presented."[52]

The day before the election, the professors telegraphed a formal complaint to the FCC calling for an investigation into WRAL's broadcast of the film. At a press conference that day, Cooley responded to a reporter's question about the FCC complaint with a long tirade against WRAL-TV. His rambling, incoherent answer recounted his version of events, including the meeting the previous Monday at WRAL and his effort to persuade the station not to air the edited film. Cooley's attack on WRAL was a mistake. He only mentioned his opponent in passing. WRAL and Helms were immensely popular with many of the voters whose support he needed. Whatever the station's role, Cooley had to defeat Gardner, not Helms. His previous public remarks had kept that reality in mind by blaming Gardner for the film.[53]

Cooley's press conference also offered Helms an opening. That evening WRAL ran Cooley's disjointed attack on *Dateline* at the top of the hour and announced that Helms's response would follow on *Viewpoint*. Helms began by reminding viewers of the station's policy of not formally endorsing candidates. "We do not propose to alter that policy today. On the other hand, there has been a strange development in the Gardner-Cooley congressional race, a deliberately trumped-up 'issue' that cries out for the record to be set straight." Helms's non-endorsement endorsement managed to support Gardner and denounce Cooley all in the name of defending the station against "false attacks." Helms said, "WRAL-Television has been deliberately and directly attacked by agents of Congressman Harold Cooley, and at least implicitly by the Congressman himself, we feel obliged to observe that the Congressman and his friends are knowingly tampering with the truth." Helms denied that WRAL had edited the film.

Moreover, WRAL had given Cooley the film on "the same commercial basis" with which they gave it to Gardner. Helms maintained Cooley could have presented his own film "calculated to enhance his image." The professors' FCC complaint was a "contrived controversy" designed to intimidate WRAL. Helms closed, "If Mr. Cooley feels that he flunked his screen test in his confrontation with Mr. Gardner at N.C. State University, it would have been more graceful for him to have chalked up the sad experience as a bad performance."[54]

To protect itself against an FCC investigation, the station borrowed a complete film of the debate from NBC and planned to run it at 11:30 p.m. At 6:15 p.m. WRAL sent Cooley a copy of the editorial with an offer of equal time. This was twenty minutes before it aired and about twelve hours before the voting started. The campaign staff called at once to accept the offer of equal time, but WRAL personnel informed them that "no one on duty was authorized to comply with WRAL-TV's offer of equal time." Despite repeated attempts, WRAL ignored the Cooley campaign's efforts to make a response for three hours. Finally, at 9:30 p.m., A. J. Fletcher called Cooley and said they would air his response at 11:30 before their broadcast of the debate. Allen Paul, Cooley's campaign manager, delivered the response. The next day Cooley lost the election by 13,000 votes—5,900 in Wake County—a victory that Helms celebrated in two *Viewpoints*.[55]

Cooley filed an FCC complaint ten days after the election. "Capitol Broadcasting Company, its officials, principals and personnel, promoted and engaged in a conspiracy," he contended, "the object of which was my defeat as a candidate for reelection to the United States Congress." Cooley made three major complaints. "WRAL-TV lent material, facilities and personnel to the production and airing of a television program on behalf of James Gardner . . . which totally and willfully distorted the panel discussion between the candidates." Cooley believed WRAL was ultimately responsible, labeling WRAL "the original producer of this film." Second, like Richardson Preyer in 1964, Cooley found WRAL's news biased and accused the station of slanting its news coverage in favor of Gardner. WRAL had covered Gardner's announcement of Housing and Urban Development's plans to build an "industrial training facility" in the district. The report, Cooley concluded, left the impression that Gardner secured the facility when the congressman was the real force behind the decision. Cooley released the details of his efforts with HUD, but WRAL disregarded them. The station also ignored campaign appearances for Cooley by conservative Democrats Governor Dan Moore and Senator Sam Ervin, while other stations covered them.[56]

And third, the night before the election, "WRAL-TV failed to provide Congressman Cooley a reasonable opportunity to take advantage of equal time to respond to an editorial attacking him broadcast by Jesse Helms." Helms's *Viewpoint*, the congressman asserted, was a "vicious personal attack" just hours before the voting began. WRAL failed to "adhere to the modicum of fairness" that the FCC stipulated. The station had ignored requests for equal time until it was too late for Cooley's campaign to respond in anything like an equivalent timeslot. WRAL ran Cooley campaign's response at 11:30, when few people were watching.[57]

Helms and WRAL approached the FCC investigation as they had the one in 1963. WRAL demonstrated that it ran half as many stories on Gardner as it did on Cooley, who was after all the incumbent.[58] But the noncoverage of rallies with Governor Moore and Senator Ervin implied a pattern to the omissions that the FCC missed. Moore and Ervin were powerful members of the conservative wing of the North Carolina Democratic Party. Cooley was a moderate. He needed Moore and Ervin to say that Cooley was okay with them. Helms routinely associated conservative Democrats like Moore and Ervin with Republicans. He privileged ideology over party, while the conservative Democrats put party first, at least during general elections. Helms's limited coverage of conservative endorsements for Cooley while covering the support of moderates like Sanford was a subtle way of undermining his candidacy.

The station documented that it had no role in producing the film, as Helms and the Fletchers had insisted from the beginning. WRAL supplied an affidavit from Gardner's publicity director, Earl Cox, stating he produced the film. Cox had acquired film from WTVD and WRAL and edited it at WTVD's studios in Durham. His account is especially credible, since he was a former WTVD employee already familiar with that station's equipment. Despite the fact that WTVD also supplied film to the Gardner campaign and the film ran on WTVD first, Cooley and his associates persistently conflated WRAL's role in filming the debate for their news coverage and the actual production of the campaign film. Cooley let his anger at Helms and WRAL lead him into an attack on the station the day before the election. He lost sight of his purpose—defeating Gardner. Cooley's focus on WRAL revealed the extent to which Helms got under Democrats' skin. They blamed Helms and the Fletchers for their political losses in eastern North Carolina. In a post-election letter to a friend, Cooley charged that WRAL-TV was "out to destroy the Democratic Party." He added an observation about Fletcher that he could have also made of Helms: "'A. J.' came up the hard way and he believes that everybody else should come up the hard way." In fact, that was not a bad summary of much of Helms's outlook.[59]

The most serious charge, and the one that would stick, was the failure the night before the election to allow Cooley to respond to *Viewpoint* in a timely manner. The executives' explanation of their unavailability was unconvincing: "It was the dinner hour and none of the station's officers was at the station."[60]

WRAL's license was up for renewal in December 1966. The issue the FCC faced was whether to have a hearing investigating the complaints against the station or simply renew WRAL's license. Congressman Gardner kept Helms apprised of the mood in Congress regarding the Fairness Doctrine. Several Democrats, including Speaker of the House John McCormack, wanted aggressive enforcement. But Gardner judged they lacked the support to apply sufficient pressure to the FCC. Still, Helms was cautious. When Gardner asked him to speak at a fund-raiser, Helms put him off "until this company's travail with the bureaucrats has been settled."[61]

The FCC's decision was divided three to two in WRAL-TV's favor against any further inquiry. Secretary Waple wrote for the majority that Cooley and the other petitioners had not advanced "substantial and material questions of fact . . . which would warrant an evidentiary hearing." The majority agreed that WRAL acted properly in not censoring a paid political ad and noted that the station offered Cooley equal time and supplied him the film on the same terms. The commissioners also understood that the station had not produced the edited film, and it accepted the station's contention that it had given Cooley twice the coverage of Gardner. But the commissioners faulted the station for not allowing a timely response to Helms's *Viewpoint*. "Since time was of the essence, we do not believe that WRAL-TV fully met its obligation. . . . [I]t should have held itself open and ready to facilitate petitioner's reply." Commissioner Kenneth Cox wrote a dissent from the majority opinion. He rejected the application of the "no censorship" rule to political advertisements "concocted by editing and splicing film," noting that this was the "first time" the commission had applied the rule in this way. Cox observed, in sympathy with Cooley, that "if someone manufactures a carefully cut and spliced series of filmed sequences," then it "is very hard to counteract because it requires much detailed explanation, and, above all, the impact of this kind of thing on the public is incalculably greater than the candidate's mere spoken statement." He recognized that the FCC could not make licensees responsible "for every bit of film" they ran, "but surely it is not too much to ask him to investigate when the opponent shown in the film complains." Cox also wanted to know more about the production of the film and about the unavailability of WRAL officials the night before the election. Moreover, WRAL's past record made him suspicious: "We have had problems with this station before."[62]

Helms had stretched what he could get away with to the absolute limit. The FCC renewed the station's license, but WRAL had to wait for the decision until July 1967. During the wait, Helms told an audience in Miami that the Fairness Doctrine validated "the censorship—and that's what it amounts to—practiced both subtly and overtly by the FCC." A year later, when Meredith College invited him to speak on the topic of censorship, Helms had softened a bit. "I happen to be in that part of the communications business where the government does practice intimidation, if not actual censorship," Helms averred. He went on with effusive sarcasm, the "FCC will tell you, in a few thousand well-chosen words, that it does not believe in censorship. No, sir! And, for a fact, I cannot say that we—at my station—have ever been successfully censored. But we have been in hot water almost constantly." But he judged that others had self-censored in response to the FCC's pressure. And in an understated admission, Helms acknowledged, "We haven't gone that far in our efforts to comply with the 'Fairness Doctrine.'"[63]

Could Helms take credit for Gardner's win? On the one hand, Cooley had been in trouble weeks before Helms's *Viewpoint* attacking him. After learning of WRAL's license renewal, Cooley protested, "My one great complaint was that a public service record was destroyed."[64] Cooley had repeatedly made this lament. Today this concern over the sanctity of a political debate seems naive. Cooley and his campaign appeared unprepared for a tough political challenge in an era of television and two-party competition. Cooley had spent his decades in office mastering the arcane legislative process and rarely faced a serious challenger, but the state was changing. Gardner won the district's cities, where voters had no direct stake in the agriculture legislation Cooley oversaw. Moreover, Cooley associated himself with the national Democratic Party, especially President Johnson. This strategy had served him well before, but the fall in Johnson's popularity due to civil rights issues, the Great Society, and the Vietnam War meant the national party and the president were liabilities. Gardner's campaign employed Earl Cox, who had a background in television. The campaign recognized the potential impact of contrasting their young candidate and the sixty-nine-year-old Cooley in a year when voters were dissatisfied with the status quo.

On the other hand, Helms took credit for Lake's winning Wake County in the 1964 gubernatorial primary—a victory he interpreted as an anti-Sanford vote. WRAL was responsible for that vote, he believed, "because we kept pounding Sanford."[65] Helms had hammered away at Cooley for years. If Helms's undermining of the governor led to an anti-Sanford vote in a year when Sanford was not on the ballot, then his attacks on Cooley had a potentially greater impact. Gardner picked up Helms's themes and ran an effective campaign in a year when the political cycle favored him. In addition to attacks on the congressman, Helms was responsible for undermining Lyndon Johnson through his questioning of civil rights, the Great Society, and the president's conduct of the Vietnam War—all critical to Gardner's victory. In fact, Helms's attacks on the Great Society and the war on poverty developed many of the issues conservatives would use for decades. Gardner's election was the first significant fruit of Helms's conservative alternative. The victory demonstrated the viability of a conservative Republican candidate in eastern North Carolina—the state's most heavily Democratic region. The west already had two Republican congressmen, Charles Jonas of Charlotte and James Broyhill of Lenoir. Now it seemed a conservative Republican could win a statewide race. Helms saw his political ideas vindicated in the election and was more tempted than ever to run for office. Gardner benefited from the backlash, and it would only grow.

In 1968 Helms was a factor again in the state's elections. He supported Richard Nixon, with a nod to Alabama governor George Wallace to keep Nixon conservative. Gardner, with Helms's encouragement, ran for governor. In fact, Helms was significant enough to the congressman's plans for him to put off making the decision to run until he conferred with Helms. While praising him on WRAL, Helms advised Gardner on fund-raising and other issues. One *Viewpoint* questioned the *News and Observer* for criticizing Gardner and Senator Sam Ervin. The linking of the Republican and the conservative Democrat was strategic. Helms explained to Gardner, "I thought well of tying you and Senator Ervin together." Helms also attempted to undermine Gardner's eventual opponent in the general election, Lieutenant Governor Robert Scott. Scott, Helms reminded voters, had won the "bloc votes" in his previous elections. But Scott reacted differently from other moderate Democrats who had felt Helms's heat. Rather than file an FCC complaint, he maneuvered to protect his right flank. After the election, he courted conservatives, including Helms. Moderate Democrats recognized that Helms and his conservative alternative were part of the political landscape. Complaining to the FCC would not rid the state of Helms and might even redound to Helms's benefit. Helms had demonstrated not only that he could turn the station's policy of airing dissent to conservatism's advantage but also that he could defy the Fairness Doctrine without repercussions. Republican Earl Butz suggested "it would be a good stunt" to write "Brother Cooley" to express WRAL's gratitude: "I think the Station is indebted to him."[66]

Figure 1. Jesse Helms (*third from left*) in his naval uniform at Josephus Daniels's 80th birthday party in 1942. Courtesy of the North Carolina State Archives.

Above: Figure 2. Jesse Helms (*first from left*) at the North Carolina Bankers Association in 1955. Courtesy of the North Carolina State Archives.

Left: Figure 3. Jesse Helms as member of the Raleigh City Council in 1957. Courtesy of the North Carolina State Archives.

Figure 4. Democratic nominee for governor Hargrave "Skipper" Bowles and Republican nominee for Senate Jesse Helms share a laugh in a tobacco warehouse during the 1972 campaign. They were childhood friends. The North Carolina Collection, University of North Carolina at Chapel Hill Library.

Figure 5. Jesse Helms speaking at Young Republicans Convention in 1973. Courtesy of the North Carolina State Archives.

4

Backlash

The Great Society, Vietnam, and Conservative Solutions

Before the 1964 election, President Johnson began using the term "Great Society" to sum up his domestic agenda, including the war on poverty, Medicare, Medicaid, civil rights, education, and the environment. Johnson's Great Society committed the federal government to advancing social justice. The passage of Great Society legislation from 1964 to 1966 left Helms despondent. "I wonder," he wrote fellow conservative commentator Clarence Manion, "if all of us aren't wasting our breath." LBJ's conduct of the war in Vietnam was another reason for despair. "And isn't it wonderful that Barry wasn't elected in November!" Helms wrote James Gardner in 1965. "If it weren't for Lyndon, we wouldn't be enjoying all that peace in Vietnam."[1]

In the years after Johnson's landslide, white voters in eastern North Carolina and the rest of the South grew increasingly disenchanted with liberalism. Helms recognized that racial backlash and the unpopular war presented conservatives with their best opportunities in a generation. After half a decade on the air, pious incitement gained traction. Helms's pious incitement proved central to Republican victories in 1966 and 1968. The things that upset him the most allowed Helms to make the case against Democrats. He stoked viewer unease over black voters, the Great Society—especially the war on poverty, the Watts riot, the Black Power Movement, the Cold War, the University of North Carolina, and the sexual revolution. Since the Cold War entailed a series of indecisive clashes, Helms repeatedly accused Democrats of failure. He defended literacy tests and portrayed African Americans as menacing.

Helms also enlarged his religious and moral provocation, which he had begun with the Supreme Court rulings on prayer. American attitudes toward sex and morality were gradually shifting. In 1960, the birth control pill gave women increased control over their reproductive lives. Numerous developments from magazines like *Cosmopolitan* and Hollywood films to the counterculture's Summer of Love in 1967 challenged traditional attitudes toward sex and morality. These developments—the beginning of the sexual revolution—upset conservative Christians.[2] Helms injected allegations of sexual licentiousness into his attacks on the civil rights movement, welfare, and the liberalism of the University of North Carolina. Although his charges were often unfounded, he succeeded in politicizing disapproval of the sexual revolution and connecting it to liberals.

Helms, though, did not just criticize liberal efforts. He advocated the values of the small-town South as a conservative alternative. He played a role in building private schools and private charity and even proposed a private affirmative action plan—all alternatives to the government-based action championed by liberals. Helms's solutions would leave local elites in control and keep out the federal government. Change in race relations would occur slowly if at all. And Helms demanded that government follow the same model as his private charity—which was only for the "deserving."

Despite the backlash, liberal influence seemed pervasive to Helms, even in a southern state like North Carolina. "I am a Baptist and about the only charitable thing I can say about the Baptist leadership is thank God I'm not a Methodist." Southern Baptist leaders attempted to shift the church in a liberal direction on racial and social issues during the 1960s. Helms resisted.[3]

The 1965 Voting Rights Act, the Watts Riot, and Black Power

Helms's concerns about the civil rights movement had always centered on black voters. Lyndon Johnson's landslide victory in 1964 seemed to confirm Helms's worst fears regarding black voters and liberal Democrats. Johnson's coattails swept into office one of the most liberal Congresses in history. And voting rights violations remained widespread in the South, so the full potential of African American voters had not been realized. After the 1964 election, the civil rights movement garnered national attention for voting rights. Helms's unfettered pious incitement blamed the violence of southern law enforcement and Klansmen on civil rights activists, King, and President Johnson. But his charges were not limited to racial provocation: he added sensational allegations of sexual depravity. Helms was determined to convince viewers to vote against Democrats. But as long as the media focused on the nonviolent movement in the South, conservatives gained little ground nationally. When the Watts riot followed the Voting Rights Act in August 1965, media coverage shifted and the backlash accelerated. The Black Power Movement received national attention in 1966. The national stories harmonized with Helms's local narrative.

Early in 1965, Martin Luther King Jr. and other civil rights leaders chose Selma, Alabama, for voting rights protests. Selma was 60 percent black, but less than 1 percent of African Americans were registered. Like Birmingham, Selma had a volatile law enforcement official, Sheriff Jim Clark. After a state trooper killed a protester, Jimmy Lee Jackson, activists organized a memorial march from Selma to Montgomery for Sunday, March 7, 1965. Sheriff Clark, his deputies, and state troopers charged the marchers at the Edmund Pettus Bridge. The televised assault on peaceful marchers, labeled "Bloody Sunday," outraged the American public. But Helms attributed the brutality of Alabama law enforcement to the marchers. "Martin Luther King repeatedly refers to his 'non-violent movement.' It is about as non-violent as the Marines landing on Iwo Jima, and it is a 'movement' only in the sense that mob action is moving and spreading throughout the land."[4]

Public opinion and the congressional mood shifted toward action. On March 15, in a televised speech to Congress, the president urged the passage of voting rights legislation. Johnson astonished his audience with the lines from the movement's anthem: "Because it is not just Negroes, but really it is all of us, who must overcome the crippling legacy of bigotry and injustice." Pausing to let the drama build, he chimed, "And we shall overcome." Senators, House members, and Supreme Court justices rose in an ovation. President Johnson "made clear that he addressed not an independent Congress," Helms contended, "but one that—by whatever circumstance—would do his bidding." To Helms the applause demonstrated subjugation. A government and a nation supporting African American voting rights made Helms think of Nazis. "The pages of history are filled with the orations of monarchs who talked of justice while riding the crest of passions and emotions. Hardly anyone challenged the Third Reich."[5]

Helms expressed faith in Governor George Wallace's assurances that Alabama would register voters "on a non-discriminatory basis," but he also admitted that "foolish laws" sometimes denied "Negroes their right to vote." Still, he valued literacy tests. Helms warned southern states to change their most abusive practices before the federal government required all states to "register everybody" even if they could not "read and write." Ending literacy tests would mean "more of what Southerners call 'bloc voting.'"[6]

On March 21, the March to Montgomery resumed. Led by King and other civil rights leaders, thousands of marchers from all over the nation participated in the five-day journey to Montgomery. The evening the march ended, an Alabama Klansman shot a white Detroit woman, Viola Liuzzo. On *Viewpoint* Helms wondered if the four Klansmen arrested for Liuzzo's murder were "acting as Klansmen or as individuals. The larger question, and America may as well face it, is why and how did the rage of these men become so great as to prompt them to commit such an outrage?" National leaders deserved the blame. "Let Lyndon Johnson and Hubert Humphrey and Martin Luther King, and all the rest, probe their own consciences. Can it be honestly said that there was no deliberate provocation of violence in Alabama?"[7]

Helms found particularly infuriating the support of clergy for civil rights and the Montgomery march. On *Viewpoint* he praised the opposition of conservative clergy. Dr. Kenneth Goodson, a Methodist bishop in Alabama, described the march as a "disservice to freedom," and "equally prominent" rabbis and Catholic and Episcopal priests agreed with him. Moreover, a congressman charged "that shocking sexual activities and general depravity went on constantly during the nighttime hours of the March to Montgomery." King had just ignored the congressman and others making such allegations. "Yet the press and the radio and television continue to portray this monstrous violation of human decency as a gallant bid for freedom."[8]

Rev. W. W. Finlator of the Pullen Park Baptist Church in Raleigh defended the marchers against allegations of "immorality and sexual depravity." Finlator and Pullen Park Baptist, located near North Carolina State University, were known for liberalism. On *Viewpoint* Helms advised Finlator to stick to the "facts." "But perhaps one cannot really expect fairness of a minister making a political speech." Little incensed Helms more than ministers who failed to see the conservative light. Because of its support for civil rights, he painted the National Council of Churches as an extremist group. Helms and his pastor at the First Baptist Church of Raleigh, where Helms was a deacon, clashed over church funding for the NCC, but Helms gave no ground. "I have told my own pastor, he does not have the right to withhold from his congregation the full story of the National Council of Churches." He accused his pastor of "out-Finlatoring Finlator." By 1966 his dissatisfaction had grown sufficiently that Helms and his family moved to Hayes Barton Baptist Church. "My last Sunday at First Baptist was on the occasion of the declaration from the pulpit that one cannot be a Christian unless he supports the United Nations. That was merely the *final* straw."[9]

In August 1965 the Voting Rights Act passed, and black voter registration in the South climbed steadily. Helms dreaded black voters' impact: "I fear we have reached the point that unless one has an assurance of the Negro bloc vote, he may as well not announce." If Democrats could hold onto a significant portion of the southern white vote along with the increased black vote, then moderate Democrats would be dominant in the South. Goldwater's defeat in seven southern states suggested it was feasible. Helms confided to a viewer, "I have some friends in Mississippi who have actually purchased land in Australia. . . . Of course, in the case of Mississippi, that will be soon a Negro republic (or a Negro dictatorship)." But Helms knew that gaining black support and keeping enough white voters in the South to win a majority would be difficult. For decades southern candidates who campaigned for black votes had faced calls for white unity. Such calls had defeated Richardson Preyer in 1964 and Frank Porter Graham in 1950. That, after all, was why Helms reported on the "bloc vote."[10]

Eight days after Johnson signed the Voting Rights Act, a white policeman arrested a black man for drunk driving in Watts, a black ghetto in Los Angeles. The man's mother called for help, and a crowd began throwing rocks and bottles. For the next six days Watts burned. The riot ended with four thousand arrests, thirty-four deaths, and the neighborhood gutted. Some participants demonstrated a political consciousness behind their mayhem, denouncing living conditions and police brutality. That the riot occurred so soon after the Voting Rights Act gave Helms a macabre reason for optimism. In the coming weeks he repeatedly returned to the riot on *Viewpoint*. It was the political opportunity the right needed to counter decades of liberal influence. "Ours is a generation that has condoned, if not encouraged, a sense of irresponsibility that is now engulfing our way of life."[11]

Helms's pious incitement over Watts and later riots resembled his attacks on the civil rights movement and crime. Since the Freedom Rides, Helms had called peaceful demonstrations mobs and denounced protesters for police and vigilantes' assaults on them. After Watts he conflated rioters with protesters and made King and the president responsible for both. "The President may talk of his 'Great Society' and Martin Luther King can talk of his 'non-violent movement,' but the American public has distinct awareness of what really was the source of the shocking violence and bloodshed at Los Angeles." Helms's approach might be similar, but Watts was different and he knew it. He saw "hopeful signs" after the riot that Dr. King was losing influence. "Most of the country laughed earlier in the week when this presumptuous man announced that he was going to California on a mission of 'love.'"[12]

Helms interpreted Watts as a vindication of conservatism. Watts, he thought, discredited unemployment benefits and other social welfare programs. "If idleness is the devil's workshop," Americans should reconsider "the mad desire of the nation to create even more idleness" through federal unemployment payments. Government had taught "vast numbers of Americans . . . that loafing is an honorable career. It is government policy to pay people not to work." He connected unemployment benefits and welfare directly to the riot. "How many of these, one might well wonder, did a day's work prior to spending the night in such a riotous and angry frolic?"[13]

"We are witnessing a breakdown in law and order." Watts made that evident. Police forces, Helms charged, were neutralized "by mobs claiming that they are protesting 'police brutality.'" This insolence, which led the nation to the verge of "chaos," had two causes. First, the federal courts "have so broadened what they call the 'constitutional rights' of criminals" that police are afraid to defend themselves. The second was Dr. King's "dangerous theory" that "certain citizens may resist what they choose to regard as unjust laws." The president merely echoed King. Johnson welcomed "a group of beatnik law violators recently" as "fellow revolutionaries."[14]

Helms castigated Jonathan Daniels and liberals for their "society-is-to-blame thesis" with regard to riots and crime. In an editorial, Daniels blamed the "racial violence" in Orangeburg, South Carolina, on local conservative elites for ignoring the 1964 Civil Rights Act.[15] But it was not a question, as Helms suggested, of personal responsibility versus blaming society. Helms only blamed different elements of society—liberals and activists. The president, Dr. King's movement, and Democrats' programs beginning with the New Deal, Helms reasoned, were responsible not only for riots but also for the murder of Viola Liuzzo and everything else wrong in the nation.

Watts and later riots received the kind of expansive coverage afforded the civil rights movement, but they cut the opposite way. No longer were African Americans fighting southern oppression. The issues were complex and malleable to conservative ends. Media coverage of Watts—the first televised riot and the worst since World War II—and riots later in the decade shifted white opinion rightward. The tone of civil rights coverage shifted, too. King's slide was apparent, Helms suggested, in the *Washington Post* headline "Northern Negroes Cool to King's Campaign." The *Post* usually "helped inflate King's self-importance."[16]

King faced challenges from "other Negroes," Helms suggested, because they wanted "the publicity and the financial rewards that go along with the 'leadership' of the race." Notwithstanding his refusal to take seriously the goals of black activists, Helms was correct that other leaders, particularly younger men, were challenging King. Although he dismissed it as "pretense," Helms recognized that King opposed violence. And he knew that the younger activists' rhetoric made them easy targets for conservatives.[17]

This contest for leadership came out into the open after the wounding of activist James Meredith. In June 1966, the day before an election, a white supremacist shot Meredith as he marched across Mississippi to call attention to ongoing voting rights violations. Helms called the violence absurd, idiotic, hotheaded, and reckless but insisted that "Meredith was only superficially flecked by a teaspoonful of buckshot. Many a chicken thief has paid a heavier penalty." The incident, Helms suggested, was a boon for Meredith because it would revive the "lagging" sales of his book. Helms maintained that black Mississippians were "disinterested in the business of registering to vote, and even less interested—as Tuesday's election proved—in going to the polls." He ignored the climate of intimidation in Mississippi, which the shooting aggravated.[18]

Within a few days, other activists and organizations—King and the Southern Christian Leadership Conference, Floyd McKissick of the

Congress of Racial Equality, and Stokely Carmichael of the Student Non-violent Coordinating Committee—picked up Meredith's march. The marchers intended to demonstrate Mississippi authorities' noncompliance with the Voting Rights Act. But the march also revealed sharp generational divisions among civil rights leaders. Young activists like Carmichael expressed dissatisfaction with King's nonviolence and ties to liberal Democrats.[19]

A turning point came with Carmichael's June 16 arrest in Greenwood, Mississippi. At a rally after his release, Carmichael raged, "We been saying freedom for six years and we ain't got nothin'. What we gonna start saying now is Black Power!" The crowd began chanting "Black Power" with him. Black power's meaning was ambiguous, but it questioned the movement's nonviolence and ultimately integration's value. The phrase "black power," King argued, "would confuse our allies, isolate the Negro community, and give many prejudiced whites, who might otherwise be ashamed of their anti-Negro feeling, a ready excuse for self-justification."[20]

Helms seized on the news of "the just-concluded 'march' in Mississippi" as evidence of "belligerent demands for 'freedom.'" His commentary tied together riots, civil rights, and the Ku Klux Klan. What was the "thread" that linked the "trouble spots"? "In Watts in Los Angeles, in Harlem, in Chicago, in Mississippi, violence has been encouraged—even provoked deliberately—in the name of non-violence and on the pretense that freedom has been denied." And Helms asserted, "An unlawfully pitched tent by Negroes in Mississippi is no less an affront to society than, say, efforts by the Ku Klux Klan to set up camp on the lawns of Broughton High School in Raleigh."[21]

As Klan activity spiked in North Carolina, WRAL treated Klansmen and civil rights activists as moral equivalents. On *Viewpoint*, Helms complained that "the Ku Kluxers got from the news media an expected and perhaps deserved working-over," while the newspapers let King "come and go" without demanding "straight answers to some important questions." Governor Moore successfully blocked Klan rallies in the state, while the highway patrol protected civil rights protesters. WRAL's news department pressed the governor on his alleged double standard.[22]

Carmichael's assertion of black power made him a national figure. He addressed students in Berkeley, California, in October 1966. Black power, he explained, meant self-definition, collective action, and black racial identity as the means to liberation. "We are oppressed as a group because we are black." The only escape from oppression lay in wielding "the group power we have." Carmichael equated African Americans' situation to the position of nonwhites around the world. "If South America were to rebel today, and black people were to shoot the hell out of all the white people there, as they should, Standard Oil would crumble tomorrow."[23]

Carmichael's visibility led Helms to assail him. In 1966 the Nobel committee would not award a Peace Prize. Helms sniffed, "Martin Luther King got the prize last year," so the decision was a relief. "Perhaps it was too difficult for the committee to choose between Stokely Carmichael and Ho Chi Minh."[24]

In many respects, Helms and Carmichael represented a polarization of the nation in culture and politics. They differed in obvious ways: race, generation, and ideology. But what carried the most significance for the nation were their similarities. Both men castigated the national media. Both rejected moderation and targeted liberals. Both expressed rage through violent, angry rhetoric. And both called urban riots rebellions. Helms and Carmichael tapped into raw emotion. Whites resented guarantees of black rights, and blacks resented having to struggle for constitutional rights that whites took for granted. Black rage grew out of centuries of oppression and the reluctance of the white majority to acknowledge it. After centuries of privilege, whites felt that privilege was their right. Carmichael's righteous rage, no matter how legitimate, made Helms's predictions of doom seem prescient to WRAL's white audience. His substitution of moral superiority for white supremacy drew the support of both segregationists and conservative advocates of a color-blind America. A new era in American politics dawned in the late 1960s, in which politics revolved around divisive symbols. It favored conservatives like Helms and Richard Nixon.

After years of experimentation with racial and cultural politics, Helms was ready to exploit white backlash. "When Stokely Carmichael takes his rabble-rousings to a campus," Helms complained, "the press associations report without qualifications that he was given a 'standing ovation' and that his mouthings were 'interrupted several times by applause.' We are seldom told that a minority stood, and that a minority applauded." Helms contended that media coverage of Carmichael represented a conspiracy. "It almost had to be planned that way—this device to create distrust and misunderstanding." And he asked, "Who will profit from all of this? And the answer is inescapable: Those who wish to see America destroyed!"[25]

The Cold War and Vietnam

Helms's *Viewpoints* advanced an aggressive interventionist unilateralism. He transformed traditional American isolationism into a rejection of co-operation and compromise with other nations. He cast the Soviet Union and China as the sources of an infectious evil that spread through contact. Helms expected other nations to defer to the United States, acknowledging its power as a wealthy capitalist nation and its moral authority deriving from Christianity and the constitutional tradition. Helms most of all recognized that the frustrations of the Cold War offered opportunities for conservatives. American leaders' failings, he thought, contrasted unfavorably with America's preeminence. The commentator cast liberals as soft on communism no matter what their actual policies and achievements. Recognizing no limits on American power, not even the Soviets' nuclear arsenal, he framed Cold War conflicts in a symbolic language. Compromise and negotiations were anathema, and liberal efforts always fell short because they could not deliver total victory. The United Nations, with its global efforts at cooperation and commitment to multilateralism, embodied everything he disliked about diplomacy: the same multilateralism made it an easy mark.

During December 1961, in a hopeful tone, Helms raised the possibility of the UN's "collapse," which, he averred, was "far from remote." The UN's "failure must be laid at the doorsteps of those who have insisted that peace can be achieved by negotiating and debating and compromising with murderers, thieves, and liars." The Soviet Union's veto in the Security Council forced negotiation and cooperation with communist nations and precluded any efforts to use the UN against communism. "Russia and the rest of the communist bloc in the United Nations," Helms alleged, "have repeatedly used the U-N as a tool of deceit and delay and doubletalk." But the Soviets were not the only troubling aspect of the UN. The United Nations had grown since its creation in 1945. New nations in Asia and Africa joined as they gained their independence from European empires, and many refused to take sides in the Cold War. Viewing these new nations through a racial prism, Helms denounced them as "irresponsible—morally, financially, and in terms of intelligent leadership."[26]

Helms lacked sympathy for anticolonialism and wanted the drive for independence from European empires suppressed. The *Viewpoint* eagerly anticipating the UN's collapse was a response to India's seizure of Goa, part of its territory ruled by Portugal. Goa had been a Portuguese colony for centuries. After years of mounting tensions, India seized Goa in 1961. The Soviets blocked any efforts at the UN to interfere. "In all this, the United Nations," Helms protested, "has served no purpose except to prevent the United States from lending aid to one of our allies."[27]

Helms was, predictably, dismissive of African nations. "Africa is largely uncivilized." He asserted, "The United Nations has moved too rapidly in creating nations on that continent which are not ready for independence." His evidence for this assertion was racially loaded. "For example, the president of the newly independent country of Gabon is a man named Leon M'Ba, who served four years in prison for eating his mother-in-law." Helms, however, was especially partial to the white government of Rhodesia. Southern Rhodesia's white colonial government declared its independence from the British Empire in 1965 to forestall black majority rule. Africans and Europeans were segregated in Rhodesia: whites ran the economy for their benefit. Helms relished Rhodesia's success "in making monkeys of both Great Britain and the United States." His commentary celebrated Rhodesia's economic growth despite the international sanctions against it. "The trouble with our posture in opposition to Rhodesia is that it has been phony from the start. . . . Voting laws are fair, equally applicable to all." Helms even claimed that "the black man in Rhodesia is satisfied with the way things are going."[28]

White Rhodesians fooled no one except the willing. Rhodesia disguised the racist nature of its constitution with property requirements. The white government also banned African political parties and only allowed token black representation. The widespread scorn for Rhodesian fictions angered Helms. "I have made contact with Prime Minister Ian Smith's office," Helms wrote an ally, "and I, too, am receiving some interesting material on Rhodesia. It is amazing to note the things we aren't being told." Helms maintained regular contact with the Rhodesian government. Besides pro-Rhodesia *Viewpoints*, Helms arranged to show films on WRAL that the Rhodesian government provided.[29]

Helms found arms control treaties with the Soviet Union even more troubling than the United Nations and resistance to colonialism. The Cuban missile crisis left Soviet and American leaders alarmed at how close they had come to nuclear war. The ratification of the Nuclear Test Ban Treaty in 1963 reduced tensions but led Helms to claim, "Our leaders talk about fighting communism, but our record is one of appeasement." Even conservatives like North Carolina senator Sam Ervin voted for it. Helms turned the senator's words against him. The treaty, Ervin "said, 'should never have been negotiated.' It will not, he said, 'enhance in any degree the capacity of the United States to defend itself.' . . . Yet, Senator Ervin voted in favor of ratification." Helms painted a fearful image of ratification's implications: "And if we have taken 'the one small step toward peace' we've heard so much about, it may be the kind of peace that is found in tyranny and subjugation."[30]

Helms welcomed a chance to confront communism militarily in Vietnam. "If it's an ill wind that blows no good," Helms suggested, while Congress prepared the Tonkin Gulf Resolution in August 1964, "then perhaps the weird attack by the North Vietnamese PT boats has served to bring us to our senses." He affirmed that "politics stop, as always they must, at the water's edge." Whatever he said to the contrary, however, Helms was not about to suspend politics. The "cohesiveness of a nation" did not require we forget "past mistakes." "History must indeed record the ironies of our involvement in Vietnam, lest future generations repeat our errors in the vain belief that we can defeat a declared enemy by appeasing him." The "real force that struck at our naval vessels this week" was the Soviet Union. "Khrushchev need not commit even one of his troops to armed conflict. He pulls the strings of puppets, first here—then there; in Cuba, in Vietnam, at the Berlin Wall."[31]

Like many Americans, Helms found the limited war that the Johnson administration pursued in Vietnam frustrating. "What Mr. Johnson said . . . is that henceforth we shall have to run harder to stand still in Vietnam." Helms demanded an unrestrained war. "The 125,000 men who will be fighting an undeclared war in Vietnam deserve to be assured that they have not been sent to fight and die in a war they will not be permitted to win." President Johnson, who never considered just withdrawing, faced two options: all-out war or limited war. As it had in Korea, the first option could draw the Chinese into the conflict and might even lead to a nuclear confrontation. It also could destroy the country that the United States was trying to save. Since the risks of the first option were so grave, the only remaining option was a limited war designed to force the Vietnamese to accept division of their nation.[32]

Helms thought aggressive action would lead to victory in Vietnam and against the "single worldwide force" of communism. In 1967 he proclaimed, "Our failure to do what was necessary long ago to *win* in Vietnam is simply a re-run of a tragic era in American history. For we *could* have won, a long time ago in Vietnam." But liberals, he lamented, refused. "Clearly Vietnam seems destined to become another Korea which was, as General MacArthur described it, 'a war we could not afford to lose and which we were not permitted to win.'" Helms's analysis of the war was superficial. But it was good politics. Many Americans found the idea that the United States could easily win plausible. The United States had prevailed during World War II against stronger nations. The situation in Vietnam was complex and bewildering, and the failures were maddening.[33]

Despite his abhorrence of the Democrats' war, Helms reserved his harshest criticism for protesters. In a letter to a viewer he divided Americans into three groups, two small and one large: the saintly, the bad, and the passive. "One of the small groups consists of people who wish to preserve America; the other small group is made up of the rabblerousers who want to destroy and refashion our way of life." Anger at protests was pliable to conservative ends. "The rabblerousers are winning, however, because of that large third group, consisting of the people who just don't give a damn."[34] Helms wanted to make the third group angry enough to vote conservative. His dark warnings denied any integrity to protesters and narrowed the range of legitimate political discussion. Advocating peace, protesting inequality and poverty, and advancing black power were unacceptable to him.

Mr. Johnson's Troubles

When President Johnson outlined his plans for a Great Society in his 1965 State of the Union address, Helms pounced. He contrasted President Johnson with Senator Johnson: the senator feared "the destruction of personal freedoms in his land. There was a day when he knew the difference between civil wrongs and civil rights." Now nothing ailed America "except those troubles for which the Great Society has already sought and found a solution."[35]

Johnson's Great Society programs included something for everybody, but the majority of the benefits and the federal spending went to the middle class—to federal funds for education, student financial aid for college, Medicare, farm subsidies, and increased Social Security benefits. Those with the greatest need—the poor and minorities—received proportionally less than the middle class because they were politically less influential.

Johnson, however, declared a war on poverty and fervently advocated civil rights. Helms and other conservatives exploited Johnson's concern for the poor and minorities to persuade voters that the Democrats had abandoned them. "An effective war against poverty" required distinguishing "between those who can't work, and those who won't work," he insisted. His assault on welfare and other Great Society programs fed the backlash against Democrats.[36]

Welfare was the perfect vehicle for Helms's theme of liberalism gone wrong. The war on poverty made Democrats and the Great Society easy marks. Welfare recipients lacked the power and the votes to defend themselves. Helms cast welfare recipients with their myriad problems and limited influence out of the moral community along with their liberal advocates. In Cleveland, the "hired help," Helms alleged, stole the "office equipment" from "a little War on Poverty program known as Community Action for Youth." Yet Helms bemoaned, "Congress appropriated nearly two billion dollars recently to continue Lyndon Johnson's War on Poverty."[37]

Racial politics, Helms knew, could undermine the president's Great Society programs. He even found a way to use race against Medicare. In 1965, during the congressional debate over Medicare, the station devoted two *Viewpoints* to doctors with opposing views. The advocate for Medicare was black and the opponent white. The white doctor appeared the same week as the vote in Congress and two weeks after the black doctor. The introduction of the white doctor carefully identified the previous Medicare supporter as a "Negro physician." The white doctor attacked Medicare as a tax and insisted that America has "the finest system of health care ever known." The black doctor, Dr. E. A. Eaton, was an articulate spokesman for Medicare, but Helms counted on racial prejudice preventing many viewers from hearing his arguments.[38] The choice of doctors associated African Americans with government programs and liberalism to discredit them in the eyes of white viewers. Helms could always point to Dr. Eaton's *Viewpoint* as the station complying with the Fairness Doctrine requirement to cover both sides of controversial issues. The FCC commissioners would miss such a manipulative misuse of the doctrine.

Racial politics was most effective, however, with programs that did not benefit the middle class. "If you think *you've* got troubles," Helms proposed, "consider the case of James C. Johnson," who faced an unsympathetic "domestic relations" judge. Johnson, Helms emphasized, was a "Negro." His weekly income at a poultry processing plant was $53. Johnson and his wife had four children. "But his wife has three other children by two other men." His "mistress," Johnson admitted, had borne him seven additional children. "In her spare time, this woman has had four other children by three other men." But that was not all. "Johnson has still another woman friend, who happens to be married to a man in prison." She had five children. Of these twenty-three children, "12 are Mr. Johnson's—four legitimate and eight illegitimate. All three of the mothers are receiving welfare checks representing substantial sums of money." The "welfare department" decided that Johnson should pay "$5 a week for each of his legitimate children and four dollars a week for each of his illegitimates." His total was $52 from his weekly earnings of $53. Johnson protested that "he could not live on love plus $1 per week." This *Viewpoint* dripped with Helms's sarcasm—voters undoubtedly laughed at Mr. Johnson and Helms's telling of the tale, but Helms's main point was a lesson for taxpayers regarding the unworthiness of the African American poor. "Meanwhile, the taxpayers will continue to pay an enormous sum to provide the real support for Mr. Johnson's three women and their 23 children." The final joke, however, was on the "taxpayers." Johnson explained: "There will soon be 24."[39]

Conservative Solutions

Helms could be callous in ridiculing welfare beneficiaries. He was nothing, however, if not consistent in the values he expressed on *Viewpoint* after *Viewpoint*. Despite a rhetorical emphasis on freedom, he valued obedience to authority, order, and hierarchy more than liberty. Helms held that tradition and duty restricted everyone's choices to a straight and narrow conservative path. Throughout his life, Helms remained within the moral universe of Monroe, North Carolina. He abided by this moral code and expected government and private institutions to maintain the same small-town values. Helms worked to establish conservative private institutions, profit and nonprofit, that would engage in charity work, espouse conservative political perspectives, and support conservative candidates. On *Viewpoint* he advocated private schools and charity and praised the politicians who met his standards. But he also demanded that government share his conservative agenda. Federal, state, and local government must preserve tradition.

Helms especially distrusted the federal government, because forging national policy required compromise. The influence of big cities on American culture and politics seemed to Helms an especially difficult hurdle. Although he routinely visited Washington, D.C., and New York City on business, he detested them. Their influence as centers of national government and media infuriated him. New York City was peopled, Helms complained, with "newspaper and television personalities" who preached "about what's wrong with the South."[40]

Helms believed that the small-town South, not big cities, should serve as a model for the nation in race relations, welfare and labor policies, and myriad other issues. "It is not in the South that gangs of hoodlums terrorize city streets. It is not in the South that treason flourishes and is protected. It is not in the South that racial violence is most frequent. . . . It is not in the South that labor racketeers have taken over political power. It is not in the South that patriotism has become a dirty word." The nation should follow the South's example, because it was the only region "which has not turned its back on reality" to embrace "an all-powerful government."[41]

Helms believed the South had preserved its values and traditions because parents, teachers, ministers, and other elites enforced them. He explained to A. W. McAlister Jr. that "civilization is scarcely more than discipline." Authorities had to impose discipline. McAlister was a wealthy admirer who became a friend and partner in charity activities. Contrasting contemporary Monroe unfavorably with the town of Farmville, Virginia, Helms expressed disappointment over the changes in his hometown. "The spirit and principles of Farmville are what I remember about Monroe when, for example, my first grade teacher, Miss Lura Heath, led us up to the monument on the courthouse square on confederate Memorial Day." He regretted that "the little ones of today are not really guided to love anything much, let alone their country or their heritage. But in Farmville, they still are."[42]

Helms's hopes for the future lay in private schools. McAlister solicited Helms's advice regarding donations to conservative causes. He asked Helms to assess efforts at establishing private schools in the Carolinas. Wade Hampton Academy was "a thriving, high-class" school. The school succeeded, Helms judged, not only because parents rejected "forced integration" but also because it provided an excellent education. Helms warned against private schools created only to avoid "association with Negroes."[43]

As a local TV personality, Helms saw many opportunities for charity activities and sometimes turned to McAlister. A letter from Rozella Brower seeking a hearing aid for her mother touched Helms. Rozella lived with her mother, who was nearly blind and deaf. "It would mean a lot to her to be able to hear radio and TV. And to be able to talk on [the] telephone," she wrote. Helms asked McAlister to investigate. "I have a tender feeling in my heart for people who are struggling to make ends meet, and who refuse to turn to the government for welfare." McAlister and Helms shared a concern that charity only go to the "deserving."[44]

McAlister's investigation revealed an appropriate candidate. Blindness and hearing loss almost entirely isolated Brower's mother, Mrs. Monroe, and the Browers "both work for Burlington Industries." They were "a nice family and Mrs. Monroe is a real sweet and deserving person." Monroe spent her evenings alone with her dog while her daughter and son-in-law worked the second shift. McAlister gave Helms the credit. "I told Mrs. Brower that the hearing aid would be a gift from you" and others who would remain anonymous.[45]

Helms applied the same standard of refusing government aid in his personal life. In 1963, Helms and his wife, Dot, adopted a nine-year-old boy, Charles, with cerebral palsy. Helms turned to Dr. Lenox Baker, a surgeon at Duke University Medical Center, to evaluate Charles and eventually to operate on his legs. Baker, a conservative admirer and friend of Helms, recommended he rely on the State Board of Health for funding, since the adoption was not yet final. Helms refused. "Dot and I think we should take care of Charles's expenses privately."[46] Few people shouldering responsibility for a child with cerebral palsy would reject the government's payment of medical bills. Although the Helmses were well off, they were not wealthy.

Helms and McAlister's joint charity activities revealed Helms's fundamental approach to social and economic problems. Local authority figures exercise their power privately to ensure appropriate behavior, order, and discipline. Only the "deserving" receive charity. Helms recognized that racial change was happening and hoped conservatives could get control of it. Applying his private charity model, he proposed a conservative alternative to the civil rights movement and federal intervention in the South: a privately directed affirmative action plan.

In 1965, Helms wrote an African American businessman, A. T. Spaulding, president of the North Carolina Mutual Life Insurance Company in Durham, with his idea. "I think it likely that, behind all of the conflict and disagreement and unrest today, there is actually a general agreement among people of all races about the errors of the past and the proper goals of the present and future." With pride and a clear conscience, Helms pointed to black employees at WRAL-TV whom he had hired and promoted. "We now have Negroes operating our film center, for example, and our very best film editor is a Negro. . . . So far, so good. But where do we go from here?"[47]

Helms proposed a "Department of Racial Development" at WRAL with the specific objective of promoting black employment, and he asked for Spaulding's support. He proposed "a regular program" that would describe "job opportunities for Negroes" and "have qualified Negroes" describe their qualifications. He wanted not just to exhort African Americans to work but to facilitate hiring of blacks in positions typically reserved for whites. He also hoped to make examples of successful applicants and expected them to network within the black community and the companies that hired them. "The Negroes who have obtained jobs would then be the best possible spokesmen to urge others to prepare themselves, to stay in school, to apply themselves." Helms hoped his plan would lead to significant shifts in racial attitudes. "What I want simply said, is to create a climate of acceptance among the races—both ways."[48]

Helms recognized that his actions could easily be misconstrued. "If it's a bad idea, don't hesitate to say so." When Spaulding reacted positively to the proposal, Helms created *Opportunity Line*, a daily five-minute program designed to advance black employment. Olivette Massenburg, an African American, hosted the program. She interviewed job seekers, employers, educators, and military recruiters. The unemployed explained their qualifications, and the other guests described opportunities for African Americans.[49]

At a time when the majority of black leaders had concluded that the only effective way to address racial discrimination was to involve the federal government, Helms was consistent in his belief that government—especially the federal government—only made things worse. His private model, however, would leave control of integration to white southern elites—the same social group that had established and maintained segregation. It would also have shifted the focus of integration away from schools and public spaces to male-dominated workplaces.

Helms preferred private action to address poverty and other issues, but he realized that welfare was unlikely to go away. Any government-sponsored charity, he insisted, should follow the same model he pursued privately. Helms made poverty programs the subject of countless *Viewpoints*. He delighted in castigating "professional welfare workers" and the poor. He judged that voters agreed with the conservative perspective on welfare and that conservatives could ride the issue into office. A series of stories in a Greensboro newspaper defending the effectiveness of welfare and welfare workers caught Helms's attention. "The articles probably did nobody any good—except, perhaps, the ego of professional welfare workers who sometimes seem galvanized in their determination to travel a one-way street in conducting what has come to be known as the 'war on poverty.'" Helms thought the newspaper erred in assuming "that the public does not understand what is going on." The "American people," he believed, grasped the problem of poverty "better than the newspapers and the welfare workers."[50]

Helms zeroed in on the reporter and a social worker's visit to a welfare home. The reporter "described in detail the filth, the squalor, the swarming flies, the hordes of dirty children." Helms expressed astonishment that both overlooked the filth. "The mother of the household was sitting idle on the front porch when the reporter and the welfare worker arrived. Suppose this woman had been presented with a broom and mop, and sufficient soap and told to get to work under pain of losing her welfare." Welfare programs that tolerated "filth" and immorality and ignored the need for productive labor endangered "the stability of the nation." Helms next connected welfare and riots. "If it were necessary for them to work in order to eat, they would perhaps have neither the time nor the energy to spend their nights in destructive frolics. At the very least they should be required to keep themselves clean and their homes clean in order to qualify for welfare checks."[51] Helms's connection of welfare and riots served as a racial marker, if the subject of welfare alone were insufficient.

Three weeks later, a response from the Guilford County welfare department to Helms's criticism of the "idle" mother ran on *Viewpoint*. The department's director, L. M. Thompson, revealed that there was in fact much that Helms and the general public did not understand. He explained, for example, why cleanliness had to be a "secondary concern." Demands for cleaning would destroy "the working relationships" between welfare workers and aid recipients. The welfare department aimed for a larger goal than a clean house. "Adults can be led—not driven—toward self-help and independence." The children's fathers contributed more than the taxpayers. The six children were born before she received any government assistance, so welfare "did not cause or encourage" their births. Welfare workers had persuaded her to accept "sterilization." The four-room house for seven people only had two rooms heated, and those by a wood stove. The Salvation Army sought a refrigerator and furniture for her. Thompson clarified that this woman's case was especially difficult because she had "a wooden leg." The department had arranged for a new prosthetic leg and for job training. The hope was that she would find employment. Helms, however, did not back down. His response emphasized the "filthy, fly-infested home" and the "illegitimate children."[52]

Helms eventually discovered a welfare official he could praise, Dr. Bruce Blackmon, "a respected physician of Buies Creek." Helms's most often expressed worry about poor women regarded their sex lives. The doctor shared his concern. Blackmon wanted "to make certain that public welfare money is distributed only among the needy and deserving," with the emphasis on deserving. As a member of the State Board of Public Welfare, Dr. Blackmon made a "practical proposal to reduce the number of children being born out of wedlock to women living on welfare." He recommended that "women on welfare bearing more than one illegitimate child be 'automatically prosecuted by the State Board of Public Welfare for fornication.'" The doctor also wanted investigations of the "illegitimate mothers already receiving checks." Helms was indignant at the criticism the doctor received as "a tyrant" and "a bumbling, presumptuous fool." "If the existing system is the model of perfection that the newspapers claim it is, and . . . if no mistakes are being made, the investigation will merely strengthen the position of those who now are operating this state's welfare program."[53]

In advocating "fornication" prosecutions of poor women, Helms intended that government maintain the stigma attached to an out-of-wedlock birth in a small town. Welfare eligibility would require keeping one's home and one's sex life tidy. The contradictions between his advocacy of government power to investigate and control the lives of the poor, especially the sex lives of poor women, and his advocacy of limited government when it came to desegregation or taxes were lost on him. Poverty meant powerlessness, dependency, loss of privacy, and public ridicule.

"Who's Afraid of Jesse Helms?"

Helms's championing of the values of the small-town South also lay at the heart of his pious incitement directed at the University of North Carolina. Helms demanded that UNC apply the values of the small-town South to the university community. He was attuned to any opportunity to advance conservatism at the university's expense. In the fall of 1966, Helms condemned the *Carolina Quarterly,* a UNC literary magazine edited by graduate students, on *Viewpoint.* The magazine's contents resembled "amateurish scrawls of four-letter words on a third rate men's room." Its publication by the university demonstrated that America was "becoming saturated with filth." And liberals were to blame. Helms asked, "Where are our church leaders? When last heard from they were off marching in some parade, or lobbying for some piece of Great Society legislation." University officials were hiding behind "that placard reading Academic Freedom." The success of Helms's cultural politics often depended on politicizing something normally outside the realm of public debate like a literary magazine. The *Carolina Quarterly* was part of the university's national reputation. The story Helms found offensive was Leon Rooke's "The Ice House Gang." Rooke, an artist in residence at UNC, had already received the O. Henry Award for another story published in the magazine. Helms's commentary was a master stroke associating the university, ministers, and Democrats with the *Carolina Quarterly's* "unadulterated trash."[54]

Helms's initial success led to additional criticism of the magazine and the university. The day after his attack on the *Carolina Quarterly*, the station began pursuing an apparently related story. WRAL had received calls claiming that a professor gave freshmen the following essay topic: "If you were a girl (boy), how would you go about seducing a boy (girl)?" When the station asked the university administration about the topic, the administration went into crisis mode. WRAL associated the theme assignment with the *Carolina Quarterly*. UNC chancellor Carlyle Sitterson wanted to limit negative coverage. WRAL's allegations triggered a six-week-long media frenzy that demonstrated the effectiveness of Helms's cultural politics.[55]

Helms's *Carolina Quarterly* attack ran on a Thursday. The following Monday, WRAL anchorman Sam Beard told UNC officials that Michael Paull had made the "seduction" assignment. To investigate, Provost Hugh Holman organized an ad hoc committee of administrators including himself, acting chairman of the English Department Raymond Adams, dean of the College of Arts and Sciences Charles Morrow, and chairman of freshman-sophomore English William McQueen. Paull was a graduate student teaching part-time and editor of the *Carolina Quarterly*. Paull assigned his students an essay on figures of speech in Andrew Marvell's seventeenth-century poem "To His Coy Mistress," not the poems and short stories in the *Carolina Quarterly*. Paull asked for volunteers to read in class. One student's paper ended with "you bet your ass." Embarrassed, Paull accused the student of using "words merely for shock value."[56]

The ad hoc committee met Monday afternoon "to find something to reply to WRAL," and came up with nothing. The story of a "professor" who assigned a "theme on seduction" ran on WRAL's *Dateline* on Monday evening. Beard explained that the papers were read in class and that at least one student found them "quite embarrassing and quite vulgar." On Tuesday the committee asked Paull a series of accusatory questions: "Did your themes deal with seduction? Is this poem not on seduction?" Although the committee's questions suggested that Paull was at fault for assigning an essay on "To His Coy Mistress," Marvell's poem was on the department's mandated syllabus for freshman English. Paull gave them the essays, but the committee did not examine the papers closely. The group's concern, McQueen later admitted, was the "welfare" of the university. The administrators agreed to recommend Paull's removal from the classroom. The university had found its reply to WRAL less than twenty-four hours after Beard's story. Chancellor Sitterson announced the decision in time for the six o'clock news. Paull, the chancellor explained, was reassigned after his students "misinterpreted" an essay assignment on Marvell's "To His Coy Mistress."[57]

The actions of Chancellor Sitterson and other administrators lent credibility to WRAL's allegations and increased the negative publicity they hoped to avoid. The mainstream media echoed WRAL's pious incitement. The *Durham Morning Herald* said WRAL reported an instructor assigned an essay "detailing the proceedings of a seduction." The state's other major papers recounted WRAL's narrative. The media coverage created the impression that Helms and WRAL had defended traditional values against a state-supported institution encouraging promiscuity.[58]

The university community responded with outrage to Paull's reassignment. It was clear to many that the administration had made Paull a scapegoat. Seventeen faculty from the English Department warned, "The suspension raises grave questions about our own professional integrity and the susceptibility of the University to outside pressures." The campus paper, the *Daily Tar Heel*, asked in an editorial, "Who's Afraid of Jesse Helms?" and answered: the university administration. Paull's students signed a letter denying he had assigned a theme on seduction. The student body president and the student government approved a resolution calling for Paull's reinstatement. Even those who initially supported Sitterson's actions were questioning them by the end of the week. Weldon Thornton, an associate professor of English, wrote Sitterson that he found it "harder and harder" to defend the reassignment of Paull. By Friday, Sitterson had reconsidered his decision and announced the English Department would reexamine Paull's case.[59]

After Sitterson's reversal, the *Greensboro Daily News* criticized WRAL for its "bullying television pundit," noting that the station "devotes too much of its time to poisonous innuendo against the university." The *Raleigh News and Observer* quoted a female student denying the essays were "vulgar" and painted a sympathetic portrait of Paull. But the newspaper coverage continued to repeat WRAL's allegations.[60] The sympathy for Paull only led Helms to assault the "young English professor" preoccupied "with sex" who denied he assigned an essay on "how to seduce a girl." Marvell's poem "had nothing to do with it." The *Carolina Quarterly* edited by Paull described "a sordid bit of fornication on a 100-pound block of ice."[61]

Helms's commentaries and WRAL's reporting gained national media attention. The wire services covered them, as did CBS, the *New York Times*, and *Life*. *Life* described Helms as "an ultraconservative who thinks academic freedom has gone too far." Helms's reaction was predictable, "But almost everybody was astonished at the university's." Although critical of Helms, the media reports inevitably conveyed his perspective. *Life* quoted a Helms commentary: "No doubt the boys enjoyed the vicarious frolic of talking about erotic matters in the presence of girl students." Helms had managed to slip pious incitement into the national media.

Many readers sided with him. Elinor Nevins of Nashville criticized the *New York Times* and others in the "liberal-socialist press" for condoning "the disgraceful actions of a sleazy character—one Michael Paull." R. C. Sims of Southfield, Michigan, wrote to *Life* that Marvell's poem "is far too potent to be suitable for a co-ed freshman class to dwell upon at length." Another *Times* reader, Edward Collins of Iowa City, Iowa, congratulated Sitterson for "transferring the instructor with the dirty mind."[62]

On *Viewpoint*, Helms reveled in the media attention: "What a show it has been." The "Coy Mistress" affair was an example of "the malignancy, which infected the press," Helms charged. The editors all had "preconceived notions" of the story they wanted. WRAL "has been labeled throughout the country as a 'rightwing' station." Helms supposed the label was meant as an insult, but the station would "cheerfully accept" it.[63]

The English Department chose a committee of five to undertake a second investigation. Reading the papers and interviewing Paull, the members of the ad hoc committee, and the students, the second committee reconstructed the assignment and the decision to remove Paull. The decisive evidence was the essays. Paull told the committee that the assignment was to use figurative language in an essay based on Marvell's poem. All but three of the original student papers contained figures of speech, while only two students understood the assignment as a theme on seduction. These two students also did not use any figures of speech. None of the papers described sex. The committee recommended that Paull be returned to teaching. Committee member Richard Lyon observed, "What most nearly characterizes the majority of these themes is an expression of a kind of breathless, sentimental adoration of someone loved."[64]

Members of the ad hoc committee admitted to the English Department's committee that they had been in a hurry to respond to WRAL. Although the essays "seemed" to be "on seduction," most members had not read them. The "Coy Mistress" essays' "sentimental adoration" were a long ways from what Helms and his reporters alleged. When Helms and Beard charged that Paull assigned "seduction themes," they had sex on their minds. The *Carolina Quarterly* story "Ice House Gang" described a sexual encounter. Beard and Helms had read the story but not the student essays. And they had a complaint about freshman English. Helms and his news department crafted a narrative of a sex-obsessed professor. The ad hoc committee allowed WRAL's news department to influence them.[65]

Twenty-three days after WRAL's initial story, Chancellor Sitterson announced Paull's reinstatement. Helms was unconcerned that his characterization of Paull as "sex obsessed" was false, or he refused to believe it. "Laughter," Helms advised, "is the best medicine" for the English Department's decision. For telling "the truth," the "'liberal' press," including *Life* magazine, CBS News, the *New York Times,* and the *News and Observer,* "scolded" the station.[66]

From Helms's perspective, WRAL's allegations were a fantastic success. Viewer reaction demonstrated the effectiveness of pious incitement. Paul Hastings thought Paull's reinstatement demonstrated the "low moral standards" of the university. He promised "to protest" the use of "my tax money" to support the institution. R. C. Souder wrote the chancellor, "My daughter until recently was considering entering your college, but after the Michael Paull episode your school is out of our consideration. . . . I guess Jesse Helms has you sized up correctly."[67]

A few days before the Watts riot in 1965, Helms observed, "About the only consolation I have these days is the old saying that it's always darkest just before the dawn."[68] For Helms the riot was the sun peeping over the horizon. It heralded the racial backlash he had anticipated for years. The Great Society and the Black Power Movement accelerated it. The Vietnam War consumed tax revenues and the attention of the Johnson administration, undermining the Great Society, especially the war on poverty. In fact, the only attention poverty programs received was negative. Shifting attitudes toward morality and sex gave conservatives traction in their attacks on liberals.

The backlash would have happened without Helms, but his pious incitement transformed anti-liberal sentiment into conservative votes. Since the Depression, liberals' political power had depended on delivering government services to people. Helms's pious incitement had taken advantage of the riots, the Black Power Movement, the Great Society, the sexual revolution, and the Vietnam War to make the case against government and liberalism. Conservative alternatives like private schools and charity had growing appeal.

Helms and A. J. Fletcher set out in 1960 to win converts to conservatism and elect conservatives. As in the "Coy Mistress" affair, viewers' reactions indicated that Helms was succeeding. W. F. Alston wrote, "It appears as though the white man has no rights. . . . As for me I have been a Democrat all my life as was my forefathers—only way I see out of it [is] vote Republican." Another admiring viewer encouraged Helms to "enter the government" in order to "use your wonderful judgment, great courage, common sense and strong convictions for the good of all." Viewer letters often bore Helms's imprint. "Negroes was who put Mr. Johnson in the White House," wrote Mrs. Atlas Tant. The government "should make them healthy young negro men and women get a job." This was as true on religion as it was on race. "Mr. Helms your viewpoints are my viewpoints," wrote Mrs. Leland Gurley. "May God keep you talking. Our, so called preachers . . . do not believe in God, but have a great form of Godliness."[69]

Republican James Gardner's defeat of Harold Cooley in the 1966 Fourth District congressional race came in the midst of racial backlash and the "Coy Mistress" incident. Gardner's victory proved the viability of Helms's racial and cultural politics in eastern North Carolina elections. Helms's influence would be even more important in 1968 and 1972.

5

Turning Off *Turn-On*

Helms as a TV Executive in the 1960s

In May 1961, the new FCC chairman, Newton Minow, spoke at the National Association of Broadcasters annual meeting. Television, he warned, had become "a vast wasteland." It was "a procession of game shows, violence, audience participation shows, formula comedies about totally unbelievable families, blood and thunder, mayhem, violence, sadism, murder, western bad men, western good men, private eyes, gangsters, more violence, and cartoons. And, endlessly, commercials." "The 'vast wasteland,'" Helms observed on *Viewpoint*, "is nonetheless popular." Helms admitted to agreeing with Minow regarding most television programming. "But there is too much evidence in a fiercely competitive field that our tastes are in a minority." In his six months at WRAL, viewers had made their preferences clear. When coverage of the North Carolina legislature interrupted *The Jack Paar Show*, a viewer complained, "I want to be entertained, not educated." But Minow, Helms believed—at least in 1961—failed to notice the real significance of television: "Between the murders and the stagecoach holdups and the variety shows, Americans—thanks in large measure to television and radio—are unquestionably the best-informed people on earth."[1]

Over the next few years, however, Helms came to expect little of television. The influence of liberalism and the civil rights movement seemed pervasive in news and entertainment. On *Viewpoint* in 1964, Helms held up three TV shows he found typical: in the first, "the hero was an atheistic college professor"; in the second, "the villain was a bigot" promoting "patriotism" and questioning the Supreme Court; and in the third, "a screwball candidate" advocated "abolishing income taxes." These shows,

Helms concluded, were dangerous efforts at painting any conservative—especially a southern one—as a "ridiculous demagogue." And he asked viewers: "When was the last time you saw a Negro pictured as having committed a crime?" Moreover, television and movies appealed "to sensuality" when they were not promoting the agenda of activists and liberals. If Americans examined their popular culture they would see a "nation going to pot." Helms, unlike many other movement conservatives, did not suffer under the delusion that the marketplace produced moral outcomes. He realized that salacious content drove profits. He tried to shape what the network offered, and when that failed he did his best to censor network entertainment and news programming.[2]

Helms faced a paradox. He was part of the cultural elite, a TV executive associated with a television network, ABC, that not only harbored liberals who treated radicals seriously but also used sex to sell. Privately, Helms wanted traditional values to restrain business. Television executives, he felt, should exercise their influence by programming entertainment and news that supported time-honored morality and promoted conservatism—the conservatism, he believed, that undergirded a free and prosperous society. Yet it was not merely liberals and activists that hindered the conservative agenda. Free-enterprise ideology also interfered. Helms battled network executives in California and New York over the sexual situations, political humor, and racial portrayals in *Peyton Place*, *The Smothers Brothers*, and *The Mod Squad*. He understood that these shows portended monumental shifts in American culture with regard to race, gender, and sexual attitudes. Driving such network programming was revenue. The fact that sexual content generated profits, Helms thought, did not make it okay. It was immoral. Although he was pessimistic about conservative efforts to stem the flow of cultural change, Helms expected unease over change to open doors for conservatives. On *Viewpoint* he castigated network executives and other cultural elites. His role as a media insider allowed him to turn cultural issues to conservative political advantage.

By the late 1960s, nothing was left of Helms's previous optimism regarding television, yet he remained convinced of the medium's power. "I have reached the conclusion that television may prove to have been the most destructive device since the invention of gunpowder. I find myself constantly ashamed of my profession." And the influence of television, he recognized, surpassed that of print. "I fear that television is more effective than the most leftwing of the newspapers. I don't know whether we will survive it."[3]

Managing WRAL-TV: A Dominant ABC Affiliate

WRAL-TV, the only station in the state capital, was tremendously influential. The news department under Helms's leadership was especially so. It supplied other stations, for instance, with coverage of elections and state government. Beginning in 1964, Helms's news department organized amateur radio operators to report local election returns from all over the state. The first broadcast was the 1964 Democratic primary. The station used an IBM 401 Tabulator, an early computer, to determine leaders and call elections. WRAL's six hours of coverage were broadcast nearly statewide, running on four other stations, including WSOC-TV in Charlotte. The station reported election results thirty to forty-five minutes ahead of competing stations and the Associated Press. Other stations monitored WRAL to get the returns. Losing candidates, including gubernatorial candidate Richardson Preyer, gave concession speeches based on WRAL's reporting. In 1968 the station's statewide election coverage was a similar success.[4]

WRAL was also the ratings leader in the Raleigh-Durham and eastern North Carolina market. Helms boasted in 1967 that WRAL-TV was "the dominant station" in the area, winning "all time categories from sign-on to sign-off."[5] The station's main competition was WTVD of Durham. Until 1962, WRAL's primary affiliation was NBC; WTVD's was CBS. It was a two-station market, so they split the best shows from ABC. ABC typically ran last in ratings. Nationally, ABC's entertainment and news programming simply was not competitive with NBC's and CBS's. But in 1962 WRAL switched its primary affiliation to ABC—on the face of it, an almost inexplicable decision. WRAL continued to carry some NBC programming, including *The Huntley-Brinkley Report* and *The Today Show*, but its prime-time programming relied heavily on ABC and local offerings. This allowed WTVD to add the strongest shows from NBC's lineup to its CBS programming. With a large proportion of the nation's highest-rated shows, WTVD seemed certain to win the ratings battle. But WRAL dominated.[6]

The key to WRAL's switch and to its continued success with a weaker network was a relentlessly local focus. Helms explained, "I daresay that no three other television stations in North Carolina perform, combined, as much community service as we do. We have award winning news and farm departments. We devote more time and money to women's affairs, education, cultural and religious programming than any other stations in our state, and perhaps in the entire south." Helms's and A. J. Fletcher's conservatism favored the local over the national. ABC's weak entertainment programming allowed the station to expand its local offerings. The local focus often meant conservative programming, and not just in news and public affairs. In 1968, for example, WRAL twice preempted prime-time network programming to carry Rev. Billy Graham's revival-style crusades for four or five nights in a row. The first crusade replaced summer reruns; the second, however, ran in the midst of the new fall schedule. But the most important local program was the news. The local news provided a station with its identity. With Helms's *Viewpoint,* WRAL was the "Voice of Free Enterprise." By the late 1960s, industry observers recognized that the local station with the highest-rated news program was usually the market's dominant station, whatever its network affiliation. WRAL's experience demonstrates that this insight applied early in the decade, too.[7]

WRAL carried ABC programming and ran films from the major movie studios. Helms's responsibility for programming meant he was the primary contact between WRAL and executives at ABC and other entertainment companies. WRAL shuffled ABC's prime-time schedule to run movies selected for the local market two nights a week. Helms regularly negotiated with ABC, especially during the planning for the fall schedule, over which network prime-time shows WRAL would run. Wednesday and Thursday nights were local movie nights on WRAL in addition to *The ABC Sunday Night Movie.* ABC pushed for the full prime-time schedule. Helms picked the shows best for the local market. Inevitably, some shows—even successful ones—were broadcast on delay, that is, appeared on WRAL at a different night and time from the national schedule. *The Big Valley* debuted in 1965 on Friday nights, two days after its national broadcast.[8]

Helms and WRAL also had significant input concerning programming from Katz Television. Katz was a New York–based advertising agency that sold WRAL's ad time to national companies. But Katz did more than simply sell national spots for WRAL and other local stations. It advised

WRAL on programming—which movies, syndicated shows, and network shows to run and when to schedule them. Katz was intimately involved in planning the fall schedule and any changes made during the year, but Helms always tailored programming to the local audience. When a Katz representative accused the station of making "a change-for-change-sake," Helms fired back that he made changes because "[I] know our market better than folks who don't live here."[9]

As this comment suggests, Helms could be caustic. In 1965 he criticized *ABC's Wide World of Sports* for its inferior production quality. "Minute cutaways last for as long as 95 seconds." Helms threatened ABC's regional manager, Nat Cavalluzzi, that to avoid looking like "chumps" the station planned to announce: "THIS IS A SLOPPY TELEVISION PRODUC-TION BY ABC." Balancing such scathing remarks were his expressions of approval. "I fuss a lot," Helms wrote Cavalluzzi. "But, all in all, I am constantly very proud of our network."[10]

Helms, however, was unbending when it came to the bottom line. He applied the same toughness to contract negotiations and programming decisions that characterized him as a commentator and news director. Early in the 1968 fall football schedule, Helms informed ABC that the network's payment for NCAA football games was inconsistent "with our contractual agreement." Since it sold ads nationally, ABC paid affiliates to carry network programming, while WRAL sold ads locally and through Katz. Often network payments made network programming preferable to locally produced or syndicated shows. For non-network broadcasts WRAL had to pay for the programming and sell ad time. But the NCAA compensation rates were less than 50 percent of WRAL's usual ABC rate for the time slot. Helms made it clear that WRAL would only run the games that had local interest if ABC refused to raise the "absurd" rate.[11]

Helms developed a reputation as a tough contract negotiator, so much so that the distributor of the game show *To Tell the Truth* complained to Katz. Helms had refused to pay more for the show than the previous contract. His threat to drop it from WRAL's schedule led to renewal at the old price. Helms read contracts carefully, despite his lack of formal legal training. An apparently standard contract with Paramount Television for movies contained a paragraph that was so "broad and vague" that its "interpretation," Helms insisted, "could be as high as the sky and run to the horizon." He deemed a verbal explanation inadequate and got a written understanding that clarified the ambiguities. Helms was just as tough with regional distributors. Show Biz, Inc., the Nashville-headquartered producer of *The Porter Wagoner Show*, had a "'special Jesse contract." Charlotte-based Jefferson Productions demanded payment for a preempted episode of *The Arthur Smith Show* because WRAL failed to give advance notice. Helms refused. The station's contract, he said, did not require advance notice for emergencies.[12]

Liberal Hollywood and the Vice President of Programming

Helms relished the opportunity to shape the news, schedule conservative content, and comment daily on events, but he found his responsibilities for programming entertainment distasteful. Network television conflicted with Helms's values, particularly his sense of TV as an "educational medium." Most entertainment originated in New York or Los Angeles. Designed to attract a national audience, it relied on sexual innuendo and often reflected liberal gender and racial views. The vice president of programming advised one disgruntled viewer, "I cannot defend much of what appears on television. . . . My own set at home is often silent because my family finds reading preferable." Helms regularly voiced the station's programming objections to network executives and—less often—on *Viewpoint*, but his efforts seemed to have little impact. He wondered if "all of the good and decency of the world is gone, or if it is just a matter of it being submerged in the trash of our civilization. My own industry troubles me. . . . We have complained and complained and complained to our network."[13]

Helms believed that elites had an obligation to ensure proper behavior. This meant that entertainment executives should prevent the airing of anything that was not, by the strictest standard, wholesome. Helms refused to run *A Man and a Woman*, an *ABC Wednesday Night Movie*, because of "a very explicit bedroom scene" with the camera focused on "a naked man and woman in bed complete with moans." Although his actions elicited student editorials condemning his censorship and complaints to ABC, Helms insisted that "I had a duty to prevent this being piped into the living rooms of homes in our area, for young people to see."[14]

Helms's concerns centered on race, sex, morality, liberalism, and respect for authority. Although violence worried FCC chairman Minow and some WRAL viewers, it did not alarm Helms. Westerns and crime dramas were the most consistently conservative programs on television. The "abnormal rate of crime, violence and appalling recklessness" in Fayetteville, North Carolina, distressed a Fort Bragg soldier. He attributed the high crime to the daring of the paratroopers stationed there, who "are either on their way to Vietnam or have just returned," and the influence of pop culture. "This constant barrage of horror, sex, malice, terror, erotacy [sic] and violence cannot help but feed the flame of violence." Another viewer requested a *Viewpoint* examining "violence on TV" and its impact on "young people." "I must be frank," replied Helms. "I'm not persuaded that violence on television is as harmful as the newspapers contend. When I was a boy, I used to go every Saturday afternoon to see Tom Mix and Hoot Gibson shoot'em up and it did not make me violent. . . . I think it taught me that crime doesn't pay."[15]

WRAL-TV removed objectionable scenes, when possible, and Helms closely managed the process. "I spent an hour in our film editing department, supervising the deletion of unworthy material. . . . Our editors do the best they can, but still don't get it all." The bedroom scene in *A Man and a Woman* was pivotal to the plot, so WRAL dropped the whole movie, but WRAL often had no knowledge of network content. Ruth Janesick, the mother of a teenage daughter, accused Helms of "talking out of both sides of your mouth" for carrying *Ski Party,* a movie with "young men dressed as girls." She asked Helms how he could run such movies on WRAL. Helms explained that he had been unable to preview the movie. Cavalluzzi, ABC's regional manager in charge of station relations, explained to Janesick that affiliates like WRAL had little control over network programming and defended *Ski Party* as a "tongue-in-cheek farce." As with many things Helms disapproved of, he attributed the risqué content of network TV shows and movies to a conspiracy: "I cannot avoid the notion that all of this is part of a deliberate plot to corrupt the minds and morals of the country."[16] But he also acknowledged that profits drove the sexual content on TV.

Conservative viewers repeatedly asked, "Why don't you discontinue the filthy *Newlywed Game*?" After watching an episode, Helms threatened ABC with cancellation. The "incredible dialogue" on *The Newlywed Game* must stop, he wrote Cavalluzzi. The emcee "inquired as to the husbands' sexual prowess on the wedding night," and "one young lady" discussed her "diarrhea." "I am going to cancel the show if this sort of thing continues." Yet he knew such banter was the key to the program's success. "It is obviously deliberate, and of course," Helms admitted, "it draws a large audience." Despite his threats, *The Newlywed Game* remained on WRAL because canceling a popular show would mean lost revenue.[17]

Helms was often dismayed at what attracted viewers. He reluctantly carried professional wrestling because of its high ratings. A viewer complained of the degeneration of the once "great sport" of wrestling so that it was unfit for teenagers to watch. "I can't understand why the wrestling commissioner puts up with dirty wrestling." Tactfully avoiding an outright admission of fakery, Helms accounted for wrestling's popularity with pop psychology: "A great deal of the things that go on are merely for show. Strangely enough, the people like what they see. Maybe it gives them an outlet for their pent-up emotions." When Helms moved professional wrestling to a less favorable time slot, the deluge of mail was so great that he reversed his decision. "We had letters and petitions by the hundreds. I recall one petition in particular—it was signed by every patient at a tuberculosis sanitarium."[18]

Helms objected to *Peyton Place* from the outset. "We just plain do not want to take the Peyton Place episodes. . . . [Y]ou fellows made a mistake in taking on something even with a connotation of that book." But WRAL ran *Peyton Place*. It was a tremendously successful show for ABC, the third-place network. The novel's reputation allowed the network to create a sensational atmosphere for its premiere, and the show's ratings briefly boosted ABC into first place during the fall of 1964. When *Peyton Place* faced criticism, ABC president Leonard Goldenson defended the show as important for the struggling network's bottom line.[19]

Peyton Place's success did not endear it to conservatives. The show's depiction of uncontained female sexuality supported the shifts under way in American values. Margaret Mayo, chair of the Lydia Circle of Millbrook Methodist Church in Raleigh, asked that WRAL schedule shows that "disregard the moral code" after children were in bed. "We as Christian parents are seeking to reduce the delinquency and promiscuousness" in society. Helms forwarded the letter to ABC's Robert Coe, vice president in charge of station relations, writing that "I think this is a matter which all of us in television should not dismiss lightly." Helms warned, "Mrs. Mayo's letter is typical of the reaction we receive." With the same reasoning Helms used in justifying violence, Coe defended *Peyton Place*. It demonstrated "clearly the penalties that ensue from wrong-doing." He dismissed Mayo as a "'fringe' type of complainer" and assured Helms that "the vast majority of people like *Peyton Place*." Helms thanked Coe with sarcasm: "We members of the 'fringe' element have been put in our place."[20]

The objections continued throughout *Peyton Place*'s run, but American values changed so quickly during the 1960s that *Peyton Place* was soon dated. To pull younger viewers back and battle declining ratings in its fifth year, ABC added a rock band, broadcast the show a half hour earlier, and introduced a middle-class black family. The black characters were controversial in the South. Ethel Jones announced that she had "cut out looking at *Peyton Place*" because of the story lines involving African Americans. "It wasn't fit to look at anyway—but now—since the brazen kinky-head had to fall in love and she with him. Why, oh why do we southern people have to have such things crammed down our throats?" Jones, an eighty-five-year-old rest home resident who ate her supper in her room so she could watch *Viewpoint*, was hardly ABC's target audience, but her reaction reflected the attitude of many southern whites to the presence of African Americans on TV. Jones objected to any depiction of dignified African Americans, even in a Crest toothpaste commercial. "This negro advertising is about to get my goat. . . . Only one cavity—she is about four years old and of course her daddy is made to have rank and distinction." Such portrayals contradicted the racial stereotypes to which many white southerners clung ferociously. Helms was no exception. "I agree with you about the absurd projection of Negroes into television commercials and programs," he wrote. "Not only is it insulting; it is unreal. My children just laugh when such things come on the screen."[21]

With few exceptions, television portrayed the United States as a white nation. *The Nat "King" Cole Show* was the first variety show with a black host. Cole, a sophisticated singer with multiple top-ten hits, was ideal for the variety-show format. The show debuted in 1956 on NBC, but the network canceled it a year later. Under constant pressure from the white citizens councils, advertisers would not sponsor the program. But the civil rights movement changed everything. Television news coverage of the civil rights movement contrasted images of African American protesters' dignity with the meanness of the whites opposing them. Among the civil rights movement's achievements was a new visibility for African Americans.[22]

The networks added black actors to existing shows and scrambled to develop shows like *I Spy* and *Mod Squad* with hip black characters. "There are some," Helms commented, "who object to Negro actors and demand that we cancel these shows. If we were to use that yardstick, we would have to cancel every show on the air." Helms was defending the crime drama *N.Y.P.D.* and the Western *The Outcasts* to a disgruntled viewer. He insisted that the shows "were quite realistic," even if they possessed "objectionable characterizations." Interestingly, the viewer letter did not mention race directly, although the shows she complained about had black co-stars. But Helms took her observation that "the people in this part of the country" would prefer these shows' cancellation as indicating the centrality of race to her disapproval.[23]

Writing to ABC's Cavalluzzi, Helms threatened to cancel shows because of racial depictions, which "incite hostility." "We are having more and more complaints about the unnecessary and totally unrealistic projection of race in ABC's productions." Helms enclosed a letter protesting a *Mod Squad* episode from "a distinguished North Carolina citizen," Judge L. J. Phipps. *Mod Squad,* a successful Aaron Spelling–Danny Thomas production, reworked the crime drama formula with an injection of countercultural elements—at least as imagined by Hollywood. The bad guys were usually white men in business suits. The title characters, "one white, one black, one blond," were hip but troubled teens who avoided prison by joining the fight against crime. Phipps objected to a scene in which the black cop, Linc Hayes, slapped a "hysterical" white woman. In the world of TV crime shows, the slap knocked her sensible. Helms insisted that ABC had an "obligation" to "control this sort of thing." But Cavalluzzi defended the portrayal. "A slap is not unusual to bring a person out of the state of hysteria and Linc, being trained as a cop, would do it naturally."[24]

Mod Squad and *Peyton Place* were protected by their popularity. When Helms terminated shows he opposed politically or morally, it was usually the least popular ones. In 1965, WRAL discontinued the ABC variety show *Nightlife* in part because of an episode that mocked William F. Buckley. Besides being politically offensive, *Nightlife* gave WRAL "no measurable audience." Cavalluzzi pressured the station to let *Nightlife* have another chance. "We are concentrating our heaviest guns on this show," and beginning in the fall it would originate from the Hollywood Palace in color. But Helms declined another look, stating that he lacked "confidence in the ability of theatrical people to interpret philosophy, political action, human relations—or just plain decency. And apparently the networks are not able to assure good taste." Color did not help *Nightlife*. The network canceled it early in the second season.[25]

A few years later, Helms advised ABC of WRAL's cancellation of *Dark Shadows*, a show that religious conservatives labeled "Satan's favorite TV show." *Dark Shadows*—a gothic soap opera with vampires, ghosts, and witches—attracted a young audience. The villains were "stern patriarchs" and "hypocritical preachers," while the supernatural beings were "tortured" romantic heroes that excited the countercultural interest in altered consciousness and New Age religion. "I am aware that this show is doing well nationally," Helms observed, "but we have had nothing but adverse comment." He did not close the door entirely. "We will be attentive to the reaction and if it appears that we have misjudged our market, we will see about reinstating it." WRAL had originally broadcast the show in the mornings when the target viewers—teenagers—were in school. *Dark Shadows* reappeared a few months later in an afternoon time slot that allowed it to build an audience.[26]

Although his threats to cancel popular shows like *Mod Squad* sometimes rang hollow, Helms knew that his demands had an effect on network programming. Helms bragged that ABC edited *Moll Flanders* "because this station refused to carry it in the originally-intended version." Often the influence of Helms and others like him was hidden. Helms also played a role in making the ABC variety show *Turn-On* the "shortest lived" TV series ever. ABC canceled it after one episode.[27]

Turn-On was ABC's answer to *Rowan and Martin's Laugh-In* on NBC and *The Smothers Brothers Comedy Hour* on CBS. *Turn-On*, like its counterparts, appropriated a countercultural sensibility. But of the three, *Turn-On* deviated the most from the traditional variety-show format derived from vaudeville. The show's premise was that a computer produced it; its sketches and jokes were taped without sets before a white wall; and rather than a laugh track, the computer added synthesized music. The only episode that aired began with a beautiful woman standing before a firing squad. The commander said, "I know this may seem a little unusual, miss, but in this case the firing squad has one last request." Helms canceled *Turn-On* the next morning. WRAL would drop "every program that plays fast and loose with moral standards," he explained, even if the station "ends up with no network programming." Helms was not alone: about seventy-five ABC stations refused to broadcast another episode.[28]

The widespread rejection of *Turn-On* stemmed from a combination of the unconventional format, political humor, and risqué jokes that overstepped the bounds of good taste for America in February 1969. But American culture was changing. *Turn-On* "originated in Hollywood," Helms explained to outraged viewers, "and, I suppose, represents the kind of sick humor that seems to have permeated so much of the entertainment industry." Just as surely as this "sick humor" offended some people, it attracted large audiences when packaged in the right way, and America's new sense of humor made its way into other ABC shows. A few months after the cancellation of *Turn-On*, Helms threatened to pull the plug on the "once-fine" *Hollywood Palace* during its fifth year "if the former quality is not resumed." *Hollywood Palace*, staged as a revival of vaudeville in a renovated theater, had already elicited objection. In early 1968, just as President Lyndon Johnson's popularity reached its lowest point, viewers flooded ABC with complaints regarding a skit by Milton Berle. The level of dissatisfaction prompted the network to send an apology to each complaining viewer. The network assured them that Berle and ABC did not intend "to ridicule the President of the United States, nor offend any religion" but rather "to comment on the world in general in a form of satire recently made popular."[29]

Helms's own attitudes were an indication of how difficult it was to tell where good taste and legitimate political comment ended and offense began. When they took on President Johnson, comedians affronted Helms, whether establishment figures like Milton Berle or young counterculture-identified comics like the Smothers Brothers, yet Helms's commentaries compared Johnson's power to that of the Nazi Party.[30] Network programming that relied on sex to sell often offended Helms, but he also exploited the selling power of sex. For the premiere of his talk show on WRAL, Helms asked ABC to have Dick Cavett tape promos. "Something along the lines of . . . Dick Cavett here. Why don't you be a nice guy and join me, here on WRAL-Television. . . . Bring the wife. Or the girlfriend. But, for Heaven's sake, not both!" Helms hired a female sports reporter, Jane Steppe, away from an Atlanta station. When announcing her arrival at WRAL-TV, Helms remarked, "You may be interested in her wardrobe. The men folk surely will be."[31] This contradiction's resolution lay in Helms's sense of authority: it was inappropriate for entertainers to challenge authority, but it was a conservative commentator's responsibility to challenge liberals.

A joke regarding an extramarital affair or a TV show using a striking woman to attract viewers was acceptable—and the news was ultimately only a TV show. But political comedy undermined authority, raising disquieting questions about the uses of power. The firing-squad sketch unsettled even more. By leading viewers to imagine what the men wanted, it sexualized death and violence and questioned authority. The powerlessness of the condemned woman and the soldiers' guns implied gang rape, and a viewer's uneasy laughter implicated him in their desire. Was the request really a demand? Could men with guns and the power of life and death keep order? These questions were deeply disturbing in the midst of the Vietnam War. Reacting to *Turn-On*, a preacher's wife escalated from housekeeping imagery that advocated cleaning up a dirty show to a violent rage: "In my opinion it not only needs to be cleaned up, but cleaned OUT, HUNG, SHOT—And Buried."[32]

Helms added a preemptive strike to his threats to cancel *Hollywood Palace*. When he learned that ABC might pick up the *Smothers Brothers Show,* he wrote Cavalluzzi that WRAL "will not carry it."[33] In 1969, CBS canceled *The Smothers Brothers Comedy Hour* largely for its political humor. The Smothers Brothers, Tom and Dick, injected jokes about drugs, religion, sex, and politics into the exhausted variety-show format. They attracted younger viewers who were tired of Ed Sullivan and Dean Martin. By their third season, they were in a constant fight with CBS over politics. "We've come a long way since that first Thanksgiving dinner in Plymouth," Dick observed, "when the pilgrims sat down at the table with the Indians to eat turkey." Yeah, Tom added. "Now we're in Paris, sitting down at a table with the Viet Cong, eating crow." Tom took their conflicts with CBS public. The press coverage of the network's cutting of Pete Seeger's antiwar song "Waist Deep in the Big Muddy" forced CBS to reverse the decision. Although *TV Guide* endorsed the network's "right to preview what it will telecast," most of the coverage sympathized with the brothers. With NBC's *Laugh-In* doing better, CBS decided the brothers were not worth the trouble. Tom felt the turning point was Nixon's victory. "If Humphrey had won we'd still be on."[34]

ABC announced in the spring of 1970 that the "celebrated singer-comedians," the Smothers Brothers, were back. The network wanted them to attract a young audience. Helms demanded "specific assurance" that the Smothers Brothers would not "use ABC and consequently our station, to resume their vulgar and unfair political ridicule of America." On CBS the Smothers Brothers were everything Helms hated about entertainment and the counterculture—challenging authority, winking at drugs and sex, and politically left.[35]

The network judged the comedy team sufficiently chastised to cooperate. ABC met Helms's demands, including the chance to view the show in advance. Vice President Richard Beesemyer assured Helms, "I sincerely believe you will not find any program material offensive to your market." Even *TV Guide* found the Smothers Brothers safe. They possessed, the reviewer felt, something "old-fashioned" and uncommon, "taste." But no one apparently wanted a tasteful Smothers Brothers. ABC dropped them. The demands brought by Helms and others left the Smothers Brothers with little of their original appeal. Although *Rowan and Martin's Laugh-In* on NBC contained political humor, the series caused less controversy. Dan Rowan summed up his show's differences with its rival: *Laugh-in* "used politics as a platform for comedy," while *The Smothers Brothers* "used comedy as a platform for politics."[36]

Canceling the Network News

Helms found network news just as unsettling as entertainment. "A great percentage of the news people in this country today are not interested in reporting the news as it is," he said, "but in swaying public opinion to their own point of view. A look at any of the real issues of our time, and the way the news media have handled the coverage of them, and it all comes out baloney." The network news shows as Helms saw them were unrelentingly liberal. Helms ensured that WRAL framed the news from a conservative perspective. But he did not find his efforts to sway public opinion biased. Helms insisted that he could define the station's "philosophy" in "one word": "TRUTH." His derision of other perspectives stemmed from this virtually religious faith that conservatism was the truth. No other perspective mattered. Many people found Helms's certainty comforting.[37]

Helms chafed at his lack of control over network news. He regretted, for example, that network crime reports missed opportunities to undermine the civil rights movement. The national media "are ignoring the trial of a 29-year old Negro in New York who has acknowledged that he killed three women." Helms protested, "All three networks reported the killing at the time it was committed. . . . But none of the networks indicated that the killer was a Negro." Helms's commentary shifted from the murder story to the supposed failure of the Congress of Racial Equality to interest New York ghetto residents in a plan to clean up their neighborhoods. By placing these two stories together in his five-minute commentary, Helms insinuated that these unconnected stories illustrated rampant immorality among African Americans.[38]

Despite its switch to ABC in 1962, WRAL-TV continued NBC's evening news program, *The Huntley-Brinkley Report. The Huntley-Brinkley Report* worked well for the station. It was the number-one-ranked news show nationally, and co-anchor David Brinkley was from North Carolina. But in 1963 WRAL switched to the *ABC Evening News.* This was a strange move, since ABC news came in a distant third in the ratings and was struggling to catch up to the other networks in quality.[39]

Helms's primary reason was ABC's limited news coverage. The network retained the fifteen-minute national broadcast that had been the norm since network evening news began in the late 1940s. Both CBS and NBC had shifted to a thirty-minute format in 1963. All three network news departments ran deficits, but ABC could not afford major sacrifices for a prestige program like the news. ABC lost money throughout the decade. During the mid-1960s the network converted to color, an expensive undertaking for the third-place network. The fact that ABC had a limited budget and a fifteen-minute broadcast suited WRAL's interests. Going with *ABC Evening News* reduced by one-half the network news over which Helms had no control. In the early 1960s, the networks' coverage made the civil rights movement a national story. Network reporting on civil rights was a major factor in pushing the federal government to take action. At a critical juncture in the Birmingham campaign, King reminded a packed Sixteenth Street Baptist Church that *The Huntley-Brinkley Report* was covering their marches: "Don't let anybody make you feel we are alone." Network news made African Americans' plight visible.[40]

Under Helms's direction, WRAL-TV news overhauled *Dateline*, its 6:00 p.m. news hour. Within the hour, WRAL's local news preceded and followed the *ABC Evening News,* with sports and weather coming after the national broadcast. The *ABC Evening News* began at 6:20.[41] In the late 1960s ABC made changes. The network expanded its newscast to a half hour in 1967, and in 1968 it made Frank Reynolds the *ABC Evening News* anchor. ABC, unlike other networks, allowed the anchor and correspondents to deliver commentaries on stories immediately after reporting them. Howard K. Smith was a regular contributor as a correspondent and commentator. Smith welcomed the label "hawk" and became the only news man the Nixon administration trusted. Despite Smith's role, Helms objected to the changes. Reynolds's and other commentators' liberalism outweighed everything else. Helms used viewer letters to pressure the network. Dr. Donnie Jones protested to Reynolds, "I don't appreciate being called a YAHOO. Nor do I appreciate your inferring that Mr. George Wallace is a YAHOO."[42]

Helms wrote John Gilbert, ABC's vice president of affiliate relations, with WRAL's conditions for continuing *ABC Evening News*. His conditions centered on Reynolds and other liberal-to-moderate voices on the station. Helms demanded that commentaries appear "separated from the news and features" so that the station could eliminate them "without production awkwardness." He also required the text twelve hours before broadcast of any commentary to allow WRAL to decide whether to air it.[43]

If ABC complied with these conditions, Helms and his news department would be able to delete commentaries without the audience's knowledge. When ABC went with a thirty-minute program, WRAL began the 6:00 news at 5:45 and continued to include the *ABC Evening News* within *Dateline*, running the network news at 6:20. Since the local news preceded and followed the network's broadcast, variations in the length of *ABC Evening News* would not be obvious. Helms stressed "our intent to control, according to our own best judgment, the 'balance' of commentaries carried by our station." Consciously or not, the executive vice president's quotation marks around "balance" indicated his discomfort with the idea. WRAL claimed in its conflicts with the Federal Communications Commission that its local news and commentaries balanced the network's liberalism. But Helms intended to silence the liberals and the moderates on ABC. Lack of "production awkwardness" would mean few FCC complaints.[44]

John Gilbert rejected Helms's conditions. No one at ABC knew twelve hours in advance what would be on the evening broadcast. Gilbert insisted that the program maintained "fairness" and "balance," broadcasting "views from 'liberal' to 'middle-of-the-road' to very 'conservative.'" *ABC Evening News* met "the fairness requirements" for "balance of news and commentary." Despite its financial situation, ABC was trying to distinguish its news from its rivals'. Gilbert felt ABC's "departure from the norm" was its strength. "The very fact that it's controversial and yet fair, and is bringing a great deal of reaction from the audience, indicates that we are on the right track."[45]

Helms responded that continuing *ABC Evening News* would conflict with "our duty." WRAL-TV resumed broadcast of *The Huntley-Brinkley Report*. The NBC newscast maintained the traditional organization with commentaries and features at the end, allowing local edits to go unnoticed. But WRAL's shaping of network news was well enough known for a college student to question Helms about it for his sociology paper on censorship. Helms explained that any deletions of "network news specials or public affairs programming" resulted from the network's "losing sight of 'balance.'" By the end of the summer of 1968, WRAL-TV was in the singular position of carrying news broadcasts from all three networks. In additional to *Huntley-Brinkley* in the evenings, the station carried the *CBS Morning News*. Since WRAL-TV was an ABC affiliate, ABC provided its daytime news broadcasts and special coverage, including the Democratic and Republican conventions.[46]

Helms was unhappy with most of it. Shortly after his cancellation of the *ABC Evening News*, the 1968 Democratic convention and the media reaction fueled his frustration. Ten thousand activists arrived in Chicago to protest the Vietnam War. Mayor Richard Daley, a Democrat, ordered his police officers and the Illinois National Guard to stop the protests. The network coverage switched from Humphrey's acceptance speech to the mayor's suppression of protests. Network commentary condemned Daley and the police. Helms wrote Nat Cavalluzzi that correspondent Jim Burns's "sweeping indictment of police officers" was "an emotional tantrum." "I dislike our station having been used to circulate such comment." Helms even considered eliminating the network evening news and preparing "our own national and international news summary."[47]

Helms found NBC's *Huntley-Brinkley Report* just as intolerable. He complained on *Viewpoint*, "The United States, to hear these 'news' makers tell it, is 'imperialistic' and a 'warmonger'—there is no 'freedom' here, only 'oppression' and 'discrimination' and 'racism.' Finally Chet said goodnight to David, and the bewildering spectacle was over for another evening."[48]

In 1970, Helms demanded a transcript of NBC correspondent John Chancellor's report on the Nixon administration's go-slow approach to school desegregation. Chancellor noted that Nixon's policies differed from those of his predecessor. "It used to be said in the White House that 'we shall overcome.' What is being said now is that 'we must enforce the law; we must cope with difficult situations' but that 'we shall not, in the immediate future, overcome our school problems.'" Helms thought the transcript, which was "bad enough," was inaccurate. "Unless my ears have gone completely haywire, that ain't the way John Chancellor read it."[49]

Worse, *The Huntley-Brinkley Report*'s ratings also fell. When Helms abandoned the NBC broadcast in 1963, it was the highest-rated evening news. By 1968 Walter Cronkite's *CBS Evening News* had moved to the top, but Helms expected *Huntley-Brinkley* to best CBS in the local market because of Brinkley's ties to North Carolina and WRAL's dominance. To boost ratings, he tried in October 1969 to secure Brinkley for the Raleigh Chamber of Commerce's annual dinner. "Your personal appearance in Raleigh would immeasurably help us against the CBS newscast across the way. At present time, Cronkite wins the time period in this market." Brinkley declined.[50]

The Huntley-Brinkley Report's second-place finish was part of a general ratings slide. WRAL remained ahead overall, but WTVD was eroding its dominance. WTVD's rise in the ratings began in the fall of 1967. The Durham station nearly doubled its ratings over the fall of 1966 at 5:00 p.m. with reruns of *Perry Mason* preceding the news. "More importantly, in my opinion," a frantic Oliver Blackwell of Katz Television observed, "is the inroads they have made at 6:00 p.m. in the news." WTVD's local news saw an 80 percent increase against WRAL's *Dateline*. The ratings for a station's local news usually affected the ratings for the whole evening. WRAL, after all, had been winning the ratings battle with ABC's prime-time programming and movies. WTVD carried CBS plus the best of NBC—the two highest-rated networks—during prime time. Blackwell recommended immediately making changes for the two hours. Running *The Flintstones* at 5:00 p.m. against *Perry Mason* would "set up a conflict in the home," which "the kids will win." *I Love Lucy* at 5:30 could hold the kids and pull in adults just before the news, but this change would be hard to accept. It meant cutting the local news from forty-five minutes to a half an hour. WRAL would carry a conventional half hour of local news and a half hour of network. Blackwell wanted to institute these changes before the next ratings period in February–March 1968 and warned that failure to reverse WTVD's gains would lead to "serious sales problems for the remainder of 1968." Helms accepted the "accuracy" of Blackwell's reasoning but initially rejected the proposal. By the fall of 1969, however, WRAL-TV had cut back its local news to thirty-five minutes beginning at 5:55 p.m. *The Flintstones* and *I Love Lucy* ran in the 5:00 hour and *The Huntley Brinkley Report* in the conventional 6:30 time slot.[51]

These changes were insufficient to reverse WRAL's fall-off in audience. Katz Television next proposed that WRAL consult Frank Magid Associates, which specialized in audience surveys as a basis for remaking local news programming. By the 1970s, critics blamed the company for what they disliked about local news broadcasts: chatty, young, and attractive on-air personalities, "sensational crime and accident stories," and big, flashy news sets and graphics. With Katz's input, the station suggested that the survey focus on the impact its "editorializing has on its News audiences" and reminded Magid to ensure "proper racial balance." Almost a third—29 percent—of WRAL's viewing area was African American. Katz's recommendations a few months after the survey are revealing. Blackwell endorsed substantial modifications: starting the news at 6:00, not 5:55, and dropping *Viewpoint* from the 6:00 newscast.

Blackwell clearly believed that Helms's commentaries undermined WRAL's ratings and affected profits. Helms's commentaries must have left black viewers cold. As the voice of WRAL-TV, Helms probably soured many to the whole station. But black viewers were unlikely to account for the shift away from the station in the late 1960s. Helms had been on the air for eight years. The committed WRAL viewer who waited every day for his commentary remained loyal, but a significant number of viewers had changed the channel. Perhaps they had grown tired of shifting back and forth between network newscasts and the odd start times or were drawn by Cronkite's reputation. Helms's aggressive, confrontational style undoubtedly alienated some viewers, particularly with the nation so divided in the late 1960s. The local news as a station's identity cut both ways. Without changing *Viewpoint*, WRAL shifted to a conventional half hour of local news at 6:00.[52]

Opening the Culture War

By the late 1960s, Helms recognized that efforts to halt shifts in American values on race, morality, and a host of other issues were failing. He knew that A. J. Fletcher was not going to cancel *Viewpoint* or run it only on the eleven o'clock news. Yet the station's ratings slide was one more indication for Helms that television had failed him. Even if *Viewpoint* rarely acknowledged it, he recognized how free enterprise undercut tradition. Profits drove entertainment programming, and liberalism, although challenged, remained strong. Countercultural values seeped into the American consciousness through mainstream media. Despite his pessimism over the medium's impact, he believed television could be a potent weapon against change. His own ideas for programming would reinforce tradition. These realities could be turned to conservatives' advantage. Helms's *Viewpoints* pointed the way toward a new cultural politics. Viewers' response to Vice President Spiro Agnew's 1969 attack on the network news demonstrated cultural politics' effectiveness. A focus on cultural issues addressed the problem of voters' support of liberal candidates and policies not only by changing the subject but also by weakening support for liberalism.

Helms's support for tradition left him open to charges of duplicity while WRAL profited from Hollywood. Bill Morrison, who wrote a *News and Observer* column on culture and entertainment, observed that Helms's moralizing and WRAL's programming led to ridiculous juxtapositions. Channel 5 ran a "trailer from *The Liquidator* . . . showing a passionate young couple falling into the sack." The "dirty little teaser" followed Helms's *Viewpoint*, "where *The Carolina Quarterly* was recently decried as being 'worse' than 'unadulterated trash.'" Morrison affected sarcasm similar to Helms's when he supposed *Peyton Place* managed to "make something wholesome out of illicit sex." The columnist admonished the whole industry: "This hypocrisy reflects that corrupted state of the advertising medium known fondly as 'the tube.' The dollar qualifies principle."[53]

Helms responded to these accusations by protesting his lack of control. He believed media executives had a responsibility to censor popular culture and support tradition. There is every reason to believe he would have done just that if he possessed the means. Helms's occasional recommendations for national programming would have reinforced traditional values and the authority of elites, nuclear families, and Christianity while denying media coverage to protesters. In the days after the assassination of King in April 1968, he recommended ABC arrange for Rev. Billy Graham to address the nation. Graham was the only "man who could go on national television and command at once the respect and the attention of the American people."[54]

In the summer of 1968, Helms convinced ABC, or thought he had, to cover the seventy-mile "pilgrimage" of a thousand Boy Scouts from an air force base in Goldsboro, North Carolina, to the state's oldest church in Bath. The march's "purpose is a very frank effort to lead the boys in a serious rededication to God." Helms hoped for extensive coverage of the march, including a Billy Graham sermon, various churches' choir concerts, and the determination of a "little fellow with one leg." His appeal to ABC president Leonard H. Goldenson won the CEO's support. Sydney Byrnes, ABC's assignment manager, stated the march was "the upbeat kind of news story we so sorely need these days." But an ABC news producer declined to use the film. Instead, the *ABC Evening News* focused on "the so-called Poor People's thing in Washington." The Poor People's Campaign was a march from Mississippi to Washington, D.C., to draw attention to economic justice issues. Before his assassination, King had planned the march to push for passage of a poor people's bill of rights. ABC news made the opposite choice from Helms. From Helms's perspective, substituting coverage of the Boy Scouts for coverage of the Poor People's Campaign would have had a double benefit—reinforcing traditional values while suppressing coverage of dissent.[55]

When it came to entertainment, Helms preferred variety shows. He would have rejected reliance on youth culture, particularly the comedians and rock bands that the networks programmed. His favorite was *The King Family Show*. The King Sisters had a series of hits during the 1940s. After a 1966 appearance on *The Hollywood Palace*, ABC offered them a show. The Kings hosted with appearances by their entire extended family: brothers, husbands, cousins, nephews, nieces, and children. Even their seventy-nine-year-old father could sing and dance. A King husband did a patriotic narration on "The Square." WRAL-TV used a clip of the "The Square" to promote the show's patriotism. In conjunction the station gave away lapel pins that declared, "I'm a square and proud of it." The North Carolina Young Americans for Freedom, which Helms advised, distributed the pins. Helms expressed his hope that *The King Family Show* would establish a new commitment to family entertainment for the networks. ABC canceled *The King Family Show* in its second season.[56]

ABC largely ignored Helms's programming suggestions. When executives preferred profit to tradition, Helms wanted government intervention. The "best legal minds of America" have warned that the Supreme Court "has been making law under the guise of interpreting the Constitution." The Court had "demolished" the people's ability "to protect themselves against a tidal wave of pornography," while the "filth-mongers" grew "bolder and richer."[57] Conservatives threatened censorship. Justice

I. Beverly Lake of the North Carolina Supreme Court expressed his concern to the presidents of all three networks over the possible "tragic loss" of free speech if their industry's irresponsibility necessitated government involvement. For all their anti-regulation rhetoric, conservatives favored government enforcement of traditional morality. Helms pointed to California governor and movement conservatives' favorite for president, Ronald Reagan. "Reagan lamented the situation on television a few weeks ago—acknowledging that California is 'first' in its production and, thanks to Fortas and the rest of the Supreme Court, very little can be done to stop it." If Reagan became president, his Supreme Court appointments might reverse the decisions, or they might not. But Reagan, like Helms, recognized the efficacy of cultural politics, even if they had little practical effect. The Nixon administration grasped them, too.[58]

In the fall of 1969, President Richard Nixon delivered a speech calling for unity behind his plans to bring the Vietnam War to a satisfactory conclusion. The network commentaries following the president's address were uniformly skeptical. Helms telegraphed the White House to protest ABC's special coverage. Their discussion was not only "biased, inane and provocative" but also "prejudiced to the point of tragic absurdity."[59] To Helms's delight, Vice President Spiro Agnew voiced his concerns a few days later in a nationally televised speech.

Before a cheering Republican audience in Iowa, Agnew accused the network news broadcasters of abusing their power: "No medium has a more profound influence over public opinion. Nowhere in our system are there fewer checks on vast power." He especially attacked the networks' coverage of protest: "How many marches and demonstrations would we have if the marchers did not know that the ever-faithful TV cameras would be there to record their antics for the next news show? . . . [H]as more than equal time gone to the minority of Americans who specialize in attacking the United States?" Agnew closed with a challenge to television viewers to "let the networks know that they want their news straight and objective."[60] His deft questioning of the integrity and motivations of anchors and reporters gained ground for the Republican Party, especially its conservative wing.

The next *Viewpoint* glowed with approval for Agnew: "What the man said . . . is absolutely true." Helms relished the outpouring of public support for the vice president. "No, sir, the left-wing crowd no longer snickers about Spiro Agnew." Agnew, Helms felt, had pinpointed the media's role in the nation's crises: "There is no question, as Mr. Agnew said, that the news media have created much of the violence and turmoil now threatening to strangle this republic. . . . [T]hey have glorified the welfare state almost to the point of driving a stake through the heart of the free enterprise system."[61]

Helms broadcast Agnew's speech twice, once live and then again the next day. Local viewers let the networks have it. "We agree 100% with Spiro Agnew." "The good guys, the squares, the establishment get the short end." "We would appreciate hearing the news each day as fact only and without someone else's opinion." "You are destroying your freedom and ours by . . . exaggerated coverage of disruptive activities of minority groups such as the SDS [Students for a Democratic Society]." Several letter writers took advantage of the opening Agnew gave them to defend the South. "The biased news coverage as presented on your network is a slander on many of America's great institutions [particularly] . . . the grossly one-sided story given to the American people of the entire Southern region." The comments ranged from naive advocacy of broadcasts limited to the facts to acknowledgment of the complexity of television production. "TV news is not news. It's staged the same as *Tom Jones* and only slightly less apt to make a normal person regurgitate." "Our local TV Station (WRAL in Raleigh) has changed networks and newscasters several times . . . in an effort to reduce the stench." The networks' "Czars of Public Opinion" "do create news. They did in Chicago, and they did the same in Selma, Alabama."[62]

Conservative eastern North Carolinians recognized that Agnew mirrored Helms, and they praised WRAL for its "fair and unbiased news." "If it were not for WRAL the people of this area would never know the truth." "Brave! Brave! Brave!" "WRAL has always been just and fair in their broadcasting."[63] These viewer letters reflected not only Agnew's plea to let the networks know but also Helms's message for nearly ten years. He had coached them. Even their language as applied to television—"biased" and "unbiased," "fair," "just," and "truth"—they learned from Helms. They shared his sense that the civil rights movement victimized the white South and that elites had an obligation to support tradition and quash dissent. Helms and Agnew tapped into a mountain of discontent with the networks and the divided state of the country.

Nevertheless, a few viewers disagreed with WRAL and the vice president. "I think the national newsmen do a commendable job." "WRAL news is biased, and I think your bias shows up consistently. . . . Helms has an unpleasant manner that somehow makes even some of his good opinions sound sort of sour." But this opposition was rare. Helms hoped the lack of popular support for the networks would "jolt the pipsqueaks."[64]

Helms and Fletcher lost no time using the reaction to Agnew's speech to push ABC rightward. They supplied viewers with the addresses of network executives and forwarded choice letters to ABC, the other networks, and Agnew. Helms warned Nat Cavalluzzi that the vice president had pummeled the networks. "The count in favor of Agnew is running about 200-to-one." Fletcher applied pressure to ABC president Leonard Goldenson. "Agnew pointed up the very things that necessitated our dropping the ABC newscast," Fletcher explained. The nation "is fed up with the TV publicity given to Stokely Carmichael, Rap Brown, Eldridge Cleaver and his wife, and James Foreman, and other protesters and revolutionaries."[65]

Neither Goldenson nor other network executives conceded any need for change. After all, the networks broadcast Agnew's speech criticizing them, so the whole nation saw it rather than a few Iowa Republicans. In the summer of 1969, months before Agnew's speech, ABC had made the relatively conservative Howard K. Smith co-anchor of the *ABC Evening News* with Frank Reynolds. Smith was one of the few network commentators who expressed some sympathy with Agnew. He accepted the invitation from the Raleigh Chamber of Commerce that David Brinkley turned down. Helms approved his speech in advance, and it received an enthusiastic reception. Even with *The Huntley-Brinkley Report*'s ratings slide and Smith joining Reynolds, WRAL stayed with the NBC newscast until Reynolds left. In December 1970, Harry Reasoner replaced Reynolds. WRAL resumed broadcast of the *ABC Evening News* with Smith and Reasoner within a month of Reynolds's exit.[66]

There was little that Helms or even a president and vice president could do directly about the liberal perspectives in the media, let alone the era's social and cultural transformations. But cultural politics allowed Helms and his fellow conservatives to mobilize a conservative base. Helms's pious incitement pioneered cultural politics, mixing religious moralizing with racial incitement and red-baiting over issues like civil rights and prayer. Pious incitement began with attacks on the mainstream media in the 1950s. Helms's experience at WRAL—especially his years of reading viewer mail—taught him that the path to power involved assaulting the changes in America later summed up as "the sixties." This cultural politics helped conservatives control the GOP, win over the white South, and defeat Democrats. Once movement conservatives won power, Helms hoped, they could defend tradition.

On *Viewpoint* Helms continued to find fault with network programming, not because his disapproval made the news or entertainment more conservative but because it was good politics. "There was this big, burly bearded fellow," he complained, "on network television the other night identified as a Harvard professor speaking at a so-called 'peace rally', who was permitted to run on and on in a tirade against the American military." The professor accused the country of possessing an "obsession for war" and concluded that the military establishment was "fascist." "Yet the television networks portrayed him as some sort of authority. There was no one to offset his comments or even mildly disagree with them."[67]

Network executives, Helms explained on *Viewpoint*, "roll their eyes to the heavens in injured innocence" when they are criticized for the "rank propagandizing" in TV shows. ABC's film *Paris Blues* "was one of those typical propaganda pieces in which the white characters were all bad and the Negro characters all good."[68] The same bias showed up on the news. The networks, he accused, unfairly targeted the South: "What about other sections of the country? The major news media are struck suddenly deaf, dumb and blind!" In Trenton, New Jersey, schools closed because of "racial violence" and "cross-town busing." If this had happened in Charlotte, "can't you just hear the major news media talking about 'discrimination' in the south? But not a word about Trenton."[69]

Helms depicted an epic battle of tradition versus dangerous new values. When he raised racial issues, he focused on crime and welfare. He started with race early in the decade and never let up. But many cultural issues that would later be staples for Helms and other conservatives received scant attention: gays and lesbians, feminists, and abortion. Abortion debates took place at the state level before *Roe v. Wade*, while gay and lesbian activists had a limited profile before the 1970s. When Helms discussed gay rights, abortion, or feminism, his views anticipated the kinds of stands that movement conservatives would make in the 1970s. Helms was deeply homophobic. This showed up in his attacks on Bayard Rustin throughout the decade. In a 1971 *Viewpoint* on the liberal definition of "opportunity," he pointed to an "outraged lady" who "protested a federal grant of $9,000 to a group of young homosexuals to 'educate the public' on the 'normalcy of their perversion.'" This group was no doubt part of the gay rights movement emerging around the country. Helms admitted that he had no idea whether the allegation of federal funding was credible, but he used it as "a measurement of just how perverted are the present-day ideas of 'opportunity.'" He was convinced that the nation was homophobic enough that any support for gay and lesbian rights would benefit conservatives.[70]

Unlike gays and lesbians, feminists were active and visible during the late 1960s. Feminists received considerable media attention, and their protests gained national coverage. Given Helms's assault on feminism later in his career and his attention to liberals and radicals in the 1960s, his failure to comment on feminism's resurgence seems odd. But Helms simply did not take feminism seriously. The professional women he knew he found nonthreatening. The most prominent was Jane Dowden, president of Show Biz, Inc., the leading producer of syndicated variety shows in the nation. The company produced *The Porter Wagoner Show* and gave Dolly Parton her big break. But Dowden was in other respects a traditional woman. She and her family visited the Helmses. Helms's daughter Nancy was especially impressed. Helms wrote Dowden that "my Nancy was simply thrilled to see a *lady* president" and warned that after college she might come to Nashville looking for a job. Although Helms considered Dowden an appropriate role model for his daughter, this did not indicate support for a reconstruction of American gender relations. Dowden was acceptable because she otherwise made traditional choices. He also expected career women like Dowden and Jane Steppe, the female sportscaster Helms hired, to remain rare. In fact, his hiring of Steppe was something of a gimmick, as his comments about her acknowledged. An NBC executive wrote asking Helms: "How fast can she do the hundred .. . with full equipment?" Helms responded, "I dunno about 'the hundred,' but the little gal will hold her own in about any other contest."[71]

Despite his apparent respect for Dowden, Helms, like many of his colleagues, thought that feminists were ridiculous. His comments on radical feminists protesting a beauty pageant in 1970 reveals his attitude: Bob Hope "sized up a gang of 'women's lib' demonstrators who barged in on the Miss World contest" with 'Who are those uglies?'" Feminists, particularly the radicals protesting beauty pageants, challenged traditional conceptions of femininity and gender roles that even their male colleagues in the civil rights and antiwar movements clung to. Helms's lack of interest stemmed from the near unanimity on gender roles among men regardless of their ideological perspective. Once feminism's challenge to traditional roles for women gained traction during the 1970s, Helms took feminists seriously and helped build a backlash against them.[72]

One of the key issues for movement conservatives and feminists in the 1970s was abortion. In the 1960s, American public opinion had supported women's access to abortion for the life or health of the woman, for fetal deformity, and in cases of rape or incest. States began changing their laws in the late 1960s. The Roman Catholic Church opposed abortion in all cases, but most Protestant leaders, including many evangelicals, accepted the changes. So did many Democrats and Republicans, including some prominent movement conservatives like Senator Barry Goldwater. Governor Ronald Reagan signed California's abortion liberalization law in 1967, although he later regretted it. Helms agreed with the Catholic Church. Before *Roe v. Wade*, North Carolina had legalized abortion to protect a woman's health and in cases of rape and incest. Helms accused the legislature of violating Moses' "Commandments" and claimed that the measure resulted from the "relaxation of moral standards." He blamed "a permissive society, obsessed with the idea that there should be no restraints on human behavior." Once in the Senate, he would repeatedly support limits on abortion, including constitutional amendments without exceptions for the life of the woman or in cases of rape and incest.[73]

By the early 1970s, when he wrote these *Viewpoints* on Miss World protests and abortion, Helms was restless, even unhappy, at WRAL. He had honed pious incitement into a potent new ideology drawing on movement conservatism and rooted in the South's racial politics. His career at WRAL had allowed him time to experiment with what worked and what fell flat in a way that no politician could. Anxious to test his ideas in an election, he waited for an opening. He seriously considered a run for governor in 1968 but decided the field was too crowded. The decision to wait was fortuitous. His run for the Senate in 1972 came at just the right time in national and state politics.

6

The Dawn of a Conservative Era

Gaining Power, 1968 to 1972

Since the 1950s, Helms had alternated between premonitions of an America doomed by an immense conspiracy and a nation saved by conservatism's ascent. At the end of the decade he labeled the "sick Sixties," Helms concluded that America would either choose conservatism or succumb to the left-wing conspiracy that had been stalking the nation for decades. "The longer I live," Helms wrote Dr. Peele, his John Birch Society contact, "the more persuaded I become that there is a definite, perilous conspiracy far beyond anything imagined even by Robert Welch. And there is an incredible organization ready to pounce upon anybody who mentions it." In a similar vein, Helms painted an image of sinister forces steering the nation before a high school chapter of Future Farmers of America. "I am unalterably persuaded that even the best-intentioned people of America have been—and are being—misled." But there was always the hope the nation would turn to conservatives: "You live in an era when many are beginning to come alive to the fact that they have been subjected to three or four decades of brainwashing."[1]

Conspiracy theories had been a key feature of pious incitement since the 1950s. Helms admitted to Peele that it was "next to impossible" to find proof that a left-wing conspiracy existed.[2] The lack of evidence, however, did not undermine conspiracies' political value. Helms equated radicals, liberals, and moderates with Cold War enemies. He accused activists of violence to justify using violence against them. His tendency to lump everyone to his left into a single category fueled his suspicions. Although establishment liberals like Lyndon Johnson and Hubert Humphrey and radicals in black power and antiwar movements viewed each other with disdain, Helms believed that liberals and radicals were complicit. Conservatives could turn the upheavals of the decade to their benefit. In the early 1960s the mainstream media had focused on the heroic civil rights struggle in the South. Vigilantes and southern law enforcement targeted decorous protesters for sitting in the front of a bus or ordering a cup of coffee. This story was a simplified version of the issues at stake, but it was an attractive story for news media, especially television. The protests of the late 1960s—antiwar and black power—did not lend themselves to the sort of simple morality tale television favored.[3]

In retrospect, 1968 was the year a conservative era dawned. After the disastrous Democratic convention in Chicago, Helms surmised, "All of a sudden, it's no longer unpopular to be a rightwinger." Even the liberals admitted that voters were fed up. The year was so promising that Helms considered a run for governor. But a shift toward conservatives was far from certain. Helms feared that Republican nominee Richard Nixon would run as a moderate out of political expediency. Helms used WRAL to push the debate as far to the right as possible during the election and after—never hesitating to criticize Nixon.[4]

From 1968 until Helms's election to the U.S. Senate in 1972, urban riots, the failing effort in Vietnam, continued liberal influence, and the activism of the black power, antiwar, and feminist movements made his prognostications of doom seem plausible. Events aided his efforts to further the backlash against Democrats no matter how moderate. By 1968 his audience had expanded to forty weekly papers and fifty radio stations in North Carolina alone, and more than two hundred thousand people had written or called in response to Helms's commentaries. Nationally, *Viewpoint* appeared in ten daily papers and aired on radio stations as far away as Oregon. *Human Events* and the *Citizen*, the magazine of the white Citizens' Council, reprinted *Viewpoints*. And *Viewpoint* continued growing to two hundred newspapers across the country and seventy radio stations over the next few years. By 1972, three hundred thousand people had written.[5]

Two decades of mixing his media career with politics culminated in Helms's entrance into the 1972 Senate contest. But Helms was not a politician. He was first of all a media insider—a news director, a reluctant entertainment executive, and a conservative television personality. He had refined pious incitement for eleven years on WRAL. Conservatives encouraged him to run, and voters responded favorably because of *Viewpoint*. Helms's years addressing civic clubs and students made him an effective public speaker. But he disliked it and only reluctantly engaged in the retail politics of handshaking and barbecues. Along with his campaign manager and close friend Tom Ellis, Helms used pious incitement in a massive advertising campaign to depict his opponent—Congressman Nick Galifianakis—as an out-of-touch liberal.

Funeral Pyres for the Republic

Although Helms recognized that conspiracy theories made good politics, his private correspondence suggests he really believed his allegations.[6] The 1968 presidential race was a fight for the survival of the nation, and a conservative shift in American public life was the only hope for the future. Helms knew the public had grown weary of liberals and activists like King, Kennedy, and the president. But he feared voters would fail to understand what was at stake in 1968 as they had in 1964.

In the summer of 1967, Helms blamed Martin Luther King Jr. and Bobby Kennedy for the riots in Newark, Detroit, and other cities because they told "certain elements of society" they could ignore the law. In "a time when funeral pyres for the republic have been lit," King's and Kennedy's solutions resembled the guidance "the village arsonist" would give "the fire department." They had recommended expansion of federal programs to ease ghetto conditions. If "their advice" was rejected, Helms charged, King and Kennedy predicted "more riots." He insisted that riots were the visible edge of communist designs: "We have been carefully following the communist blue print, with scarcely a deviation. There are chuckles in the Kremlin these days" because things "are going according to form." Helms's pious incitement insinuated that King and Kennedy were at the very least "apologists" for those trying "to destroy America." Among King's "top lieutenants" was Bayard Rustin, who had "communist connections" in addition to pleading guilty to "a crime against nature." The crisis required an end to federal programs and "enough law enforcement, whatever the cost, to put down any further rebellion."[7]

The riots in the summer of 1967, the ongoing backlash against civil rights, the Great Society, and Vietnam—all made him confident that Johnson would be beaten. After the president's 1968 State of the Union address, Helms explored Johnson's vulnerabilities on *Viewpoint*. As a senator Johnson had opposed "so-called 'civil rights' laws," but as president he switched his position "in hot pursuit of bloc votes." Now the president was posing "as the original law-and-order man," Helms complained. "Not once—for a change—did he mention the words 'civil rights.'" President Johnson, Helms surmised, hoped the voters had forgotten his "open invitation to rebellion" when he "thundered: 'We shall overcome.'" Johnson had also campaigned as a guarantor of peace in 1964. Helms reminded viewers that Johnson had implied a limited commitment of American forces to Vietnam. "Remember?" he asked. "The president said, 'We don't want our American boys to do the fighting for Asian boys.'"[8]

Johnson was even more vulnerable—particularly on Vietnam—than Helms realized. The Tet offensive at the end of January 1968 shifted public opinion against the president and the war. After Johnson struggled in the New Hampshire primary, Bobby Kennedy decided to challenge him for the Democratic nomination. Helms reacted with disappointment to Johnson's withdrawal from the presidential race in March. He feared Johnson's retirement would deny conservatives the chance to define liberalism as the nation's problem. The president "is the symbol of the strange war in Vietnam" and "the nation's folly in dealing with racial strife." He embodied the instability that resulted from "too many compromises with pressure groups, too much deficit spending, and the rash imposition of unwise, dangerous federal controls."[9] If the conservatives faced Bobby Kennedy or Hubert Humphrey in the fall, voters might decide that Johnson was the problem, not liberalism.

King also seemed vulnerable to Helms in 1968. Helms reckoned the nation recognized King "for what he is—a sham, an agitator, a fellow traveler." When King pressed for programs addressing urban poverty, a law prohibiting housing discrimination, and an end to the Vietnam War, Helms accused him of extortion. "Failing to get all of this, the Negroes of America plan to take to the streets this summer in 15 major cities and countless smaller ones. 'Our nation,' the Reverend Doctor King threatened in—what does he call it?—his non-violent way, 'will sink deeper and deeper into the tragic valley of chaos.'" Close by, Stokely Carmichael "just grinned."[10]

Helms told WRAL viewers that King's concern about a right-wing takeover was a revealing "slip." King's fear of police violence demonstrated "that the black power movement thrives on the nation's timidity." Helms pleaded with viewers to understand that the "internal torment" was "carefully contrived" to undermine "our resistance to the spread of communism." The ongoing antiwar and civil rights protests across the nation should convince anyone of "this conspiracy." "Black power movements are festering on Negro campuses, and among Negro and white beatnik students on integrated campuses." The students were merely "puppets" controlled by America's enemies. "Law enforcement officials are aware of this. With proper support from the public and politicians, they could—and would—restore safety and sanity to the republic." But indifferent voters distracted by "trivialities" and politicians "too concerned" about reelection failed to support police action.[11]

Helms wanted an aggressive police presence for two reasons. First, he favored police suppression of protests. Second, he believed it would benefit the right politically. The police could curtail demonstrations, and many—perhaps most—Americans would back the authorities. Police repression would attach a stigma to the protesters. If a law enforcement crackdown triggered more riots, the distinction between protesters and rioters would be further confused.

Three days after Johnson's withdrawal from the presidential campaign, King was assassinated in Memphis. Helms condemned the "senseless murder" as "insanity" and then implied that King was at least partially culpable. "The suggestion was often made during Dr. King's career that violence stalked his heels, that indeed he provoked it," but it should make "no difference that Dr. King may have participated in the creation of an atmosphere of terrible tension at Memphis." Helms mixed pleas for moderation with warnings to African Americans to remain calm. The commentator hoped that King's death meant an end to protest. "Martin Luther King's death, as we say, now ironically provides the sternest test of his often contradictory advocacy of non-violence. If somehow it can cause the country to turn away from its apparent obsession with social conflict, then much good can emerge."[12]

In 1968, Senator Bobby Kennedy's visibility rose as he sought the Democratic nomination for president. Kennedy seemed to be the Democrats' best hope. His stance on the war had evolved into opposition. Kennedy's victory in the June 5 California primary made him the almost certain nominee. His assassination the same evening as his victory in California shocked the nation.

Helms's response to Kennedy's assassination—"awesomely regrettable"—resembled his reaction to King's. The "waves of violence" in the United States were due to "the deviltry of a frenzied minority, provoked and agitated by pious and self-serving architects of various movements that have as their goal the absolute destruction of all of the fundamental principles of America." Kennedy, like King, shared some of the blame for his assassination. "Candor compels the observation that Robert Kennedy himself played a substantial role in the provocation of unrest in this country." Helms then turned to speculate that King was assassinated to incite riots: "And though 'white society' has been roundly condemned for killing Martin Luther King, a very acceptable case can be made for the theory that it was a carefully-contrived conspiracy designed to set off a violent wave of racial disorders across the land. Certainly that was the result of it."[13]

Helms was confident enough that 1968 was a year of conservative opportunity that he considered running for governor. He shared his political ambitions with Republican ally Earl Butz, former assistant secretary of agriculture under Eisenhower. Butz was dean of Purdue University's school of agriculture. Like Helms, he was politically ambitious, entering the governor's race in Indiana in 1968. Well respected by A. J. Fletcher, Butz raised the possibility of Helms running for governor to WRAL's founder. But Fletcher dismissed it.[14]

Helms was bitter over Fletcher's reaction. "I sometimes feel that I am being resented because of the public attention that naturally would come to anybody doing the sort of work that I do." Helms decided to pursue his ambitions, even if it meant quitting his job. He promised Butz to leave "no stone unturned." In the end, though, Helms decided against running for governor. The GOP primary was crowded. Two well-connected Republicans announced: Jim Gardner, the first Republican congressman from eastern North Carolina since the turn of the century, and a "Stickley fellow" who was a protégé of Congressman Jonas. Helms supported Gardner and planned "to help him privately."[15]

The GOP nominated Gardner, and Lieutenant Governor Robert Scott defeated Mel Broughton in the Democratic primary. Gardner's personal appeal in the east along with the GOP's usual strength in the west meant he would be a strong statewide candidate. "Scott could not win the Governorship," Helms contended, although "Gardner could lose it." During the primary, Broughton had claimed the mantle of conservatism. To Helms's deep frustration, the defeated Broughton endorsed his opponent. On *Viewpoint* Helms complained that Broughton's rallying around his party nominee blurred the lines between "contrasting philosophies" and contributed to voter "cynicism." It made the "politics" of the state resemble that of the nation. When conservative Democrats "survey[ed] the field of Humphrey, Bobby Kennedy, and McCarthy," they found "a choice of bad, worse, or worst."[16] Scott was significantly more conservative than the national candidates, but Helms cast him as a liberal whose supporters wanted to "conceal" his "Negro" support.[17]

After Bobby Kennedy's assassination, the leading contenders in the presidential race were Richard Nixon and Hubert Humphrey, with George Wallace as an independent candidate. Helms feared that the influence of liberal Republicans—particularly Nelson Rockefeller—at the GOP convention in Miami would lead to "a Nixon-grown-timid." The commentator cautioned Republicans that "a compromising Richard Nixon will have all the public appeal of a stale cup of yesterday's coffee. . . . The rising popularity of George Wallace, and the repeated ovations given Governor Ronald Reagan, ought to be instructive about the mood of the people." Helms hoped that pressure from Wallace on his right flank would lead Nixon to "return to the fighting posture that years ago won for him the hatred of the leftwing." If the parties did not provide a conservative al-. ternative, Helms hinted, Americans might seek change outside the law: "If the people cannot reverse the trends of their government by political means, then none should be surprised if they turn to other means."[18]

In Helms's assessment, Nixon delivered "a masterful acceptance speech" at the GOP convention. Helms expressed his hopes to conservative editor Bill Sharpe: "I've known him a long time, and this was by far his best effort. If he could somehow decide to be his own man, and not try to cater to Rockefeller and the rest, he might give the country a choice." Nixon's speech put Helms in a rare optimistic mood. The disastrous Democratic convention lifted him to jubilation. "Happiness," he pronounced, "is a Republican watching the turmoil of the Democratic National Convention on television."[19]

The divide between activists and the liberal Democrats of the Kennedy presidency had grown into a chasm by 1968. Humphrey had championed civil rights throughout his career and advocated the Nuclear Test Ban Treaty, Medicare, and the Peace Corps. But activists saw him as the establishment candidate. Several thousand protesters arrived in Chicago with different backgrounds and agendas, but all were against the war. The war also divided Democrats inside the convention. Ignoring the counsel of other Democrats, Mayor Richard Daley deployed force to halt the protests. Conflict came to a head the day of Humphrey's nomination. The police and Illinois National Guard met protesters chanting "Peace Now, Peace Now" and marching down Michigan Avenue. The authorities attacked—swinging clubs, firing tear gas, and losing track of who was a protester, who was a reporter, and who was an uninvolved pedestrian. The networks cut away from Humphrey's acceptance speech to the live conflict. NBC anchorman Chet Huntley charged that Chicago police went "out of their way to injure newsmen and prevent them from . . . gathering information about what was going on." A *New York Times* reporter detailed the indiscriminate police behavior, noting that even "elderly bystanders were caught in the police onslaught." Liberal columnist Tom Wicker mused, "The truth was these were our children in the streets, and the Chicago Police beat them up." The cutaway from Humphrey's speech not only denied the candidate a national audience but inadvertently associated Humphrey and the rest of the Democrats with the chaos.[20]

Press reports on the Chicago demonstrations enraged Helms. The issue for him was how to interpret the beating police delivered to protesters and reporters. "The public has been subjected to a steady stream of tearful accounts of how various reporters were cracked across the head by police during efforts to disperse mobs of dirty, smelly hippies threatening to take over the city." The police action, the commentator believed, was what the nation needed. "If newsmen . . . want to continue to help provoke and encourage violence," Helms declared, then "a cracked skull" was "what they deserve."[21]

In the wake of the Chicago convention, Helms drew tenuous conclusions regarding antiwar demonstrators. The "leftwing crowd never refers to *communism* when discussing violence" because communism "to them is at least implicitly equated with 'peace.' One understands, therefore, what is meant by 'peaceful demonstrations,' and the clamoring, agitating 'peace organizations.'" Instead of Wicker's children, Helms saw communists. The "major news media," he alleged, concealed a "groundswell of evidence" of communist infiltration. Helms quoted a "liberal" news photographer who covered the Chicago convention: "The disorder created by the hippies and the peaceniks was 'carefully planned and executed by admitted communists.'"[22]

Helms used the Chicago convention to depict the vice president as a dangerous radical. Humphrey "has long been the symbol of the far left . . . even now, though in camouflaged semantics, he boasts of his 20-year record of promoting forced integration, endless government controls, greater government spending, and higher taxes." Humphrey may "serve as the country's chief executive for the next four or eight years," but "history will record it as an event conceived in an era of planned anarchy and brought forth in an atmosphere of conspiratorial riots." Helms's description of Humphrey as a "far left" candidate nominated during "conspiratorial riots" associated Humphrey with protesters demanding "Dump the Hump," as if he were their candidate. Helms's commentaries blurred the distinctions among everyone to his left, whether an establishment liberal like Humphrey or radical antiwar protesters such as the Yippies.[23] Helms was right, however, that the convention was a disaster for the Democratic Party.

In the Chicago convention protests, Helms saw not only political opportunity but a vindication of conservatives. "The architects of destruction are not through—yet. But there is an encouraging stirring among the people" because of what they "saw on television." The disruption of the convention was more than just another opportunity to write liberals and activists out of the moral community. Helms recognized it as a major turning point in American politics. For conservatives it was "a glimmer of light and hope." Helms mused, "If the sun is setting on the charlatans who have for so long sought to undo the republic, then it may be rising again for the American dream of decency, responsibility and progress. Let us all hope that this is indeed the beginning of the dawn of a new era. The old one has been a nightmare."[24]

After the conventions, Nixon maneuvered adroitly to draw as many racial conservatives into the Republican Party as possible without alienating moderates. In September 1968 he gave an interview in Charlotte, North Carolina, in which he expressed his support for school desegregation but questioned federal authority to achieve it. "I think to use that power on the part of the federal government to force a local community to carry out what a federal administrator or bureaucrat may think is best for that local community—I think that is a doctrine that is a very dangerous one." He settled on a formula that would serve Republicans well for two decades, expressing support for racial equality while attacking Washington liberals and their programs seeking equality. The candidate ignored the parents in Charlotte who actively sought integrated schools.[25]

Nixon's statement echoed Helms. But Helms applied pressure to push the presidential candidate as far right as he would go. He relayed rumors circulated by Nixon supporters that a President Nixon would rein in "the arbitrary high-handedness of the Department of Health, Education and Welfare with respect to forced school integration," but he wanted to hear it from the candidate. "It would be more comforting, and certainly more persuasive, if Mr. Nixon himself would declare his intentions in unequivocal terms." Helms cited a case in Nash County, North Carolina, as indicative of the issue. Local school officials declared they had done all they could to integrate, but Health, Education and Welfare (HEW) officials insisted that the efforts were inadequate. "It matters not to HEW," Helms railed, "that the substantial integration already achieved in Nash County has been detrimental to all children—and most detrimental to Negro children." HEW believed the high dropout rate among black students in the "previously all-white schools" resulted from local authorities' failure to create "a suitable climate." Helms blamed the African American students. The "Negro pupils" dropped out because they were "forced to compete beyond their capabilities." Keeping the pressure on the candidate, Helms asserted that "Nixon would do well to make clear his intent on this question. George Wallace already has."[26]

Helms believed that Wallace was critical to conservatism. When conservative ally A. W. McAlister disclosed that he had donated "substantially" to the Wallace campaign, Helms replied, "We're on the same team." Wallace would make Nixon "at least a little more conservative. And I am persuaded—regardless of what anybody says to the contrary—that Wallace will be getting votes that Nixon wouldn't get," especially in eastern North Carolina. Expressing similar sentiments on *Viewpoint*, Helms maintained that many white working-class Wallace voters disliked Humphrey but would not vote for Nixon. This demonstrated, Helms insisted, that "a vote for Wallace is a vote for Wallace."[27]

In late October a worried Helms assessed the Wallace phenomenon for editor and friend Bill Sharpe. Predicting Wallace would win North Carolina with Nixon second and Humphrey third, he conceded, "I would bet no sizable amount of money on it." Helms explained that a friend "down east" looked up the license plates of cars with "Wallace stickers" and "less than 50 per cent of them were even registered to vote." Helms concluded, "It's a baffling situation. . . . [T]here is so much silence, and so much 'undecided' vote. I remember how supremely confident I was in 1948 that Truman would lose."[28]

Nixon was stronger than Helms suspected, but otherwise the commentator was on target. Nixon won North Carolina, but Wallace carried the racially conservative but solidly Democratic eastern part of the state. Many eastern North Carolinians who had supported Johnson in 1964 voted for Wallace four years later. Nationally, Nixon won 43.4 percent of the popular vote to Humphrey's 42.7 percent, with Wallace receiving 10.5 percent. The combined Wallace-Nixon vote delivered a solid defeat to liberalism. In the governor's race, the Democrat Scott defeated Gardner. Helms praised Gardner in a post-election *Viewpoint*: Gardner's strong support "has indeed established a meaningful two-party system in this state." But privately Helms was not satisfied with Gardner's performance. "Gardner has had it," Helms concluded in late October. "The Republicans have blown a perfectly good opportunity to establish a permanent two-party system in North Carolina." Enough people voted for Wallace and Scott to give the Democrat the win.[29]

Helms's own interest in running for office must have deepened his disappointment with the North Carolina GOP and Gardner's missed opportunity. After the election, Helms wrote Earl Butz regarding his ambitions for future officeholding and his discontent at WRAL-TV. He planned to travel to Washington as often as possible to "renew and rebuild my contacts." In January he felt that "problems" continued between him and Fletcher. "I respect the gentleman, and intend to continue to do the best I can for him and the company. But it is not always pleasant." Over time his relationship with Fletcher improved, but Helms's political ambitions did not fade.[30]

Nixon and the Conservative Turn

The presidential election had proved a referendum on liberalism—exactly what Helms wanted. Humphrey did not successfully distance himself from Johnson on Vietnam and was just as closely identified with the liberal social and racial policies of the Democrats as LBJ. The national mood on race had shifted, as many whites regardless of region came to share at least some of Helms's racial anxieties. An offhand remark to a friend captured the white voters' mood in 1968. "I see in the paper," Helms grumbled, "where the white folks are to blame for everything. What are we going to do about us?" Three years before, LBJ had appropriated civil rights slogans to identify his presidency with black aspirations, but Helms started 1968 using "We Shall Overcome" to stoke white voter resentment.[31]

In the midst of racial backlash, voters who feared change heard law-and-order rhetoric as a promise to halt social transformation. The voters' conservative mood was stronger in North Carolina and the rest of the South than in other regions. The newly elected Governor Scott—from the moderate wing of the state's Democratic Party—recognized that reality. "I've been very proud of the Governor," Helms observed to Tom White. "I would not try to kid either you or him: I did not support him. His conduct these past eight weeks makes me wish I had." Among the most pleasing actions to Helms was Scott's selection of White as his chief legislative counsel. White, a Helms ally, had been an advocate of the speaker ban in the general assembly and served on the university system of North Carolina's board of trustees. Scott's rhetoric indicated a tough policy toward the university. White gave Helms a direct avenue to the governor.[32]

Helms was not content, however, with the shift toward conservatism at the local or national level. He wanted a reversal of the policies of recent decades. He worried over liberal influence on Nixon—this time from Congress and the federal bureaucracy. "Nixon has the capacity to serve the republic well," Helms wrote Edward Annis, but it would require "vigilance on his part to avoid being mesmerized by the liberals." Only a couple weeks after the inaugural, Nixon had disappointed him.[33]

Helms wasted no time before criticizing the president. He lashed into the president for his stand on the nonproliferation treaty. "In Russia's planned conquest of Europe—and let no one pretend that this is not on her schedule—the communists seek to reduce all possible resistance to Russia's 'conventional' weapons." It was critical, Helms believed, that Western European nations develop a "nuclear umbrella" to deter the Soviets. The "real question" regarding the treaty, he maintained, was "When—not if—Russia decides to move against Western Europe, how is Europe to be defended?"[34]

Helms hoped that conservative criticism would shift policy rightward, especially with a sympathetic president. Few Nixon policies maddened Helms more than the president's opening to China. Recognizing there were limits to American power, Nixon envisioned a world of five major powers: the Soviet Union, the United States, Western Europe, Japan, and China. But the United States had refused to have diplomatic or other ties to the People's Republic of China since the Chinese Revolution in 1949. Establishing normal relations with China, Nixon believed, would mean increased global stability and allow the United States to exploit the rift between the Soviets and the Chinese. In 1969 the division between the two communist powers led to fighting along their vast border. Nixon decided to reverse a policy that amounted to the United States favoring the Soviets over the Chinese. But Helms expressed bewilderment at Nixon's Chinese diplomacy: "It is one of history's ironies that Richard Nixon, who first attracted public admiration through his strong stand against communism, should now be the President to lead his nation into an alliance with communist China." Helms could not fathom the reasons for Nixon's shift. An appeal to the left, accepting the inevitable, a misguided effort to reduce Chinese aggression—these reasons all ignored "the morality of the matter." Nixon's change meant appeasing the world's "most brutal and ruthless communist regime." Helms supposed that admitting China to the UN could not make the institution "worse." "The United Nations has never, in its most remote action, served to benefit either the United States or the cause of freedom." What Helms feared, however, was that U.S. allies would "interpret it as a surrender to communism."[35]

Nixon's China policy infuriated Helms, but the most important foreign policy issue the administration faced was Vietnam. Helms rejected the peace talks the Johnson administration pursued during the 1968 presidential elections. Insinuating that the negotiations were treasonous, he cited casualty figures as though deaths only occurred during peace talks. "And in the period of May 13 through the middle of November, 6,914 Americans died in Vietnam. May 13 is the day, you recall, that those 'peace talks' began in Paris. One can only imagine how heavy must be the hearts of the mothers and fathers of American boys who are dying while our government 'negotiates' with the communists." Helms hoped the "new President will bring the country to its senses—and, in doing so, save the lives of countless thousands of Americans. Mr. Nixon need only ask: Why not win?"[36]

Helms's private correspondence on the war demonstrated a more nuanced understanding than his commentaries. In a 1972 letter to a viewer who had doubts about Nixon's Vietnam policies, Helms described himself as "one who more than a decade ago opposed our entry into this Asian mess on the ground." This private reference to a long-standing opposition to the war—at least the ground war—would surprise WRAL-TV viewers, since *Viewpoint* was relentlessly hawkish. Helms's reaction was even more sympathetic when a conservative Christian mother wrote him that she did not want her son, a high school basketball star and a B-plus student, "sent off to fight a no-win war." Helms responded, "You're on sound ground concerning your son and the Vietnam situation."[37]

Helms's misgivings about the war sometimes crept into his commentaries. Citing MacArthur, Helms insisted that the United States should have limited its commitments to support for "those already effectively fighting communism in Vietnam." Helms shared with some hawks, including Ronald Reagan, doubts about the wisdom of America's original involvement in Vietnam. But he believed victory essential once the commitment was made, a position that compounded one mistake with numerous sequels. No matter how badly the war went, Helms encouraged aggressive military action and blamed failure on the antiwar movement and timid Democrats. "A united America, determined to win, could and would have won the Vietnam war years ago had it not been for the militant voices and political pressures," he insisted, "which gave aid and comfort to the enemy."[38]

Despite recognizing no limits on America power and insisting on the ease of victory in Vietnam, Helms limited his criticism of Nixon on the war. The nation "may wish" Nixon would instruct the military to "win in Vietnam, and then get out," but people "give the President credit for making every other possible overture for peace." The Nixon administration's approach to the war was Vietnamization. This meant replacing U.S. combat troops with South Vietnam's forces. Vietnamization had Helms's tentative support. Nixon, he noted, had withdrawn sixty thousand troops, and U.S. casualties were down. Helms gave the president wide latitude on Vietnam for several reasons. For one thing, letters to WRAL demonstrated that many conservatives were sick of the war. But perhaps most important were the continuing protests and the Nixon administration's response. Helms understood that the protesters and the nation's war fatigue restricted the president's options. And Helms loved the administration's tough stance on demonstrations. In the spring of 1969, Helms castigated the American Association of University Professors for their "bewildering condemnation" of the Nixon administration. What, Helms asked, had the professors so upset? "Why, it was the announcement in Washington last week that the Justice Department plans a crackdown on student militants." The administration's tough law-and-order stance toward protests would build support for conservatism. "The country better make haste to rally in support of the President and the Justice Department," Helms warned viewers, "for, at last, the law-abiding citizens of the republic—the ones who foot the bill—have something going for *them*."[39]

In a similar tone, Governor Scott signaled that his administration possessed limited tolerance for dissent, particularly from students at state universities. Shortly after his inauguration, Scott sent a memo to the state university presidents acknowledging that although "peaceful picketing and demonstrating" were legal, "picketing or demonstrating must not jeopardize public order" or "interfere with the regular classroom, laboratory or office activity." He reminded the presidents that police did not need their permission to enforce the law on their campuses. The memo was a not-too-subtle warning to subdue the antiwar demonstrations on state university campuses. The federal courts had ruled the communist speaker ban unconstitutional, but many in the state remained uncomfortable with the challenges to authority at the University of North Carolina at Chapel Hill and other schools. Helms expressed strong approval of the governor's actions. Governor Scott has "always been a 'liberal,'" Helms wrote a friend in Tennessee, "but he has taken an astonishingly hard line on the campus creeps. The leftwingers are about to throw up—and we conservatives, who thought we had lost our shirts, are cheering madly." The governor received equally glowing praise on *Viewpoint*: "Governor Robert Scott, bless him, continues to stand undaunted in his apparent determination that the campuses of state-owned colleges and universities in North Carolina shall not be surrendered to the arrogant absurdities of a loud minority. . . . As the saying goes, the university officials were chicken; Bob Scott wasn't."[40]

After Helms joined the advisory board for the North Carolina Young Americans for Freedom in 1966, his involvement in the state's colleges and universities grew. For many the advisory board was honorary, but Helms helped YAF raise money, gain media coverage, and secure speaking engagements at civic clubs. He advised YAF on strategy and drew them into his own projects. One of several endorsements of YAF activities on *Viewpoint* led to seven new branches and five hundred dollars in donations. Helms won a national YAF award for Outstanding State Advisor. With Helms advising, the North Carolina YAF gained widespread attention. In the fall of 1969 the organization received coverage in a dozen AP and UPI stories, which half the state's daily papers carried, in addition to numerous local stories. CBS news also reported on the North Carolina YAF's efforts.[41]

At UNC, conservative students won significant victories. Conservatives, including YAF, persuaded the student body to reject affiliation with the National Student Association. On *Viewpoint*, Helms celebrated this development, noting that the organization had "been active in student uprisings across the country." But not all students were going to accept the governor's demands for obedience. The editorial staff at UNC's student newspaper, the *Daily Tar Heel*, asserted their independence just as the spring 1969 semester ended. The state legislature considered an amendment that would require student members of the board of trustees to have "a clean shave" and a "normal businessman's haircut." The amendment failed, but the *Daily Tar Heel* ran an editorial titled "Go to Hell" that condemned the measure. "The point is that any bigot who feels qualified enough to judge another human being on the basis of, say, his looks, or his color, or whatever, is out of the range of the appeal of this newspaper, and can simply go to hell."[42]

The Chapel Hill YAF turned to Helms for help in responding. He recognized an opportunity for conservatives. "Senator White and I have entered into a little conspiracy (not the first one, I might add)," Helms wrote Harvey Harkness, a YAF leader at UNC. We hope to "be of assistance to you." Attending a board of trustees meeting in Charlotte, White introduced a resolution condemning the *Daily Tar Heel*'s editorial language and cutting off the student fees that supported the newspaper. The trustees substituted a mild resolution that criticized the editorial's language but left the paper's funding alone.[43]

On *Viewpoint*, Helms praised White and took the *Daily Tar Heel* and the trustees to task: "Former State Senator Tom White, by making sense himself, has once again emphasized the functional absurdity of the backslapping mutual admiration society known as the board of trustees of the University of North Carolina." White, Helms admitted, knew his resolution would fail. In fact, White introduced the measure to allow Helms to criticize the "squirming" trustees along with the *Daily Tar Heel*. Helms also rebuked campus authorities for doing nothing about the "barnyard language" in the *Daily Tar Heel* and the *Technician* at North Carolina State University. "How long must one wait before *somebody* in authority warns the immature little boys with the nasty minds—the ones who have been writing and publishing the obscene campus editorials—that this kind of irresponsibility will not be tolerated?" Although the trustees protected the student newspaper's freedom of expression, Helms saw the issue from a different perspective. "What could be a greater example of freedom than to allow each student, according to his own choice, to decide whether he *wants* to help finance the publication of . . . *The Daily Tar Heel*?"[44]

For YAF and other conservatives at UNC, the "Go to Hell" editorial was just one in a series of battles with the *Daily Tar Heel*. The paper sometimes published conservative commentaries or letters and covered the conservatives' efforts, but the editorial staff was supportive of campus activism against the war and for civil rights. YAF threatened to sue the school over the student fees, which supported the paper. Helms solicited advice from White, a UNC law school graduate. The conservative students, Helms concluded, "have the kooks and the UNC administration off-balance." White recommended that YAF recruit "some negro student with a greatly underprivileged background" to join the lawsuit against the *Daily Tar Heel*. White thought this would push the university administration rightward. YAF was following Helms's lead with the *Daily Tar Heel* lawsuit. Two weeks before the "Go to Hell" editorial, he asked "why students at all universities don't protest their being forced to contribute to the financing of such publications." Little seems to have come of the lawsuit beyond publicity. Helms felt, however, that the students "made their point."[45]

In the fall of 1969 Helms drew YAF into his own project. "Confidentially," he explained to state YAF chairman Harold Herring, "we are about to be successful in persuading Bob Scott to launch an investigation into the textbook and collateral reading material being fed to high school and college students." Herring, a student at Atlantic Christian College in Wilson, North Carolina, was a fervent Helms supporter. Herring contacted YAF members—especially those on state-supported campuses—and asked for reports on the readings assigned in their classes. Helms was particularly interested in "obscene books, such as that trash produced by James Baldwin," "leftwing books such as Michael Harrington's essay on socialism," books "slanted to the left in economics, government, philosophy," and "other materials which disclose an obvious attempt to orient students' minds toward the left." Helms wanted "details"—not just "the books" but also "the courses, the professors, [and] the library-card numbers." The students embraced the assignment. Harvey Harkness, the Chapel Hill informant, reported, "The list is not as damaging as I would like, since almost all texts in these departments are very 'liberal' but relatively few are 'hard left.'" YAF members supplied lists of books, courses, and professors from UNC, North Carolina State, and Duke. Helms sent them to Governor Scott.[46]

Helms's satisfaction with Governor Scott lasted about a year. Scott apparently took no action on Helms's and YAF's textbook report. The primary cause for Helms's break with Scott, however, concerned school desegregation. During Scott's term, a decade and half after the *Brown* decisions, North Carolina had exhausted its resistance to desegregation. Scott was inclined to follow federal law on desegregation, but busing was unpopular. The governor, Helms protested, enjoyed "lavish praise" from liberals for giving in to the federal requirement "that the southern states—and the southern states only—begin massive busing of school children to achieve instant integration." Faced with a choice "between the citizens" and "the federal oppressors," Scott sided with "the oppressors." A week later, Scott had reconsidered his position. Helms, though, was in no mood to praise his reversal. The governor planned to withhold funds under a state law for the "busing of school children 'until'—and he laid unusual stress on the word," Helms observed—the courts declared it unconstitutional. Helms acknowledged that Scott judged correctly that the law could not withstand legal scrutiny. This court battle should just be the beginning of state resistance. The legislature could pass new laws expressing "the will of the people." Finally, "if need be, the legislature can take the public schools out of the transportation business altogether."[47]

Helms was no happier with President Nixon on public school desegregation than Scott. A month after Nixon took office, he bristled at the suggestion it was "'too early' to begin questioning the policies and judgments of President Nixon." On *Viewpoint*, Helms pointed to Nixon's statements concerning public schools in his acceptance speech at the Republican National Convention and on a campaign stop in Charlotte. "So, Mr. Nixon—the candidate—favored not only freedom-of-choice, but he also favored returning policy-making decisions concerning schools to the local communities. But Mr. Nixon—the President—has now appointed as his Secretary of Health, Education and Welfare, Robert Finch, who has flatly rejected freedom-of-choice." His commissioner of education, Dr. James Allen, numbers "among the nation's most zealous advocates of forced integration." Helms concluded, "Maybe George Wallace was wrong when he commented . . . that there isn't a 'dime's worth of difference' between Mr. Nixon and Hubert Humphrey." But judging Nixon on these appointments, Wallace's "dime" seemed about "right."[48]

The war on poverty, which continued under Nixon, and the president's guaranteed income proposal also drew withering criticism. Nixon's "proposal to establish a guaranteed annual income for everybody—by whatever name it may be called—would be a giant step in the wrong direction," Helms fumed. "It flies in the face of logic, sound economics and human nature." The president admitted that his proposal "would double the present number of welfare recipients." His work requirements appeared sound at first, but the "loopholes there are so gaping that the Civil Liberties Union could drive city buses through them." Helms lamented, "The simple truth is that no government has the ability to solve the personal problems of all of its citizens." Nixon only helped "galvanize the false notion that the government 'owes' everybody a guaranteed annual income." Private initiative would do a better job if the federal government would stop preempting "personal charity and compassion in America."[49]

Helms was profoundly dissatisfied with the continuities from Johnson to Nixon—or for that matter from the New Deal to Nixon. The commentator recognized that Nixon was more conservative than any likely Democrat and that the conservative movement wielded more influence through the GOP than among the Democrats or in a third party. Certainly, Helms would have criticized Johnson or Humphrey more harshly and more often than he did Nixon if they had proposed a federally guaranteed income or recognized the People's Republic of China. Listening to his commentaries, one might conclude that Helms had so many differences with Nixon that he agreed with Wallace's assessment. But Nixon—really Nixon-Agnew—earned Helms's admiration and support on a key point: cultural politics. Nothing excited Helms like Agnew lashing out at the media. The same is true of Scott's getting tough on state universities at the start of his term. Helms celebrated Scott for demanding order, but there was not a substantial change in policy. The state universities remained largely autonomous.

Helms had contemplated switching parties for years. When he considered campaigns against Congressman Cooley in 1962 and Senator Jordan in 1966 and for governor in 1968, he expected to run as a Republican.[50] But during Nixon's presidency he finally switched parties. The deciding factor was Nixon's rhetoric, which Helms judged correct even if his policies hewed too close to the center. At Kansas State University in September 1970 before an audience of sixteen thousand students with a live network broadcast, Nixon declared that a stable peace in Vietnam required continued fighting and demanded law and order; he blamed lax university officials and the liberal establishment for the nation's troubles. "We all know that at some universities small bands of destructionists have been allowed to impose their own rule of arbitrary force," the president intimated. He then departed from his prepared address. "That may be true in some places, but not at Kansas State." The students gave Nixon a standing ovation. The speech so excited Helms that he praised the president on two consecutive *Viewpoints* and attributed his change in party registration to it.[51]

"Wednesday at Manhattan, Kansas, may very well have marked the time and place of the making of a President," Helms reckoned. During the speech, the "television network cameras" searched out the "clusters of hippies moving through the crowd like shaggy spiders" with the intention of disrupting the president's address. The protesters "visibly" shook the president. But the majority of students came to his rescue. These "young people" gave "an ovation of thunderous support for the President clearly unlike anything he had experienced before. He hesitated, then smiled, and to the delight of his audience, he began to talk about decency and courtesy. He talked about freedom—how it can be preserved and how it can be lost."[52]

After hearing "your splendid address" and seeing "the magnificent response" of the students, "I went downtown and changed my registration from Democrat to Republican," Helms wrote Nixon. "I thought I ought to put my registration where my mouth is," Helms explained to Harry Dent, a former aide to Senator Strom Thurmond and Nixon's chief southern adviser. "Anyhow I am now a Republican."[53]

Proving a Conservative Could Win: The 1972 North Carolina Senate Election

Ever since the 1950s, conservatives had encouraged Helms to enter the political arena. Helms had considered runs for Congress in 1962, for Senate in 1966, and for governor in 1968. His reluctance had more to do with financial and family obligations than the lack of ambition. In December 1971 he wrote Earl Butz, Nixon's secretary of agriculture, that he "would be interested" in conservatives' suggestion that he challenge Jordan in 1972 on "one condition." Helms wanted Fletcher's assurance of a job if he lost. Under pressure from friends and political allies, particularly Tom Ellis, Fletcher relented.[54] In late January 1972, a month before the filing deadline, Ellis sent out a letter soliciting support for Helms's candidacy. Publicly, Helms dubbed the prospect of his running "far-fetched." If he harbored any real doubts, the response to the letter erased them. It brought fifteen thousand letters of support and twenty thousand dollars. Helms valued the letters as much as the money because, like viewer letters, they indicated deep support.[55]

The *Goldsboro News*, an eastern North Carolina paper, sized Helms up as Senator Jordan's "most formidable opponent," but few believed he had a real chance. Republicans had not won a statewide election in seven decades. Helms sought the votes of Republicans and the conservative Democrats who had supported I. Beverly Lake and George Wallace. Lake lost his two bids for governor in 1960 and 1964. Nixon won North Carolina with a plurality of votes in 1968. Wallace came in second, denying Humphrey the conservative Democrats he needed for victory. Nixon's and Wallace's combined votes amounted to an anti-liberal majority in the state and nation. But enough white voters chose Scott to elect him governor over Republican Jim Gardner. Any candidate who could draw Republicans and conservative Democrats together would be daunting, but no one had done it in a statewide election. Helms was relatively unknown in the region of greatest Republican strength—the piedmont cities and mountain towns west of WRAL's viewing area. Moreover, a division in the North Carolina Republican Party between longtime party members and former conservative Democrats like Helms and Gardner was a potential stumbling block. But key endorsements from Congressman Charles Jonas and former GOP state chairman Sim Delapp helped Helms sail through the primary.[56]

The year 1972 proved to be fortuitous for Helms to run. The issues he emphasized—busing, crime, and welfare—had moved to the center of voters' concerns. President Nixon was immensely popular in North Carolina. George McGovern, the Democratic nominee for president, never mounted a strong challenge to the president and became a liability for other Democrats. In an upset primary victory, the North Carolina Democratic Party chose Durham congressman Nick Galifianakis over the incumbent, Everett Jordan. Although a moderate in a national context, Galifianakis was more liberal and less well known than the seventy-five-year-old Jordan, and he was far more vulnerable to Helms's pious incitement.[57]

Helms, with Ellis as campaign manager, assembled a strong statewide organization. They relied on conservative Democrats and Republicans for county managers, most of them political veterans. The campaign also drew on YAF for staff, including Harold Herring, a past chairman of the North Carolina YAF and a member of the YAF national board. Hundreds of other YAF members worked for the Helms campaign. Helms bragged that "the average age of our staff" is "22½." The campaign cooperated with the other statewide Republicans, including President Nixon and gubernatorial nominee James Holshouser, only when it seemed advantageous. The three campaigns coordinated voter-canvassing projects in the seventy counties of the central and western parts of the state, but in the thirty eastern counties the Helms campaign canvassed alone. The east was racially conservative and traditionally a bastion of Democratic strength. Helms was a familiar conservative, a former Democrat. His racial views and his broad opposition to the civil rights, student, and antiwar movements of the 1960s were well known. The central and western counties, where *Viewpoint* only appeared on radio and in small weekly newspapers, were areas of Republican strength, so cooperation with the GOP helped.[58]

Galifianakis's defeat of Jordan improved Helms's chances. But Galifianakis was a talented politician. And North Carolina voters supported liberal policies that Helms had long questioned, especially Social Security, Medicare, and farm subsidies. The congressman was a southern moderate with a good sense of how North Carolina voters felt on most issues. He had voted against busing every chance he had. He advocated tax and spending reforms over tax increases. He wanted welfare reforms that provided job training for the able-bodied and cracked down on cheaters. He supported time limits for an "orderly disengagement from Vietnam" and believed that peace talks should focus primarily on ensuring the return of POWs.[59] Through the late summer and the early fall, Galifianakis maintained a comfortable lead. The Democrat was particularly strong in piedmont cities from Charlotte northeast to Durham. One Democratic poll had him up by 25 points in September.[60]

The congressman relied on a dawn-to-dusk schedule of traditional retail politics. Helms never matched Galifianakis's frenzied pace of face-to-face events. He confessed to being "a lousy candidate because . . . all of the political hoopla just isn't my cup of tea." But Helms had practiced public speaking in front of civic clubs and graduating classes. And voters recognized him from *Viewpoint*: "I'm a strong Democrat, but I'm sure going to vote for you because you used to tell it like it was."[61] Together Helms and Ellis mastered the "wholesale politics" of fund-raising and advertising. During the summer, the campaign ran ads on the Tobacco Radio Network and in numerous newspapers—often the small weeklies that carried *Viewpoint*. Running ads where voters usually read or listened to *Viewpoint* reinforced voters' knowledge of him as a commentator. The ads in small-town papers often solicited donations of one, five, or ten dollars over a slogan: "TV or not: The answer is up to you." Helms's ads soliciting support even appeared in *TV Guide* alongside listings for WRAL news.[62]

To win, Helms had to gain the trust of regular Republican voters from outside WRAL's viewing area and convince conservative Democrats to choose a Republican. The polls showed this was proving to be a difficult task. A *Greensboro Daily News* five-part series on the election concluded, "Skim Off Rhetoric and Helms, Galifianakis Aren't Far Apart." In mid-September the Helms campaign went on attack on television, in newspapers, and on the stump. Helms's ads and his campaign raised his name recognition, connected his candidacy to Nixon, and assaulted Galifianakis—not as a Democrat, but as a liberal. But most of all, Helms turned pious incitement on the congressman. His speeches and ads identified Galifianakis with the turmoil of the 1960s: crime and inflation, the civil rights and antiwar movements, and lax countercultural attitudes toward drugs.[63]

The Helms campaign's first attack ad played on voters' concerns over drugs and crime. The ad accused Galifianakis of missing "100%" of "four major" congressional votes on drugs during the Democratic primary. "Where was Nick?" it asked. The ad expressed outrage at Galifianakis's alleged apathy toward drug dealers who sell to "teenagers." "We need a senator who *cares* about drug addiction and young people." The ad made the sort of sensational and exaggerated accusations coupled with claims of moral superiority that had characterized pious incitement since the 1950s. An apparently independent group, "Doctors Against Drug Abuse," was listed as sponsor. Galifianakis accused his opponent of misleading the voters. He had voted six times for antidrug legislation. He only missed insignificant votes on legislation that easily passed. Two of the three doctors named as members in the group denied knowing anything about it, and one of them, Dr. William Hollister, endorsed Galifianakis. Reporting on the ad was critical of the Helms campaign, and editorials condemned it. The *Greensboro Daily News* said the ad contained "cheap smears and false innuendos." The *News and Observer* called it "ugly and malicious." The *Charlotte Observer* was certain that "Mr. Galifianakis cares as much about drug addiction and young people as Mr. Helms."[64]

The media focus forced the campaign to admit writing the drug ad and paying for it. Helms conceded that it was inaccurate in part but denied approving it. The newspapers seemed certain the drug ad had backfired, yet that was far from clear. Helms's remarks emphasized "the fact" that his opponent "wasn't there 40 per cent of the time." The *Charlotte Observer*'s critical article was accompanied by a small reprint of the ad on the front page. In a public statement, Ellis accused the Galifianakis campaign of obscuring "the point" of "this week's advertisements." The "fact remains that Mr. Galifianakis missed each of the votes." The *Charlotte Observer* also carried an Ellis-penned letter on its editorial page: "Nick Missed Anti-Drug Votes." The ad's point, of course, was to cast Galifianakis out of the moral community because of his alleged insufficient opposition to drugs. Part of the effectiveness of pious incitement was to get an echo effect with sensational claims, and in this the drug ad succeeded. The congressman's explanation was coupled with coverage of the Helms campaign emphasizing Galifianakis's missed votes.[65]

Helms's most effective television and newspaper ads cast Galifianakis as part of a big-spending and busing "McGovern Radical Bloc." The ad campaign started a month before the election and linked the names of "McGovern-Galifianakis," as if the latter were the candidate for vice president. "McGovern-Galifianakis" cooperated on "WELFARE GIVE-AWAYS," "HIGHER PRICES," "CUT AND RUN" in Vietnam, and "Busing." Like Helms's commentaries, the ads stoked voters' fears: "Worried about the cost of living and higher food prices? McGovern-Galifianakis both voted for the same inflationary schemes," and Galifianakis had cooperated with McGovern in an attempt "to tie President Nixon's hands in negotiating a Vietnam peace settlement."[66]

As the *Greensboro Daily News* observed, "it is not exactly a smear" to connect a Democrat running for the Senate to his party's presidential nominee. The McGovern-Galifianakis ads relied on pious incitement's distortion to suggest that a few "coincidences" in voting meant broad ideological similarity. One ad quoted syndicated columnist John Roche as saying that Galifianakis was "in ideological terms close to George McGovern" and concluded that McGovern and Galifianakis were "ONE AND

THE SAME." Yet Roche was referring only to shared views on ending the Vietnam War—not broad similarity. The same Roche column observed that having McGovern as his party's presidential nominee must give Galifianakis "nightmares."[67]

The linking of "McGovern-Galifianakis" was part of an extensive effort to define Galifianakis as too liberal for the state. Because he was new to many voters, Galifianakis was susceptible to Helms's pious incitement. Helms especially used busing to paint the congressman as his polar opposite on race. The congressman was only "SOMETIMES against busing." The ads assured voters that Helms had "always opposed forced busing" and had "never been namby-pamby about it."[68]

The Galifianakis campaign believed they were well prepared to respond to Helms. Their research suggested significant vulnerability over Helms's criticism of President Nixon and popular federal programs on *Viewpoint*. Helms's ads claimed "Nixon Needs Helms." But Galifianakis stressed his own support for the president and their shared moderation. The congressman quoted Helms's editorials as accusing Nixon of pursuing "reckless" economic policies, making a "complete surrender to communist demands," and labeling grain exports to the Soviet Union as "trading with the enemy." Galifianakis charged that Helms's "sudden" assumption of a "pro-Nixon stance" was only "political expediency" and that it raised "serious questions about his credibility." The congressman also attacked Helms for his positions on popular New Deal and Great Society programs. Helms had called Social Security "nothing more than doles and handouts" and Medicare "socialized medicine" while opposing "price supports for all North Carolina farm products"[69]

Helms moderated his positions for the election. He pledged support for Medicare and "all programs beneficial to farmers" and advocated an increase in Social Security benefits along with raising the earnings cap for Social Security recipients. He also downplayed his past differences with the president, including his opposition to Nixon's China policy.[70]

Helms's pious incitement and eastern North Carolina Democrats' long familiarity with him provided protection against Galifianakis. Helms obscured the shifts in his positions with attacks on his opponent's trustworthiness. A Helms ad asserted that McGovern-Galifianakis had "a credibility problem" but that "You can trust Jesse Helms!" It then described Helms as standing "Four Square with our farmers." At a rally in Dunn, Helms said that Galifianakis "will say anything, will do anything to make a point." He lashed out at the congressman for quoting his editorials "out of context." "I don't resent what my opponent has said. I'm simply astonished by it. Does the man have no honor?"[71]

Helms had not changed his mind about anything. A week before he left *Viewpoint* to run for the Senate, Helms avowed, America's "destruction" had begun when "our political leadership turned to socialism. They didn't *call* it socialism, of course." Instead, they came up with "fancy slogans." "We heard about 'New Deals,' and 'Fair Deals'—and 'New Frontiers' and 'the Great Society.'"[72] But Helms knew he had to accept Social Security, Medicare, and farm programs to represent North Carolina in the Senate.

The Helms campaign formed a "Democrats for Helms" committee to convince disaffected Democrats to vote Republican. Helms announced that members of the committee were "longtime leaders of the party who this year have found themselves rudely shoved aside by a militant minority of McGovernites." As with many *Viewpoints*, his point was cultural. The announcement associated the national Democratic Party and his opponent with everything about the 1960s that made white voters uncomfortable: challenges to traditional values, antiwar protests, and the civil rights movement. Democrats for Helms sponsored ads with a similar cultural message: "SEND JESSE HELMS TO WASHINGTON TO DELIVER YOUR MESSAGE TO GEORGE MCGOVERN." The ad was an indirect appeal to the Wallace voter—the line "send them a message" was lifted straight from the Alabama governor.[73]

Prominent Democrats who joined Democrats for Helms included J. Melville Broughton Jr., former chairman of the North Carolina Democratic Party, and Joe Hunt, campaign manager for Governor Dan Moore. But the campaign also tied Helms to the most popular Democratic officeholders in the state without their permission. They ran ads linking his name to Senator Sam Ervin, so that "Helms-Ervin" appeared in contrast to "McGovern-Galifianakis." Voters were asked, "WHICH PAIR REPRESENTS YOU?" The campaign circulated a photo of Helms and North Carolina agricultural commissioner Jim Graham along with a quote from the commissioner praising Helms. Both Graham and Ervin had endorsed Galifianakis. Ervin campaigned for the congressman and declared in a TV ad, "Nick is the only really qualified candidate in the race." Graham criticized Helms for using his past ties to Democrats in "unfair and confusing ways." His praise, Graham explained, was for Helms's adoption of his son and had nothing to do with politics. Association with these prominent Democrats increased the acceptability of Helms's candidacy in a state where the Republican Party had been out of power for seven decades. It also disassociated Helms from some of his extreme positions. In Graham's case it served to reassure farmers that Helms posed no threat. When asked about Graham's complaints, Ellis stayed on message. "We recognize that Jim Graham is a Democratic office holder," he answered. "Nevertheless he knows that Jesse is a friend of the farmer."[74]

Late in the race, the Helms campaign began using the slogan "Jesse Helms—He's One of Us." It focused attention on his opponent's Greek name. The clear implication was that Galifianakis was not "one of us." In a Wadesboro newspaper, the Anson County Committee for Helms ran an ad that identified Galifianakis as "the Greek." The committee's treasurer thought it "came from state headquarters," but the state office denied any responsibility. Helms's campaign operatives later rejected the notion that the "He's One of Us" ads were about Galifianakis's Greek ancestry. They insisted the ads only reminded voters of their familiarity with Helms to make it okay to vote Republican. The Helms campaign also used "You Know Where He Stands" for this effect.[75] Their denials were half-truths, however. The power of "He's One of Us" depended on the congressman's name to define him as different from other North Carolina Democrats like Governor Scott and Senator Ervin.

Faced with Helms's media onslaught, Galifianakis expressed confidence that his opponent's negative campaign would prove ineffective "because they are editorially repudiated." The congressman was right about the papers' support of him. A *News and Observer* editorial mocked Helms for shifting his positions, asking, "Suddenly Jesse Helms Is a Moderate?" But Galifianakis overestimated the editors' influence.[76]

The large-circulation daily papers criticized Helms in editorials and regular news stories throughout the campaign, and in the end they endorsed his opponent. In "Nixon-Helms—Odd Couple: Political Expediency Makes for Strange Bedfellows," the *Greensboro Daily News* detailed the contradictions in conservative New York senator James Buckley's appearance at a Helms fund-raiser. The theme of the event, held in a gated golf club for an "affluent audience," was "Nixon Needs Helms." Reporter Ned Cline focused on Helms's criticism of Nixon on *Viewpoint*. Helms had found irony in a young Nixon's "strong" anticommunism and the president's "appeasement of the Chinese communist." He had ridiculed Nixon's revenue-sharing proposal: "What revenue does the federal government have to share?" Late in the race, the *News and Observer* ran a similar story—"Recent, Earlier Helms Views Differ"—that focused on his changed positions on Social Security, Medicare, and farm programs. In 1970 Helms had referred to Social Security as "merely another hand-to-mouth federal bureaucracy" and criticized politicians promising increased Social Security benefits, yet in the last weeks of his own campaign he was promising increased benefits. He had criticized farm programs as recently as December 1971. Reporter Leslie Wayne stressed that Helms had questioned Galifianakis's honor simply for criticizing his changed positions. Both stories quoted *Viewpoint* directly and conveyed the Galifianakis campaign's themes.[77]

Helms expected the newspapers to oppose him. And Galifianakis failed to anticipate Helms's ability to turn the papers' opposition to his advantage. Three weeks before the election, Helms charged "nine newspaper editors" with "carrying on Mr. Galifianakis' campaign for him." He refused to identify them all but pointed to William Snider of the *Greensboro Daily News* as an example.[78] Helms had been attacking newspapers for two decades. Such attacks countered criticisms of him, whether the criticism originated with an editor, a reporter, or a political opponent. Criticism of the mainstream media was central to pious incitement. By criticizing the media, Helms also shifted the terms of debate away from his changed positions and cast himself as a victim of unfair elite attacks.

The newspapers' coverage of Helms, however, was not one-sided. The papers covered his events and quoted his statements, including his criticism of them. The *News and Observer*, for example, reported on Helms's questioning of Galifianakis's honesty with straightforward stories: "Helms Declares Ad Says It All" and "Helms Scores Nick's 'Honor.'" The *Greensboro Daily News'* story "Nixon-Helms—Odd Couple" summed Helms up as believing he and Nixon agreed on the most important issues. Cline also reported Helms's sense of what was at stake in the election: "I am alarmed at the potential to destroy America." Just below Cline's story was another, "Helms Favors the Highest Price for Peanuts." Helms, the article said, wanted to keep "our peanut support price as high as possible." These stories all echoed the narrative the Helms campaign put forward in ads and the candidate's statements and speeches.[79]

By mid-October it was clear that Helms was gaining on Galifianakis, and by Halloween the race was even, with Helms leading in some polls.[80] Between early September and the end of October the Helms campaign outspent Galifianakis by more than three to one. Helms's money came from the state's leading industries—textiles, furniture, and banking—and some small donors. His two largest contributors were textile executives Hugh Chatham and Roger Milliken. Helms and Ellis also raised money from sources outside the state: the National Republican Senatorial Committee and other GOP campaign committees, the National Association of Manufacturers, and two key conservative movement organizations—the Young Americans for Freedom and the American Conservative Union. The money paid for media consultants, pollsters, and most of all for the television, radio, and newspaper ads in the final two months of the race.[81]

With Democrats tacitly conceding, Nixon would win big in the state. Helms's pollster recommended an ad campaign linking Helms to the president late in the race. Textile executive Hugh Chatham agreed to endorse a $100,000 loan to buy the media. The ads trumpeted "Nixon Needs Helms."[82] The Saturday before the election, Nixon stopped in Greensboro to support Helms and gubernatorial nominee Holshouser. Nixon's endorsement of Helms countered any sense that the two were at odds. With help from the Helms campaign, Nixon told an anecdote from the early 1950s, when Helms was Senator Willis Smith's assistant and Nixon was a newly elected senator from California. The president closed with Helms's slogan, "North Carolina needs Jesse Helms in the United States Senate. The Nation needs Jesse Helms," and "I need him."[83]

North Carolina Republicans had a blockbuster election day in 1972. Nixon won in a landslide. The state elected its first Republican governor and senator since the 1890s. Helms concluded, "The people of North Carolina had a clear-cut choice in this election and I believe they choose conservatism." Calling himself a "bipartisan Senator-Elect," Helms privately took credit for the GOP's success in North Carolina. "I think it is evident that had it not been for our campaign, no Republican would have been elected statewide." Helms even doubted whether he had been elected on Nixon's coattails. "I don't know that Nixon did us any good. In some parts of our state he's regarded as just another liberal." Helms was significantly overstating his importance. Nixon would have won North Carolina regardless of who ran for Senate. Overall, Helms won 54 percent of the vote compared to Holshouser's 51 percent, but Nixon won 69 percent. In the region west of WRAL where Helms depended on Republican votes, Nixon and Holshouser boosted him. Helms's years on WRAL, however, had laid the groundwork for Nixon and Holshouser in the east.[84]

Helms attributed Galifianakis's loss to overconfidence in the main-stream media: "Nick sat on his bohunkus, confident that what he read in the papers (that he was an affable shoo-in) was true."[85] The commentator's money advantage, the effectiveness of his campaign, and Nixon's popularity swamped Galifianakis. Helms had defined his opponent as a man with a strange name who was untrustworthy, culturally out of touch, and too liberal. In covering Helms's sensational and exaggerated portrait of the congressman, the papers conveyed that message even while criticizing it. Galifianakis's efforts to exploit *Viewpoint* failed for several reasons. Nixon's support for Helms neutralized his differences with the president. Helms's editorials attacking popular federal policies were relatively rare, while he assaulted liberalism, the civil rights movement, and the media every day. His attack on busing began in 1963.

Helms's victory meant he would take pious incitement to the Senate. He had no intention of being a Nixon Republican. He was first and last a movement conservative. Still, Helms hoped the Republican victories, particularly Nixon's crushing defeat of McGovern, would advance realignment in the state and the South. Despite his differences with Nixon, Helms believed the president and his party were moving in the right direction. Yet most of Helms's hopes for a conservative future rested on movement conservatives. He attributed his victory to YAF staffers. Without "the hundreds of young men and women" from YAF, "I have my doubts that we could have won." The difference that ideologically driven conservatives made in his campaign left Helms believing that movement conservatives could turn the nation to the right: "Nothing pleased me more than to have had a part in demonstrating that the lib'rul editors are virtually without influence—if those of us on the other side simply fight hard enough."[86]

Helms meant this literally. He believed that conservatives could govern the nation if they refused to compromise. That was what he intended to do: advocate an unbending, relentless right-wing conservatism that recognized no moderates and preferred stalemate to governing.

Epilogue

Mainstreaming the Fringe

After his victory in the Senate race, Helms wrote to William Loeb of the *Manchester Union-Leader* that voters would be "more conservative . . . if there were some concerted effort to harness their interests." Many conservatives had failed to grasp this, let alone understand how to do it. Helms's twin accomplishments on WRAL—media politics and a potent movement ideology rooted in southern conservatism—meant that he understood better than other national leaders how to connect with voters in a modern media environment. Helms arrived in Washington with the intention of transforming American politics.[1] Mastering the chamber's complex rules, he adapted pious incitement to the Senate. Helms frustrated congressional leaders by raising issues they believed settled: abortion, school prayer, détente, and the Panama Canal. Helms was confident that conservatives' day was dawning. "I sense a spirit of unity among conservatives that I haven't felt for many years," he wrote Stanton Evans of the American Conservative Union (ACU). Evans made it clear that the ACU was ready to cooperate.[2]

From the start, Helms aimed to push the nation, the Nixon administration, and Congress as far to the right as possible, but he joined a Senate under Democrats' control. He found being a freshman senator in a Democratic Congress maddening: "Things are really frustrating here now. Javits, Humphrey, Kennedy and McGovern are really cramming things down the throat of the Senate. They have the votes to do it."[3]

Many of his early efforts amounted to nothing more than isolated no votes. He was one of five senators to vote against the 1973 Federal Highway Act, one of ten against the Rural Environmental Assistance Program, and one of three opponents of Nixon's nominee for secretary of labor, Peter Brennan. Helms opposed Nixon's main foreign policy initiative—détente—and was one of seven votes against Henry Kissinger's confirmation as secretary of state. "I'm so fed up," he protested, "with playing 'footsie' with our enemies."[4]

Helms knew from Georgia senator Richard Russell's example that determined use of Senate rules allowed a lone senator disproportionate influence. During his first year in office he introduced constitutional amendments providing for school-led prayer, prohibiting busing, and reversing *Roe v. Wade* along with 138 speeches, 96 bills, and numerous amendments to legislation. For example, he offered an amendment to a farm subsidy bill that prohibited low-interest loans to communist nations buying American agricultural exports. He repeatedly introduced a bill that would take away the Supreme Court's power to rule on the constitutionality of school prayer. His constitutional amendment prohibiting abortion protected "the right to life from the moment of conception" with no exceptions. He delayed forty Nixon appointees with a hold on Helmut Sonnenfeldt's nomination to be undersecretary of the treasury. Helms filibustered the Legal Services Corporation Act, delaying its passage for months. The legislation was a bipartisan compromise providing legal services for the poor and was supported by most senators and the Nixon administration. Helms hinted that he had as many as a hundred amendments for his colleagues to consider. The *Charlotte Observer* condemned his opposition to "programs that make sense to conservatives and liberals alike."[5]

Helms sometimes succeeded in the traditional sense. He blocked something he opposed or forced changes to legislation. His amendment to a foreign aid bill prohibiting the use of foreign aid funds for abortion passed, but little of his legislation even got close to passage. Helms cast his votes and delivered his speeches for a national conservative audience, not to craft legislation.[6]

What appeared to be the wasted efforts of a marginal senator, however, proved to be the foundation for a monumental shift in American politics. Helms's purpose, which he never lost sight of, was to build the conservative movement. "You can be the leader who will save America," declared conservative activist Phyllis Schlafly. Helms made himself the heart of movement conservatism. In September 1973 the Young Americans for Freedom welcomed Helms as one of their own, repeatedly interrupting his speech with applause. "When I first got up here to Washington," he told them, "the first thing a reporter asked me was, 'Are you really the ultra right wing extremist they say you are?' And I replied, 'Beauty is in the eyes of the beholder.'"[7]

Helms was critical in the formation of the New Right network of the 1970s. First, he and Ellis organized the North Carolina Congressional Club to pay off his campaign debt and help elect conservatives. Initially they relied on traditional means—both Senator James Buckley and Ronald Reagan spoke at fund-raising dinners—but in 1975 Helms and Ellis turned to conservative direct-mail fund-raiser Richard Viguerie. Viguerie's strength was sending letters soliciting funds to computerized lists of carefully selected donors. The letters raised money, but they were also an unfiltered means of political communication. The results of Viguerie's first letter for Helms exceeded the senator's and Ellis's expectations. They were soon studying Viguerie's method. The Congressional Club made the most out of Helms's hero status among conservatives, raising millions. Helms also played an important role in building other New Right organizations. Terry Dolan, founder of the National Conservative Political Action Committee, said, "Helms for a time was on everyone's fundraising letters, and helped establish conservative organizations," including "ours." Helms also lent his name to Howard Phillips's Conservative Caucus, Paul Weyrich's Committee for Survival of a Free Congress, and Jerry Falwell's Moral Majority.[8]

Helms's YAF speech prompted the *Hickory Daily Record* to call him "an asinine reactionary" and hope he would be a one-term senator. A local supporter sent Helms the editorial as proof of what an "excellent job" he was doing. The paper's ire in August 1973 focused on Helms's opposition to Nixon after having run as the senator the president needed. Despite Helms's highly visible anti-Nixon positions, he had a strong record of support for the president. He endorsed Nixon's efforts to terminate various federal programs and his impoundment of federal funds. Most of all, he gave Nixon unflinching support during the Watergate scandal.[9]

At a press conference in August 1973, Helms declared, "Watergate is stupid." Helms backed Nixon's firing of Special Prosecutor Archibald Cox—he should not have been "hired in the first place"—and provided cover for the eighteen minutes of erased tape: "As a TV man, I know how tape machines malfunction." And he blamed press coverage. "The trouble," Helms explained, "lies with the news media," which had "hated Nixon ever since he exposed Alger Hiss." But the crux of Helms's opposition to the Watergate investigation was its ideological impact. "The only problem I have about Nixon is the obvious fact that his departure from the White House would mean an absolute take-over by the ultra-liberals."[10]

By 1974 Helms was frustrated with the Republican Party. Nixon had resigned. Conservative Democrats declined to register as Republicans, and Governor Holshouser controlled the North Carolina GOP. The Congressional Club had more money in the bank than either of the state parties in late 1974. The Congressional Club's success and his frustrations with GOP moderation led Helms to consider forming a third party. Helms and Ellis recognized during Helms's first two years in office that the Congressional Club and the fledgling network of movement conservative groups were sufficiently powerful to provide an alternative.[11]

In February 1975, Helms addressed the Conservative Political Action Conference organized by the ACU and YAF. "About 60% of the American people identity with the conservative political philosophy on a majority of issues," he explained. Conservatives needed a "coherent structure" that brought together committed conservatives and voters worried about the economy and "social issues" such as "pornography, the right to life," and "community control of schools." A third-party threat, Helms hoped, would push the GOP rightward: "There will be no new party—unless one is necessary. And if we see that a new party is necessary, then we will be ready."[12]

Republicans faced a crisis not just with conservatives: party identification was only 18 percent after Watergate, with Democrats over 40 percent. Gerald Ford had succeeded Nixon as president. At a press conference, the president insisted that the GOP "has to be a broad-based, wide spectrum party." Ford believed he needed conservatives and moderates to win the 1976 election. Helms rejected any moderation: "This broad-based thing is a bunch of hokum."[13] Ford shuffled his administration to accommodate conservatives in the fall of 1975. Although Kissinger remained secretary of state, Ford replaced him as national security adviser. But Helms and other movement conservatives found the changes inadequate. The president left détente in place. Reagan, about to announce he would challenge Ford, declared, "I'm certainly not appeased."[14]

In the summer of 1975, Helms abandoned his third-party talk to back Reagan for the Republican nomination. Helms and the Congressional Club became the dike that held Ford back. Rarely criticizing the president or the secretary of state, Reagan's early speeches failed to excite anyone.

He lost to Ford in New Hampshire and Florida. His campaign was short on morale and money when he arrived in North Carolina. Under Helms's and Ellis's influence, Reagan attacked Ford and Kissinger's foreign policy, particularly the Panama Canal "giveaway." Ellis convinced Reagan's staff, despite their doubts, to buy thirty-minute blocks on fifteen TV stations to appeal for money. The television buys and the focus on the canal worked. Drawing on his success in North Carolina, Reagan challenged Ford all the way to the Kansas City convention. Ford narrowly defeated Reagan. After Reagan's 1980 election as president, New Right organizer Richard Viguerie declared that Helms and Ellis had "saved" Reagan from retirement.[15]

Helms had gone to the Kansas City convention determined to push the party's platform rightward. Ford acquiesced to avoid a fight. When Helms and his allies finished, the Republican platform committed the party to tax cuts and balanced budgets, supported school-led prayer and right-to-life amendments, opposed gun control, championed the private sector, and abandoned environmentalism. In foreign affairs it rejected the Panama Canal treaties, called for increased defense spending, and included a "Morality in Foreign Policy" provision rejecting Kissinger's détente. Ford's people barely kept the platform neutral on the Equal Rights Amendment, which Ford strongly supported. Few people, including most Republicans, realized the extent to which the platform indicated the party's future direction. Helms demanded that Kissinger support the platform or "resign immediately."[16]

Helms was probably not very disappointed with Jimmy Carter's win in 1976. GOP moderates' failure could only strengthen conservatives. Carter was a moderate southern Democrat who campaigned as a born-again Christian. Helms expected to work with the new president on issues like pornography and abortion. His approval of Carter's progress in the Mideast peace talks verged on the ecstatic: "Your success thus far is the result of your basing the talks on prayer." Helms had many of the same disagreements with Carter that he did with Ford, particularly on foreign policy. When White House staff prepared a briefing on Helms, they assessed him as "a rabid opponent of the Panama Canal treaties."[17]

Once the treaties were signed, conservatives orchestrated a massive fight against ratification with Helms in the lead. He offered two hundred amendments to a revision of the federal criminal code simply to delay the vote. The longer Helms stretched it out, the closer the canal vote to the 1978 congressional elections and the more skittish his vulnerable colleagues became. In the spring of 1978 the Senate ratified the canal treaties with only two votes to spare. With Helms and the Congressional Club leading the charge, movement conservatives would make the treaties an issue in the 1978 and 1980 elections.[18]

While Democrats vied for the chance to challenge him, Helms expressed comfort as "Senator No." "Many times when you're voting 'no' you're voting precisely the wish of the people." Helms cast one of ten votes against creation of the Department of Energy and the only one against revising federal campaign laws. He championed defense appropriations, especially the B-1 bomber. He opposed the Equal Rights Amendment and contested the Carter administration's revocation of private schools' tax-exempt status for racial discrimination. And he reintroduced his constitutional amendments on abortion and prayer.[19]

Helms initially seemed beatable. A November 1977 poll indicated that three-quarters of voters were undecided. Democrats still had a three-to-one registration advantage and had come back strong since 1972. Robert Morgan had won election to the Senate in 1974 and Jim Hunt the governorship in 1976. But the Congressional Club and the Helms campaign raised over $8 million with Viguerie's help—the most money ever spent in a Senate race up to then. More than two hundred thousand people contributed. The Carter administration expressed a willingness to help defeat Helms, which only boosted his fund-raising.[20]

The Congressional Club's direct-mail operation relied on pious incitement and Helms's reputation as the senator whom conservatives counted on. Reagan signed a March 1977 letter warning that "Big Labor and Radical Pressure Groups" were already organizing against Helms. A Helms-signed letter followed Reagan's. Both pleaded for donations so Helms could work in the Senate instead of attending traditional fund-raisers. Conservatives needed Helms to oppose liberal attempts to "give away the Panama Canal," "repeal all state Right to work laws," and eliminate "vital" defense spending. A Phyllis Schlafly letter commended him for his opposition to the Equal Rights Amendment and "other dangerous lib legislation." After Carter campaigned for Helms's opponent, a letter over Helms's signature claimed, "I'M THE NUMBER ONE TARGET OF JIMMY CARTER, THE LIBERAL ESTABLISHMENT, AND THE UNION BOSSES." Helms's direct-mail campaign was not just fund-raising. The letters' sensational claims were a form of advertising, and they were pious incitement. They increased Helms's stature and built the movement.[21]

Helms faced Insurance Commissioner John Ingram in 1978. Ingram surprised everyone by defeating Luther Hodges Jr., a Charlotte banker and son of the former governor, to win the nomination. Helms, Ingram charged, was the "Six Million Dollar Man" and "he's not even bionic." Ingram spent less than $300,000. He hunted TV cameras, showed up at radio stations, and campaigned at cotton mills and strip malls. The *News and Observer* called Ingram's campaign a "farce," and many of the state's Democratic leaders were noticeably unenthused. Helms's ads charged that Ingram would support the canal treaties, reduce defense spending, and harm tobacco farmers. Helms had a spending edge of thirty-two to one against a weak candidate and only managed 55 percent. Still, another term meant growing power.[22]

With the rechristened National Congressional Club's financial resources, Helms and Ellis established multiple organizations to finance travel, pay aides' salaries, and conduct research supporting conservatism. Helms's reelection, the Congressional Club's fund-raising prowess, and the foundations increased his influence. By August 1979, Helms sensed that Carter was vulnerable: "I believe that 1980 is time for conservatives to go all out. The country is in a conservative mood." The National Congressional Club raised nearly $2 million in 1979.[23]

Helms switched to the Foreign Affairs Committee after his reelection, and this gave him an opportunity to advocate his unilateral foreign policy. The *Charlotte Observer* described Helms's foundations as a "shadow State Department." He sent his aides James Lucier and John Carbaugh around the world to support white governments in southern Africa and right-wing regimes in Latin America. Helms rejected any cooperation with the Chinese or Soviets. The ratification of the Strategic Arms Limitation Talks (SALT II), he warned, would "mark the end of Western power." Helms was just as aggressive on domestic issues. His prayer amendment got closer than ever in 1980, but this marked its fifth loss.[24]

The Congressional Club ran an independent campaign for Reagan in 1980. Its letters played on familiar themes. Reagan could revive the U.S. economy and "end the world's ridicule of our nation," but "I am frightened," Helms declared. Because "the liberals control the news media, paid air time is the only way to reach the American people." The independent effort for Reagan brought in $4.6 million. The Congressional Club spent an additional $3 million on candidates for the Senate and House. Republicans took control of the Senate, gaining twelve senators in 1980.[25]

The benefits to conservatives of Helms's aggressive pursuit of losing votes on prayer, abortion, and the Panama Canal went beyond fund-raising and organizing. Helms forced roll-call votes on these issues that many liberal and moderate senators preferred not to cast. New Right organizations were deeply involved in the 1978 and 1980 elections. They focused on issues that Helms had repeatedly forced his colleagues to vote on. In 1980 Dan Quayle defeated Indiana's three-term Democratic senator Birch Bayh using votes against Helms. Twenty senators who voted to ratify the Panama Canal treaties lost in 1978 and 1980. Among them was North Carolina's junior senator, Robert Morgan who had been defeated by Congressional Club candidate John East. Besides Reagan, East was the club's greatest success.[26]

The conservative victories in 1978 and 1980 shifted the political center to the right, achieving the transformation of American politics that Helms had coveted since the 1950s. He was widely recognized as central to the conservative triumph. The National Congressional Club was the nation's "most successful political action committee." ABC news called Helms "the godfather of the new right." Once Reagan was in office, Helms became the most important defender of the conservative revolution. If that meant opposing the Reagan administration, he did. The Conservative Caucus's Phillips declared, "Jesse Helms has always had the courage of Ronald Reagan's convictions."[27]

Helms and other movement conservatives were worried by Reagan's transition team: "Ron," he said, had "to remember who took him to the dance." Helms wrote Viguerie two weeks after the election, "I am a bit puzzled by some of the things that are going on, but we'll just have to confront each situation as it develops." Helms vigorously opposed any Reagan appointees whom he deemed insufficiently conservative. This was especially the case for defense and foreign policy. On inauguration day, Helms and East cast the only two votes against Casper Weinberger for secretary of defense. Helms placed holds on the confirmations of undersecretaries of state and other officials. These nominees were primarily veterans of the Ford and Nixon administrations with ties to Kissinger. In the *Foreign Service Journal*, Alan Tonelson accused Helms of rejecting the "very idea" of "a foreign policy based on the systematic study of world affairs." Helms's fight gained few concessions, but it demonstrated to the Reagan White House and the movement that Helms would push Reagan to the right just as he had the president's predecessors.[28]

Governing required different skills from the opposition Helms had perfected while Democrats held power. During his first year as chair of the Senate Agriculture Committee, Helms needed to meet the Reagan administration's demands for cuts and keep North Carolina farmers happy. He ended up jeopardizing the coalition that supported federal agriculture policy. Helms held hearings on food stamp "abuses" and put forward his own farm bill. Urban congressmen opposed it. They only supported federal agriculture policy because of programs like food stamps. Farm state senators and representatives believed Helms was trying to protect programs for tobacco and peanut farmers—both important to his state—at the expense of other farmers. His actions led to a "backlash." Peanut price supports were reduced. A measure eliminating the tobacco program received forty-two votes and avoided substantial reductions by a single vote. Helms admitted that the votes left him "scared silly."[29]

Helms was even more divisive on social issues. When Senate Majority Leader Howard Baker tried to place conservatives' social agenda on hold until after the president's budget had passed, Helms refused to relent. On prayer and abortion, Helms shifted from favoring constitutional amendments to proposing legislation. His bills sought to outlaw abortion, support state-sponsored prayer, and restrict federal courts' jurisdiction regarding abortion and prayer. Helms expected legislation to be easier to pass than constitutional amendments. But tampering with court jurisdiction drew strong opposition, and both measures failed. Still, Helms's efforts on abortion, prayer, and food stamps were immensely popular with movement conservatives and helped generate money and support for the New Right. But Helms's name also appeared in the fund-raising efforts and ads of liberal advocacy groups. He became Democrats' and liberal activists' favorite "devil."[30]

The senator's performance in 1978 against a weak opponent suggested that a strong candidate could defeat him. Helms and Ellis failed to build on their successes in 1978 and 1980: all five Congressional Club candidates lost in 1982. In 1984 Helms faced popular Democratic governor Jim Hunt. Hunt had won three statewide races—two for governor and one for lieutenant governor—and had prevailed in the Republican years of 1972 and 1980. Many North Carolinians had voted for both Helms and Hunt. A moderate Democrat, Hunt also had the confidence of the conservative Democrats on whom Helms usually relied. The governor was a Presbyterian, supported school-led prayer, and opposed liquor-by-the-drink. He expressed disapproval of abortion, although he supported a state abortion fund for poor women. In several early polls, Hunt led by twenty points. The Helms campaign believed they could never "lift Helms up," so they had to "bring Hunt down."[31]

The *News and Observer* billed the contest between the "dominant political figures" in the state as "Organization vs. Money." Hunt's organization had a presence in every county: he essentially campaigned nonstop as governor. His regular schedule included more than twenty events a week all over the state. Ellis called Hunt "our greatest ribbon cutter." By 1984 Helms's political team had become the most experienced and innovative campaign organization in the country, both in fund-raising and advertising. They drew important lessons from previous campaigns. In 1978 the Helms campaign had spent several million dollars on traditional county-by-county organization, but the polls did not shift significantly until TV ads started in the spring of 1978. Ellis concluded that attack ads were the most efficient use of money and that the bulk of spending should go to television. Most campaigns relied on radio and newspapers for negative ads and assumed that similar ads on TV would harm the candidate running them. In the East-Morgan contest in 1980 the Congressional Club ran negative TV ads attacking Morgan as a liberal by highlighting carefully selected votes Morgan had cast in the Senate. The commercials proved highly effective.[32]

The Helms campaign's media assault on Hunt started in the spring of 1983, eighteen months before the election. The intention was to undercut Hunt's positive reputation with negative ads. The Helms campaign produced over 150 TV ads, both positive and negative, and ran them continuously from April 1983 through the election. The first ads attacked Hunt as flip-flopping on prayer, abortion, taxes, and unions and then asked, "Where do you stand, Jim?" Helms's commercials made this question the chorus of his reelection bid. His campaign was the first to sustain the flip-flopping allegation systematically. The ads cast Helms as a principled statesman and Hunt as an amoral politician. Simultaneously, the Helms campaign began targeting rural white voters on radio and in weekly newspapers. The ads depicted Hunt as pro-union and connected him to prominent black leaders such as Andrew Young and Jesse Jackson. The Jackson ads tied the governor to Jackson's efforts to register black voters in the state and pictured the two together in Hunt's office. Even the union ads had racial overtones with a picture of striking black schoolteachers in

Washington, D.C. A related TV ad tied Hunt to the two significantly more liberal Democrats vying to challenge Reagan: "I wouldn't vote for Walter Mondale or Jesse Jackson for president. Where do you stand, Jim?"[33]

Hunt's weekly events made the most of being governor, but Helms understood better than any other politician how to use his office to build support. In the fall of 1983 he resurrected an old opponent, Martin Luther King Jr. Since King's assassination, support for a national holiday honoring him had grown. The new holiday was poised to pass in October 1983, and Helms filibustered it. In an immediately infamous Senate speech reminiscent of *Viewpoint* in the 1960s, he injected race, bloc voting, and communism into the election. "Martin Luther King Jr. was either an irresponsible individual," the senator said, or he "knowingly cooperated and sympathized with subversive and totalitarian elements under the control of a foreign power." King's behavior suggested he "may have had an explicit but clandestine relationship with the Communist Party" and sought "not the civil rights of blacks or social justice and progress, but the totalitarian goals and ideology of communism."[34]

The Senate passed the King holiday measure by a substantial margin. Before Reagan signed the legislation, Helms sent out fund-raising letters. "The ultra-liberal news media are chortling that 'Jesse Helms has committed political suicide.' They are delirious with joy. I did my level best to stop the Martin Luther King Holiday. But there was an atmosphere of pressure and intimidation." Senators who opposed the bill feared being labeled "'racist' by the news media and liberal black establishment." Helms asked for money to help counter the voter registration drives of "Jesse Jackson and the bloc vote extremists." King Holiday ads ran heavily: "I voted against the Martin Luther King holiday. Where do you stand, Jim?"[35]

The *Charlotte Observer* dismissed his repetitious ads as posing "that irreverent question." The *Washington Post* called Helms the "stopped clock" of American politics. ABC's *World News Tonight* depicted his King holiday filibuster as essentially pointless: other media outlets agreed. Helms made the most of media disapproval in his ads and fund-raising letters. Yet the media echoed his themes as they always had. The *News and Observer* quoted his King holiday fund-raising letter extensively. Even when they gave his perspective scant attention, the criticism gained him tremendous exposure.[36] Movement conservatives celebrated Helms. *Human Events* reprinted his speech attacking King, and the *National Review* and other conservative publications praised it. New Right organizations including the Conservative Caucus, the Moral Majority, and the National Conservative Political Action Committee joined Helms in a lawsuit pressuring the Justice Department to release FBI surveillance tapes of King. Some observers believed that Helms's harsh opposition increased support for the King holiday, but it boosted his fund-raising and reelection chances.[37]

Hunt owed his early lead to both overwhelming black support and strength among North Carolina whites. To defeat Hunt, Helms had to win 60 percent of white voters. Polls showed that 85 percent of white North Carolinians opposed the King holiday. When asked about his harsh attacks on King, Helms was blunt about his political calculations: "I'm not going to get any black votes, period."[38]

By the spring of 1984—a year after his TV ads began—Helms had erased Hunt's lead. Helms also ran conventional positive ads, including a Reagan endorsement, but what was unprecedented was the relentless campaign of negative television commercials. They made the race competitive. Early on the Hunt campaign was overly cautious, trying to protect the governor's lead. When they ran their own negative ads in the summer of 1984, they were clumsy and failed to shift the polls.[39]

With the help of Reagan's coattails, Helms won the election 52 to 48 percent. He captured 62 percent of white voters. The Helms-Hunt election remained the most expensive Senate race for years after, with Hunt spending $9.5 million and Helms $17 million. Hunt recovered after his loss to Helms and won two more terms as governor—ultimately winning five of his six statewide races. The senator went five for five. Helms's ability to control such a successful candidate's image demonstrates how formidable his organization was.[40]

Today's conservative Republican Party is the institution Jesse Helms envisioned in the 1950s and 1960s and then helped to create. The 1994 midterm elections completed the South's realignment with the GOP. White southerners are the most reliable conservative voters. As the right expanded its power, Helms's pious incitement became a national strategy. White racial fears and moral outrage have remained central to Republican strategy. Conservatives have accomplished many things Helms advocated: reducing taxes, eliminating regulations, purging the Republican Party of its moderates, and making criticism of the private sector inappropriate. They took southern low-tax, bare-bones social policy national.

Presidential candidates insist on the importance of religion in their lives.[41] And after overturning the Fairness Doctrine, they created national right-wing news media: first AM radio and then Fox News.

The willingness of party stalwarts to welcome Helms and other southerners into the Republican Party in the 1960s and 1970s and, most significantly, to embrace their racial and cultural views explains the success of the party in the 1980s and 1990s and the difficulties of today's Republican Party. In winning over the white South, the Republican Party abandoned the middle ground and nonwhite voters. As the percentage of minorities in the electorate rises, the long-term viability of a political party focused solely on white voters is uncertain. The tea party movement allowed the Republican Party to retake the House of Representatives in 2010. The party's doubling down on issues like gay marriage, immigration, antiunion right-to-work laws, tax cuts, birth control, and abortion fired up the base. But these same issues, along with the conservative fringe's obsession with President Barack Obama's birth certificate, drove away other voters in 2012. The start of the Great Recession in 2008 eroded Republican advantages on the economy, taxes, and deficits while making criticism of the private sector acceptable. The future of the Republican Party that Jesse Helms helped to build appears less certain in 2012 after the reelection of Barack Obama than it did in George W. Bush's first term, when Helms retired.

Notes

Abbreviations

JCL	Jimmy Carter Library, Atlanta, Georgia
JH	Jesse Helms
JHC	Jesse Helms Center, Wingate, North Carolina
NACP	National Archives at College Park, Maryland
NCBA Papers	Jesse Helms Personal Papers, North Carolina Bankers Association, JHC
NCC	North Carolina Collection, Wilson Library, University of North Carolina at Chapel Hill
RG	Record Group
SHC	Southern Historical Collection, Wilson Library, University of North Carolina at Chapel Hill
WRAL-TV Papers	Jesse Helms Personal Papers, WRAL-TV Papers, JHC

Introduction

1. Clinton, *My Life*, 613.

2. Goldberg, *Barry Goldwater*, ix–xii, 112–13, 181–237; Andrew, *The Other Side of the Sixties*, 1–31; Farber, *Rise and Fall*, 39–118.

3. Goldberg, *Barry Goldwater*, ix–xii, 112–13, 181–237; Andrew, *The Other Side of the Sixties*, 1–31 (quote on 7); Farber, *Rise and Fall*, 77–118.

4. Carter, *The Politics of Rage*; Edsall and Edsall, *Chain Reaction*.

5. Schulman, *The Seventies*; Kruse, *White Flight*; Lassiter, *The Silent Majority*; Crespino, *In Search of Another Country*; McGirr, *Suburban Warriors;* Brennan, *Turning Right in the Sixties*. For a biography of Helms that addresses his Senate career and his role in the rise of modern conservatism, see Link, *Righteous Warrior*.

6. Farber, *Rise and Fall,* 1–38; Crespino, *Strom Thurmond's America*, 3–11, 34–126 (quote on 6).

7. Crespino, *Strom Thurmond's America*, 3–11, 34–126; Carter, *The Politics of Rage*, 7–15, 68–109, 236–40, 351–52.

8. *Viewpoint* #16, December 13, 1960; JH to Bill Sharpe, October 29, 1963, Bill Sharpe file, WRAL-TV Papers, JHC. I completed my research before Jesse Helms's papers were processed. The documents and folders cited will not change, but I was unable to cite

boxes. All of Helms's personal files from the North Carolina Bankers Association are now at the Jesse Helms Center. Helms's WRAL-TV *Viewpoint* commentaries are available at the Jesse Helms Center and in the North Carolina Collection in Wilson Library at the University of North Carolina.

9. JH to Ben Sumner, October 16, 1961, Spindale Mills file, WRAL-TV Papers, JHC (quote); Lassiter, *The Silent Majority*, 3–4; Farber, *Rise and Fall*, 72–74.

10. Crespino, *Strom Thurmond's America*, 3–11, 34–126; Carter, *The Politics of Rage*, 7–15, 68–109, 236–40, 351–52.

11. Crespino, *Strom Thurmond's America*, 3–11, 34–126.

12. JH to James Wick, July 13, 1959, Personal file, NCBA Papers; JH to William F. Buckley, May 2, May 14, 1963, and Buckley to JH, May 8, 1963, William F. Buckley file, WRAL-TV Papers, JHC; *Viewpoint* #12, December 7, 1960.

13. "Pious Incitement," *Raleigh News and Observer*, January 31, 1958.

14. *Viewpoint* #736, November 20, 1963.

15. *Viewpoint* #372, May 23, 1962 (quotes); *Viewpoint* #354, April 26, 1962; *Viewpoint* #369, May 18, 1962.

16. *Viewpoint* #372, May 23, 1962 (quotes).

17. Farber, *Rise and Fall*, 1–38 (quote on 3).

18. *Viewpoint* #504, December 14, 1962 (first quote); *Viewpoint* #1761, January 5, 1968 (second quote); *Viewpoint* #824, February 27, 1964 (third and fourth quotes).

19. *Viewpoint* #1411, August 4, 1966 (first quote); *Viewpoint* #694, September 20, 1963 (second quote); *Viewpoint* #730, November 12, 1963 (third quote).

20. JH to Charles Reynolds, April 16, 1962 (quote), and Reynolds to JH, April 7, 1962, Spindale Mills file, WRAL-TV Papers, JHC.

Chapter 1. "There Is Another Way"

1. Resume, "Jesse Helms," May 1959, and JH to Dr. Preston Scott, September 19, 1960, Personal file, NCBA Papers, JHC; "Biographical Information," n.d., Biographical Sketch file, and "Jesse Helms," December 4, 1972, Chronological file, WRAL-TV Papers, JHC; Furgurson, *Hard Right*, 30–33.

2. "Jesse Helms, Jr. Named Secretary Bankers Assn.," *Monroe (N.C.) Journal,* August 15, 1953 (quote); "Helms Says He Gave Notice to Sen. Lennon," *Charlotte Observer*, September 22, 1953; JH to J. Winfield Crew, February 8, 1954, and Crew to JH, February 10, 1954, Personal file, NCBA Papers, JHC.

3. JH to Richard Nixon, December 18, 1956, January 8 and January 28, 1957, and JH to Robert King, January 8, 1957, Personal file, NCBA, JHC.

4. JH to Richard Norton, April 28, 1964 (quote), Chronological file, WRAL-TV Papers, JHC; Furgurson, *Hard Right*, 42.

5. Resume, "Jesse Helms," May 1959, and JH to Dr. Preston Scott, September 19, 1960, Personal file, NCBA Papers, JHC; "Biographical Information," n.d., Biographical Sketch file, and "Jesse Helms," December 4, 1972, Chronological file, WRAL-TV Papers, JHC; Furgurson, *Hard Right*, 42–46.

6. Resume, "Jesse Helms," May 1959, Personal file, NCBA Papers, JHC; JH to Allen

Woodall, April 14, 1965, Miscellaneous Television and Radio file, WRAL-TV Papers, JHC; Furgurson, *Hard Right*, 42–46.

7. Resume, "Jesse Helms," May 1959, and JH to Dr. Preston H. Scott, September 19, 1960 (first quote), Personal file, NCBA Papers, JHC; Furgurson, *Hard Right*, 42–46; JH, "The Man on the Nail Keg Was Too Curious," *Tarheel Banker*, February 1956, 39 (second quote). The *Tarheel Banker* is available in Wilson Library at the University of North Carolina.

8. Pleasants and Burns, *Frank Porter Graham*, 197–201; Furgurson, *Hard Right*, 46–57; Luebke, *Tar Heel Politics*, 16–17, 127–28; Ashby, *Frank Porter Graham*, 257–73.

9. Pleasants and Burns, *Frank Porter Graham*, 197–201; Furgurson, *Hard Right*, 46–57 (quote); Luebke, *Tar Heel Politics*, 16–17, 127–28; Ashby, *Frank Porter Graham*, 257–73.

10. Pleasants and Burns, *Frank Porter Graham*, 197–201; Furgurson, *Hard Right*, 46–57 (first quote); Luebke, *Tar Heel Politics*, 16–17, 127–28; JH to Bill Sharpe, April 11, 1967 (second quote), Sharpe file, WRAL-TV Papers, JHC.

11. Pleasants and Burns, *Frank Porter Graham*, 197–201; Furgurson, *Hard Right*, 46–57; Luebke, *Tar Heel Politics*, 16–17, 127–28; Ashby, *Frank Porter Graham*, 257–73.

12. Crespino, *Strom Thurmond's America*, 91–94.

13. JH to Polk Moffett, August 18, 1969 (first quote), Chronological file, WRAL-TV Papers, JHC; JH to Rev. Owen Norment Jr., December 12, 1961 (second quote), Critical Mail file, WRAL-TV Papers, JHC; JH to Eleanor Short, January 23, 1969 (third quote), and JH to Mrs. G. A. Leonard, August 20, 1965 (fifth quote), Chronological file, WRAL-TV Papers, JHC; *Viewpoint* #1910, August 22, 1968; *Viewpoint* #2368, June 29, 1970 (fourth quote).

14. "How's Your Humility Lately, Arthur?" *Hereford County Herald*, November 12, 1953; Norman McCulloch, "This and That," *Bladen Journal*, September 24, 1953.

15. JH, "Bankers in Politics," *Tarheel Banker*, September 1958, 32 (first quote); JH, "Thanks Mr. Editor," *Tarheel Banker*, July 1954, 22 (second quote); JH, "A Trend of Wisdom," *Tarheel Banker*, September 1954, 24 (third quote).

16. JH, "Target for Tonight," *Tarheel Banker*, December 1953, 18; JH, "That's the Way," *Tarheel Banker*, January 1954, 16; "The Big Change," *Belmont (N.C.) Banner*, January 13, 1954; Hoover Adams to JH, June 6, 1955, Personal file, NCBA Papers, JHC.

17. Griffith, "Eisenhower and the Corporate Commonwealth"; JH, "Those Inflexible Boys!" *Tarheel Banker*, October 1954, 28 (first quote); JH, "Now Wait a Minute," *Tarheel Banker*, February 1958, 38 (second quote); JH, "Our Farm Edition," *Tarheel Banker*, February 1956, 34 (third quote); JH, "Good Farming Is Vital," *Tarheel Banker*, February 1955, 30 (fourth quote); JH, "Wherein Ray Reeve Really Nails a 'Phony,'" *Tarheel Banker*, March 1956, 39; JH, "It's the Same Old Applesauce, Warmed Over," *Tarheel Banker*, April 1956, 35; JH, "One Law Cannot Be Repealed," *Tarheel Banker*, February 1957, 38; JH, "The Backbone of America," *Tarheel Banker*, February 1959, 40; JH, "In Defense of Farmers," *Tarheel Banker*, February 1960, 46.

18. JH, "The Backbone of America," *Tarheel Banker*, February 1959, 40 (first quote); JH, "One Law Cannot Be Repealed," *Tarheel Banker*, February 1957, 38 (second quote); JH, "Our Farm Edition," *Tarheel Banker*, February 1956, 34; JH, "It's the Same Old Applesauce, Warmed Over," *Tarheel Banker*, April 1956, 35 (third and fourth quotes).

19. JH, "Death Just Couldn't Have Any Sting," *Tarheel Banker,* May 1955, 35 (first quote); JH, "Groups Indictment and Demagoguery," *Tarheel Banker,* April 1955, 28 (second quote); JH, "The Best Time Is Now," *Tarheel Banker,* January 1956, 24 (second and third quotes).

20. JH, "Much to Gain, Nothing to Lose," *Tarheel Banker,* November 1956, 32 (first and second quotes); JH, "Look under the Sheet, Quick," *Tarheel Banker,* July 1957, 26 (third quote); JH, "Truth vs. Half-Truth," *Tarheel Banker,* March 1957, 40 (fourth and fifth quotes); JH, "Defining a Windfall," *Tarheel Banker,* May 1958, 32; JH, "Thoughts for Today," *Tarheel Banker,* February 1958, 38 (sixth and seventh quotes).

21. JH, "He Was Sure Dambanker Was One Word," *Tarheel Banker,* January 1957, 25.

22. JH, "Monroe? Why That's a Place Called Home!" *Tarheel Banker,* May 1956, 33, 55.

23. Resume, "Jesse Helms," May 1959, J. T. Wright to JH, April 29, 1954, Edward Graham to JH, September 22, 1955, F. A. Arthur to JH, July 28, 1956, Personal file, NCBA Papers, JHC.

24. JH to Dr. Claude Broach, November 3, 1959, and JH to J. Everett Miller, November 16, 1959, First Baptist Church of Raleigh file, NCBA Papers, JHC.

25. JH, "The Distaff Side of Banking," *Tarheel Banker,* August 1955, 30; JH, "Office Secrets and Notes about Mr. Joe," *Tarheel Banker,* December 1958, 32 (last quote).

26. JH, "There Is Another Way," *Tarheel Banker,* September 1955, 24 (emphasis in the original).

27. Ibid.; "Silliest School Suggestion Yet," *Raleigh News and Observer*, September 6, 1955; "Private Enterprise Schools," *Winston-Salem Journal*, September 7, 1955; "The Bankers Know Better," *Greensboro Daily News*, September 7, 1955; "N.C. Has an Educational Choice and It Isn't Logically Private," *Charlotte Observer*, September 7, 1955; "Public Schools Belong to the People," *Ashville Citizen*, September 11, 1955; JH to William Snider, September 9, 1955, JH to C. A. (Pete) McKnight, September 9, 1955, JH to Mason Yeager, September 12, 1955, I. Beverly Lake to Reed Sarratt, September 9, 1955, and "Bankers Assn. Editorial Supports Private Schools," AP clipping, September 5, 1955, Personal file, NCBA Papers, JHC; Chafe, *Civilities and Civil Rights*, 49–60; "National Affairs," *Time,* September 16, 1957, 25–26.

28. JH, "There Is Another Way," *Tarheel Banker,* September 1955, 24 (emphasis in the original); "Silliest School Suggestion Yet," *Raleigh News and Observer*, September 6, 1955; "Private Enterprise Schools," *Winston-Salem Journal*, September 7, 1955; "The Bankers Know Better," *Greensboro Daily News*, September 7, 1955; "N.C. Has an Educational Choice and It Isn't Logically Private," *Charlotte Observer*, September 7, 1955; "Public Schools Belong to the People," *Ashville Citizen*, September 11, 1955; "Bankers Assn. Editorial Supports Private Schools," AP clipping, September 5, 1955, Personal file, NCBA Papers, JHC.

29. JH, "Let's Face the Issue," *Tarheel Banker,* October 1955, 28 (emphasis in the original).

30. JH to J. Winfield Crew, February 8, 1954 (first quote), Crew to JH, February 10, 1954, and JH to R. B. Carpenter, January 11, 1956 (second quote), Personal file, NCBA Papers, JHC.

31. JH, "Let's Face the Issue," *Tarheel Banker,* October 1955, 28; "Silliest School Suggestion Yet," *Raleigh News and Observer,* September 6, 1955.

32. JH, "There Is Another Way," *Tarheel Banker,* September 1955, 24; JH to A. A. Chappell, September 5, 1955, JH to Price Gwynn, September 6, 1955, Mason Yeager to JH, September 6, 1955, Personal file, NCBA Papers, JHC.

33. Geoghegan to JH, September 7, 1955, JH to George Geoghegan Jr., September 9, 1955, JH to John Foster, September 9, 1955, John Stedman to JH, September 9, 1955, and Stedman to JH, n.d., Personal file, NCBA Papers, JHC.

34. JH, "These Are Important Days for the South," *Tarheel Banker,* August 1956, 35 (first quote); JH, "That Arkansas Farmer Is Plumb Confused," *Tarheel Banker,* February 1958, 39; Chafe, *Civilities and Civil Rights,* 49–60.

35. R. K. Scott to JH, December 7, 1959, attached NAACP ad, n.d., and JH to Scott, December 2, 1959, Personal file, NCBA Papers, JHC.

36. JH to C. A. (Pete) McKnight, September 9, 1955, and JH to Mrs. Holmes Van Mater, March 30, 1956, Personal file, NCBA Papers, JHC.

37. Furgurson, *Hard Right,* 89.

38. JH to Charles R. Jonas, May 9, 1968, Charles R. Jonas file, WRAL-TV Papers, JHC; Black and Black, *Rise of Southern Republicans,* 65.

39. JH, "Quiet Effectiveness," *Tarheel Banker,* June 1954, 38; JH, "Edwin Pate: A Lengthened Shadow," *Tarheel Banker,* May 1955, 34; JH to Hodges, June 3, 1954, JH to Edwin Pate, December 8, 1955, Pate to JH, April 21, 1958, and JH to Pate, April 23, 1958, Personal file, NCBA Papers, JHC.

40. Thomas F. Ellis to JH, April 2, 1958, JH to Bob Holding, April 8, 1958, Ellis to JH, April 23, 1958, and attached draft of campaign letter, Personal file, NCBA Papers, JHC.

41. C. Aubrey Gasque to JH, January 25, 1954, and JH to Mrs. Cleo Birchett Liner, October 20, 1958 (last quote), Personal file, NCBA Papers, JHC.

42. JH, "Mr. Pate Learned about Those Hitchhikers," *Tarheel Banker,* March 1958, 41 (quote); Schulman, *Lyndon B. Johnson,* 12–14, 36–39; Gerstle, "Race and the Myth of the Liberal Consensus."

43. JH, "Caswell Street Is One Guy's Memory Lane," *Tarheel Banker,* October 1957, 33 (first quote); JH to Ralph Howland, January 13, 1956 (second quote), JH to Earl Butz, January 31, 1957 (third quote), JH to Richard Nixon, December 21, 1955 (fourth and fifth quotes), and JH to Edward McMahan, January 26, 1956 (last quote), Personal file, NCBA Papers, JHC.

44. JH to McMahan, June 11, 1958, Personal file, NCBA Papers, JHC.

45. Russell to JH, November 28, 1955, and Russell to JH, July 3, 1958, Personal file, NCBA Papers, JHC; JH, "It's the Same Old Applesauce, Warmed Over," *Tarheel Banker,* April 1956, 35.

46. JH, "It's the Same Old Applesauce, Warmed Over," *Tarheel Banker,* April 1956, 35.

47. JH, "That Important, Independent," *Tarheel Banker,* July 1956, 24.

48. Ibid.; JH to Bill Sharpe, April 11, 1967 (last quote), Sharpe file, WRAL-TV Papers, JHC; Griffith, "Eisenhower and the Corporate Commonwealth"; Phillips-Fein, *Invisible Hands,* 56–58.

49. JH, "One Law Cannot Be Repealed" (first quote), *Tarheel Banker,* February 1957, 38 (emphasis in original); JH, "In Politics, Maybe We Ought to Be Specific" (remaining quotes), *Tarheel Banker,* December 1956, 27.

50. Crespino, *Strom Thurmond's America,* 167–73.

51. JH, "We Aren't Solving Anything," *Tarheel Banker,* November 1957, 32.

52. JH, "An Interesting Question," *Tarheel Banker,* October 1956, 30 (first quote); JH's City Council Campaign Statement, [1957] (second quote), and JH to Robert Putnam, April 23, 1957 (third quote), Personal file, NCBA Papers, JHC; Jack Crosswell, "Helms Controversial Councilman," *Raleigh News and Observer,* June 3, 1959; JH, "Wherein a Fellow Muses about Politics," *Tarheel Banker,* June 1957, 30 (last quote).

53. JH to Edward McMahan, June 11, 1958 (first quote), and JH, City Council Statement on Taxes, [1960], Personal file, NCBA Papers, JHC; JH, Joe Correll, and Guy Rawls, "A Statement," [1958], JH to John Mason, February 23, 1959 (second and third quotes), and W. T. Martin to JH, April 25, 1958 (last quote), City Council City Hall file, NCBA Papers, JHC.

54. JH, "'Urban Redevelopment'—Phew," *Tarheel Banker,* October 1957, 32.

55. JH to Isabel Busbee, August 21, 1957 (first quote), Stella Barbee to JH, September 16, 1957, and JH to Barbee, September 18, 1957, City Council City Hall file, and JH's City Council Campaign Statement, [1957] (second quote), Personal file, NCBA Papers, JHC; Schoenwald, *A Time for Choosing,* 3–13, 162–89.

56. "Institute's Speaker List Resented Here, Helms Says," January 31, 1958, and "Pious Incitement," February 1, 1958, *Raleigh News and Observer.*

57. "Institute's Speaker List Resented Here, Helms Says," January 31, 1958 (quotes), and "Pious Incitement," February 1, 1958, *Raleigh News and Observer.* Ellipses are in the original.

58. "Pious Incitement," February 1, 1958, *Raleigh News and Observer.*

59. JH, "Mr. Pate Learned about Those Hitchhikers," *Tarheel Banker,* March 1950, 41.

60. "The 1958 Concern Somewhat Puzzling," *Raleigh Times,* January 31, 1958; JH to Herbert O'Keefe, January 31, 1958, Personal file, NCBA Papers, JHC.

61. Henry Dennis to JH, March 12, 1958, JH to Dennis, March 13, 1958 (first quote; fourth and remaining quotes), JH to Jack Spain, February 7, 1958, Bill Sharpe to JH, March 10, 1958, JH to Sharpe, March 11, 1958, James Dees to JH, August 27, 1959, and JH to Dees, August 31, 1959 (second and third quotes), Personal file, NCBA Papers, JHC.

62. JH to Dees, August 31, 1959, Personal file, NCBA Papers, JHC.

63. JH to Jack Spain, February 7, 1958, and JH to Dees, August 31, 1959 (last quote), Personal file, NCBA Papers, JHC.

64. Rusk, *Cities without Suburbs,* 17, 28–38, 76–78.

65. JH, "It's Time for a Change," *Tarheel Banker,* November 1955, 24.

66. Bill Sharpe to JH, January 22, 1960, and JH to Sharpe, January 25, 1960, with attached article titled "Archaic Tax System" (quote), Personal file, NCBA Papers, JHC.

67. JH to Sharpe, January 25, 1960, with attached article titled "Archaic Tax System" (first quote), and JH, City Council Statement on Taxes, [1960] (remaining quotes), Personal file, NCBA Papers, JHC.

68. George and Constance Wey to JH, June 24, 1960, and Calvin Zimmerman to JH, June 30, 1960, Personal file, NCBA Papers, JHC.

69. Frank Parker to JH, March 1, 1960, with attached Raleigh City Limits Extensions Complaint, Personal file, NCBA Papers, JHC.

70. JH, "Talk Isn't Cheap," *Tarheel Banker,* March 1958, 33 (first and second quotes); JH, "The Difference Is Important," *Tarheel Banker,* December 1959, 30 (third and fourth quotes); JH, "Right Issue, Wrong Target?" *Tarheel Banker,* November 1959, 36 (fifth quote); JH, "Compromise into Oblivion," *Tarheel Banker,* January 1959, 30 (remaining quotes).

71. JH, "Compromise into Oblivion," *Tarheel Banker,* January 1959, 30.

72. JH, "You Have Been Good to Us," *Tarheel Banker,* December 1959, 30.

73. JH, "He Was Billed for Office Rent Only Once," *Tarheel Banker,* May 1958, 33 (first quote); A. J. Fletcher to JH, July 17 (remaining quotes), July 22, September 4, 1957, and July 2, 1958, JH to Fletcher, July 19, August 28, 1957, Personal file, NCBA Papers, JHC.

74. A. J. Fletcher to JH, July 17, July 22 (first quote), September 4, 1957, and July 2, 1958, JH to Fletcher, July 19 (second quote), August 28, 1957, Personal file, NCBA Papers, JHC.

75. JH to Grady Harrell, September 30, 1958, Harrell to JH, September 28, 1958 (quote), and JH to Graham Barden, August 27, 1958, Personal file, NCBA Papers, JHC.

76. JH to J. Kemp Doughton, April 30, 1957, Fletcher to JH, January 28, 1958, and attached memo, Fletcher to Bill Armstrong, January 27, 1958 (quotes), Personal file, NCBA Papers, JHC.

77. JH to Clifton Beckwith, January 22, 1960, Beckwith to JH, January 21, 1960, and statement on state senate campaign, [1960] (quote), Personal file, NCBA Papers, JHC.

78. JH, "Thoughts about Stories, Snow—and Cloture," *Tarheel Banker,* April 1960, 37.

79. JH, "What Fools We Mortals Be," *Tarheel Banker,* March 1960, 42 (quotes); Tuck, *We Ain't What We Ought to Be,* 282–83; Chafe, *Civilities and Civil Rights,* 86–87.

80. Fred Fletcher to JH, January 8, 1960, JH to Fletcher, January 12, 1960, Sterling Booth to JH, August 3, 1960, and JH to Booth, August 11, 1960 (quotes), City Council file, NCBA Papers, JHC.

81. I. Beverly Lake to JH, January 19, 1959, and attached speech "Conservation and Development," January 19, 1959, Personal file, NCBA Papers, JHC; Chafe, *Civilities and Civil Rights,* 49–60, 103–7; Luebke, *Tar Heel Politics,* 27–29, 109–12, 156–57; Klink Cook, "Demos Decide Candidate Today: Lake or Sanford?" *Hendersonville (N.C.) Times-News,* June 25, 1960 (quotes).

82. Lake to JH, June 8, 1959, Lake to W. H. Reedy, June 8, 1959, JH to Lake, June 9, 1959, and JH to George Myrover, June 6, 1960, Personal file, NCBA Papers, JHC; George Myrover, "A Little of This—A Little of That," *Fayetteville Observer,* May 30, 1960; JH, "This Business of Being Neutral Is Dynamite," *Tarheel Banker,* July 1960, 29.

83. Chafe, *Civilities and Civil Rights,* 49–60, 103–7; Luebke, *Tar Heel Politics,* 27–29, 109–12, 156–57; "Primary Post Mortem," *Hendersonville (N.C.) Times-News,* June 8, 1960; "Sanford Adds Surry to Supporting Counties," *Mount Airy (N.C.) News,* June 28, 1960; Crespino, *Strom Thurmond's America,* 195–97; Goldberg, *Barry Goldwater,* 114–15,

142–48; "'Hidden Support' for Gavin Cited in North Carolina," *Charleston News and Courier*, August 3, 1960 (first quote); "Potter Says Nixon Backed by 7 Southern Delegations," *Charleston News and Courier*, April 7, 1960; "Republican Party Planning to Step Up 'Operation Dixie,'" *St. Petersburg (Fla.) Evening Independent*, February 11, 1959 (second quote).

84. JH, "Will Terry Sanford Win?" (quotes), and JH, "What November Will Decide," *Tarheel Banker*, September 1960, 34; JH, "The Religion Issue," *Tarheel Banker*, October 1960, 30.

85. Goldberg, *Barry Goldwater*, 142–46.

86. JH, "What November Will Decide," *Tarheel Banker*, September 1960, 34; JH, "The Religion Issue," *Tarheel Banker*, October 1960, 30 (last two quotes).

87. JH to Dr. Preston H. Scott, September 19, 1960 (first quote), JH to Hanes McFadden, August 30, 1960, and JH to G. Russell Clark, September 5, 1960 (second quote), Personal file, NCBA Papers, JHC.

88. JH to Hanes McFadden, August 30, 1960 (first quote), Personal file, NCBA Papers, JHC; memo, A. J. Fletcher to All of Our Associates on WRAL-TV and Radio, June 28, [1960] (second quote), box 107, folders 4336 and 4337, Harold Dunbar Cooley Papers, SHC.

89. JH to Robert King, March 29, 1957, Personal file, NCBA Papers, JHC.

90. Chafe, *Civilities and Civil Rights*, 103–7; Luebke, *Tar Heel Politics*, 27–29; "The Kennedy-Sanford Victory," *Mount Airy (N.C.) News*, November 11, 1960.

91. JH to A. Hartwell Campbell, January 19, 1959, Personal file, NCBA Papers, JHC.

Chapter 2. "The Voice of Free Enterprise"

1. *Viewpoint* #9, December 2, 1960. *Viewpoints* were erased and the videotapes reused.

2. *Viewpoint* #9, December 2, 1960 (first quote); JH speech, North Carolina Association of Broadcasters, Charlotte, N.C. [early 1960s] (second quote), Speech file, WRAL-TV Papers, JHC; JH to Hardy Berry, April 28, 1963, and JH to Robert Blake, April 20, 1964, Chronological file, WRAL-TV Papers, JHC.

3. JH to G. Aiken Taylor, June 24, 1966 (quote), *Presbyterian Journal* file, JH to Hardy Berry, April 28, 1963, JH to Robert Blake, April 20, 1964, JH to Paul Nesselroad, August 21, 1969, JH to Robert Pate, May 15, 1964, JH to Charles Pace, M.D., August 22, 1969, Chronological file, and JH to Steve Dunning, April 20, 1964, *The Iroquoian* file, all in WRAL-TV Papers, JHC; *Viewpoint* #2000, December 31, 1968. Although an editorial board—composed of Helms, A. J. Fletcher, Executive Vice President Fred Fletcher, and Comptroller Aubrey Moore—reviewed each commentary, the board allowed Helms a free hand.

4. *Viewpoint* #411, July 18, 1962 (quotes); *Viewpoint* #12, December 7, 1960.

5. *Viewpoint* #12, December 7, 1960.

6. *Viewpoint* #262, December 12, 1961.

7. *Viewpoint* #76, March 9, 1961.

8. *Viewpoint* #73, March 6, 1961; Federal Communication Commission Application for Renewal of Broadcast License Capitol Broadcasting Company, Reports of Fred Fletcher to Board of Directors Capitol Broadcasting Company, Incorporated, April 1,

1962, August 1963, Broadcast Station License files, File 72A451, box 502, folder WRAL-TV (1961–66), RG 173, NACP.

9. J. C. Peele to JH, October 3, 4 (first quote), and 6, 1961, Peele to Robert McNamara, December 14, 1964, Peele to Alcoa, December 29, 1965, and JH to Peele, October 6 (fourth quote), 10, 1961, May 11 (fifth and sixth quotes), July 19 (last quote), July 23, August 25, 1965, J. C. Peele file, WRAL-TV Papers, JHC.

10. *Viewpoint* #628, June 11, 1963.

11. JH to Bill Sharpe, February 13, 1968 (quote), Sharpe file, WRAL-TV Papers, JHC; Farber, *Rise and Fall*, 70–72; Andrew, *The Other Side of the Sixties*, 1–10; McGirr, "Piety and Property"; Schoenwald, *A Time for Choosing*, 3–13, 162–89.

12. *Viewpoint* #1078, April 12, 1965 (quotes). On the Klan see *Viewpoint* #610, May 15, 1963, *Viewpoint* #1383, June 27, 1966, and *Viewpoint* #1411, August, 4, 1966, and JH to Joseph Dunn, March 23, 1966, and Dunn to JH, March 17, 1966, JH to Gertrude Price Hood, March 25, 1966, and Hood to JH, March 25, 1966, and attached *Raleigh News and Observer* clipping, Chronological file, WRAL-TV Papers, JHC.

13. *Viewpoint* #8, December 1, 1960.

14. *Viewpoint* #1, November 21, 1960 (first quote); JH to Hillard Wolfe, April 7, 1961 (second quote), Wolfe file, WRAL-TV Papers, JHC.

15. *Viewpoint* #54, February 7, 1961 (first and last quotes); *Viewpoint* #382, June 6, 1962 (second and third quotes); see Arthur Schlesinger Jr., "Speaking Out: The Failure of World Communism," *Saturday Evening Post*, May 19, 1962, 13–14; *Viewpoint* #54 criticized a Schlesinger speech, while #382 condemned the *Saturday Evening Post* article, which elaborated on the same themes.

16. *Viewpoint* #9, December 2, 1960 (first quote); *Viewpoint* #21, December 20, 1960 (second quote); *Viewpoint* #12, December 7, 1960 (third and fourth quotes); *Viewpoint* #89, March 28, 1961; *Viewpoint* #615, May 23, 1963 (fifth quote).

17. *Viewpoint* #74, March 7, 1961.

18. *Viewpoint* #660, August 2, 1963 (remaining quotes); *Viewpoint* #688, September 11, 1963 (fourth quote).

19. *Viewpoint* #8, December 1, 1960 (first quote); *Viewpoint* #54, February 7, 1961; *Viewpoint* #382, June 6, 1962; *Viewpoint* #413, July 20, 1962 (second quote); *Viewpoint* #531, January 23, 1963 (remaining quotes); on liberalism and the New Deal as socialist see especially *Viewpoint* #22, December 21, 1960.

20. JH speech, "Problems in the Procedures of Broadcast Relicensing," Fact Finders Forum, Miami, Florida, April 6, 1967 (first quote), Speech file, WRAL-TV Papers, JHC; *Viewpoint* #1761, January 5, 1968 (remaining quotes); Helms made similar, although less detailed, critiques of Social Security earlier in the decade: *Viewpoint* #69, February 28, 1961 (repeated as #385, June 11, 1962), and *Viewpoint* #776, January 20, 1964.

21. *Viewpoint* #504, December 14, 1962.

22. Williams, *God's Own Party*, 62–67; *Viewpoint* #396, June 26, 1962 (quotes); *Viewpoint* #400, July 2, 1962; *Viewpoint* #404, July 7, 1962; *Viewpoint* #426, August 16, 1962.

23. Williams, *God's Own Party*, 62–67; *Viewpoint* #396, June 26, 1962; *Viewpoint* #400, July 2, 1962; *Viewpoint* #404, July 7, 1962; *Viewpoint* #426, August 16, 1962; *Viewpoint* #503, December 13, 1962 (quote).

24. *Viewpoint* #426, August 16, 1962 (first quote); *Viewpoint* #404, July 7, 1962 (second quote).

25. Williams, *God's Own Party*, 62–67; *Viewpoint* #633, June 18, 1963 (quote); *Viewpoint* #894, July 3, 1964.

26. *Viewpoint* #396, June 26, 1962 (first quote); *Viewpoint* #701, October 1, 1963 (second quote).

27. JH to Ben Sumner, October 16, 1961, Spindale Mills file, WRAL-TV Papers, JHC; *Viewpoint* #876, June 9, 1964.

28. *Viewpoint* #424, August 14, 1962.

29. *Viewpoint* #60, February 15, 1961.

30. *Viewpoint* #7, November 30, 1960.

31. Dallek, *An Unfinished Life,* 286–96, 292, 330–32, 380–88, 491–96, 510–14; Branch, *Parting the Waters,* 171–72, 389–92, 412–91, 528–58, 600–632, 637; *Viewpoint* #128, May 22, 1961 (first, second, third, fifth, and sixth quotes); *Viewpoint* #142, June 12, 1961 (fourth quote).

32. Branch, *Parting the Waters*, 171–72, 389–92, 412–91, 528–58, 600–632, 637; *Viewpoint* #424, August 14, 1962.

33. Robert Corsauk to JH, January 15, 1962 (first quote), Josiah Bailey to JH, December 28, 1961 (second quote), and A. Lincoln Faulk to JH, July 21, 1961 (third quote), Critical Mail file, WRAL-TV Papers, JHC.

34. JH speech, North Carolina Association of Broadcasters [early 1960s] (first and second quotes), Speech file, Joe Norman to JH, May 31, 1963, Joe Norman file, Miller to Walter Cronkite, December 28, 1961, Charles Miller to JH, October 1 and October 16, 1964, Charles Miller file, and Harry Welch to JH, April 28, 1966, Chronological file, WRAL-TV Papers, JHC; *Viewpoint* #807, March 4, 1964; *Viewpoint* #838, April 16, 1964; *Viewpoint* #2319, April 20–21, 1970 (last quote).

35. *Viewpoint* #8, December 1, 1960; JH speech, North Carolina Association of Broadcasters [early 1960s], JH speech, North Carolina Associated Press Broadcasters, Raleigh, N.C., January 18, 1961, and JH speech, "Meredith College Talk: Censorship in a Democratic Society," Raleigh, N.C., February 13, 1968, all in Speech file, WRAL-TV Papers, JHC; JH to William F. Buckley, May 2, 1963, Buckley file, WRAL-TV Papers, JHC.

36. Federal Communication Commission Application for Renewal of Broadcast License Capitol Broadcasting Company, Exhibit 6, Report of Fred Fletcher to Board of Directors Capitol Broadcasting Company, Incorporated, June 15, 1963, August 1963, Broadcast Station License files, File 72A451, box 502, folder WRAL-TV (1961–66), RG 173, NACP. *Stateline,* the 6 p.m. news program on WRAL-TV, later changed its name to *Dateline.*

37. JH speech, "Meredith College Talk," February 13, 1968.

38. JH speech, North Carolina Associated Press Broadcasters, January 18, 1961.

39. *Viewpoint* #701, October 1, 1963; *Viewpoint* #808, March 5, 1964; *Viewpoint* #862, May 20, 1964; *Viewpoint* #1025, January 27, 1965; Alice Anderson to A. J. Fletcher and Fletcher to Anderson, May 15, 1965, Critical Mail file, WRAL-TV Papers, JHC; JH to Sam Ervin, August 9, 1965, and JH to Mrs. H. C. Butler, August 9, 1965, Chronological file, WRAL-TV Papers, JHC.

40. JH to Mrs. Ted Johnson, February 6, 1969 (first quote), and JH to Leo Stanis, August 9, 1965 (second quote), Chronological file, WRAL-TV Papers, JHC.

41. Andrew, *The Other Side of the Sixties*, 29–30; Federal Communication Commission Application for Renewal of Broadcast License Capitol Broadcasting Company, Exhibit 5, Public Affairs Programming (prepared by Jesse Helms), Exhibit 6, Reports of Fred Fletcher to Board of Directors Capitol Broadcasting Company, Incorporated, May 16, 1961, April 1, 1962, and June 15, 1963, August 1963, Broadcast Station License files, File 72A451, box 502, folder WRAL-TV (1961–66), RG 173, NACP (first quote); *Viewpoint* #265, December 15, 1961 (second quote).

42. Federal Communication Commission Application for Renewal of Broadcast License Capitol Broadcasting Company, Exhibit 5, Public Affairs Programming (prepared by Jesse Helms), Exhibit 6, Reports of Fred Fletcher to Board of Directors Capitol Broadcasting Company, Incorporated, May 16, 1961, April 1, 1962, and June 15, 1963, August 1963, Broadcast Station License files, File 72A451, box 502, folder WRAL-TV (1961–66), RG 173, NACP; JH speech, North Carolina Association of Broadcasters [early 1960s], Speech file, WRAL-TV Papers, JHC; JH to William F. Buckley, May 2, 1963, Buckley file, JH to Thurman Sensing, September 22, September 28, and October 23, 1961, and Sensing to JH, September 25, October 10, 1961, Thurman Sensing file, Bill Weidlich to JH, August 9, 1963, Job Applications file, WRAL-TV Papers, JHC.

43. JH to Clarence Manion, September 12, 1961 (first quote), September 11, October 1, 1963, January 21 1966, Manion to JH, September 9, 1963, April 24, September 29, 1964, January 14, 1966 (second quote), JH to L. F. Reardon, January 17, 1961 (third quote), Emmett Mellentthin to JH, October 3, 1961, JH to Mellenthin, December 9, 1963, memo, Bob Caudle to JH, January 23, 1964, Clarence Manion file, and JH to Thurmond Sensing, May 18, 1964 (last quote), Sensing file, WRAL-TV Papers, JHC; Andrew, *The Other Side of the Sixties*, 29–30.

44. Edward Annis to JH, September 30, 1961 (quote), JH to Annis, November 2, 1961, and November 5, 1963, Edward Annis file, WRAL-TV Papers, JHC.

45. JH to Paul Kitchin, April 24, 1961, and June 20, 1962, Paul Kitchin file, JH to L. H. Fountain, October 12, 1961, April 3 (second quote), July 13, 1967 (first quote), October 4, 1968 (third quote), September 18, 1969, and Fountain to JH, October 1, 1968 (fourth quote), L. H. Fountain file, JH to Alton Lennon, June 13, 1962, August 10, 1964, January 3, 1966, and December 15, 1971, Alton Lennon file, JH to B. Everett Jordan, March 14, 1966, B. Everett Jordan file, JH to Jonas, May 15, September 12, 1961 (fifth quote), June 19, 1962, April 24, 1961, July 26, 1965, January 18, 1966, February 4, 1967, and Jonas to JH, September 6, 1961, May 13, 1963, Jonas file, WRAL-TV Papers, JHC; *Viewpoint* #688, September 11, 1963; *Viewpoint* #927, September 2, 1964 (remaining quotes); *Viewpoint* #1276, January 21, 1966.

46. *Viewpoint* #688, September 11, 1963; *Viewpoint* #1276, July 30, 1965 (first quote); Raymond Crowley, "Many Close Contests," *Free Lance–Star* (Fredericksburg, Va.), November 1, 1962; Bennett Edwards, "Across the Editor's Desk," *Anson Record* (Wadesboro, N.C.), November 15, 1962; JH to B. Everett Jordan, March 14, 1966, Jordan file, and Jonas to JH, May 13, 1963 (second quote), Jonas file, WRAL-TV Papers, JHC.

47. JH to Paul Kitchin, April 24, 1961, and June 20, 1962, Kitchin file, and JH to Jonas,

May 15, June 19, 1962, Jonas file, WRAL-TV Papers, JHC; Raymond Crowley, "Many Close Contests," *Free Lance–Star*, November 1, 1962; Bennett Edwards, "Across the Editor's Desk," *Anson Record* (Wadesboro, N.C.), November 15, 1962; JH to William Whitley, January 23, 1963 (quote), Jordan file, WRAL-TV Papers, JHC; *Viewpoint* #615, May 23, 1963; Black and Black, *Rise of Southern Republicans*, 65, 147, 195.

48. Terry Sanford to Hargrove Bowles, August 18, 1961 (first quote), Sanford file, WRAL-TV Papers, JHC; *Viewpoint* #422, August 9, 1962 (remaining quotes).

49. *Viewpoint* #422, August 9, 1962.

50. *Viewpoint* #375, May 28, 1962.

51. *Viewpoint* #468, October 24, 1962 (first, second and third quotes); Dallek, *An Unfinished Life,* 535–75 (final quote on 575); Zelizer, *Arsenal of Democracy,* 148–77.

52. Zelizer, *Arsenal of Democracy,* 148–77; *Viewpoint* #469, October 25, 1962 (quotes); *Viewpoint* #472, October 30, 1962.

53. Dallek, *An Unfinished Life,* 535–75; *Viewpoint* #472, October 30, 1962 (first and second quotes); *Viewpoint* #473, October 31, 1962 (last quote).

54. *Viewpoint* #264, December 14, 1961 (quotes); *Viewpoint* #275, January 2, 1962.

55. Memo to Members of the North Carolina General Assembly, January 5, 1963, and attached document, A Resolution and Recommendation by American Legion Post No. 6 Chapel Hill, North Carolina, September 16, 1962 (first quote), Henry Royall file, WRAL-TV Papers, JHC; *Viewpoint* #461, October 11, 1962 (second quote); *Viewpoint* #502, December 12, 1962.

56. *Viewpoint* #461, October 11, 1962; *Viewpoint* #502, December 12, 1962 (quotes).

57. *Viewpoint* #461, October 11, 1962 (first quote); *Viewpoint* #466, October 18, 1962 (remaining quotes).

58. Donovan, *Unsilent Revolution*, 3–22; Bond, "The Media and the Movement."

59. *Viewpoint* #595, April 24, 1963.

60. *Viewpoint* #610, May 15, 1963 (first quote); Donovan, *Unsilent Revolution*, 3–22; Dallek, *An Unfinished Life*, 594–606 (final quote on 594).

61. Donovan, *Unsilent Revolution*, 3–22; Billingsley, *Communists on Campus*, 44–64; *Viewpoint* #610, May 15, 1963 (quotes).

62. *Viewpoint* #638, June 25, 1963 (first and second quotes); *Viewpoint* #635, June 20, 1963 (last quote); *Viewpoint* #653, July 16, 1963.

63. *Viewpoint* #631, June 14, 1963 (quotes); William Herrick, "The Truth Was the Last Straw," review of Junius Scales's *Cause at Heart: A Former Communist Remembers, New York Times*, July 12, 1987.

64. *Viewpoint* #636, June 21, 1963 (first and second quotes); JH to Charles Reynolds, February 5, 1965 (third quote), Spindale Mills file, WRAL-TV Papers, JHC; *Viewpoint* #640, June 27, 1963; *Viewpoint* #642, July 1, 1963 (last quote); Billingsley, *Communists on Campus*, ix–xvi, 1–87, 218–20.

65. *Viewpoint* #667, July 30, 1963 (quotes). Helms repeatedly used the phrase "clear-cut choice" in advocating realignment to mean a choice between a conservative and a liberal; other examples of his use of "clear-cut choice" include *Viewpoint* #877, June 10, 1964, *Viewpoint* #890, June 29, 1964, *Viewpoint* #916, August 18, 1964, and *Viewpoint* #2447, October 29, 1970.

66. *Viewpoint* #667, July 30, 1963 (first and second quotes); Viewpoint #708, October 11, 1963; *Viewpoint* #715, October 22, 1963 (last quote); JH to T. J. Youngblood Jr., May 11, 1964, May 1964, Chronological file, WRAL-TV Papers, JHC.

67. *Viewpoint* #708, October 11, 1963 (first and second quotes); *Viewpoint* #715, October 22, 1963 (third and fourth quotes).

68. Schulman, *Lyndon B. Johnson*, 62–76, 169–73; *Viewpoint* #794, February 14, 1964 (quotes).

69. *Viewpoint* #814, March 13, 1964 (first quote); JH to Bill Sharpe, October 29, 1963 (remaining quotes), Sharpe file, WRAL-TV Papers, JHC.

70. *Viewpoint* #814, March 13, 1964.

71. JH to Bill Sharpe, July 21, 1964, Sharpe file, WRAL-TV Papers, JHC.

72. William Shires, "Around Capitol Square: Want Jonas' Word," June 4, 1963, and "Changes Have Been Wrought," November 14, 1962, *Richmond County Journal* (Rockingham, N.C.); "GOP Tug of War: Goldwater Adherents Hold Key Republican Positions," *Eugene (Ore.) Register-Guard*, October 8, 1963 (reprinted from the *Congressional Quarterly*); JH to Jonas, September 12, 1961, and Jonas to JH, May 13, 1963, Jonas file, WRAL-TV Papers, JHC.

73. Luebke, *Tar Heel Politics*, 108–12, 157–60; Chafe, *Civilities and Civil Rights*, 161–63; JH to I. Beverly Lake, December 2, 1963, I. Beverly Lake file, JH to James Pou Bailey, July 29, 1963, and H. D. Harrison Jr. to JH and other committee members, July 20, 1963 (first quote), James Pou Bailey file, JH to Charles Reynolds, December 26, 1963, Spindale Mills file, WRAL-TV Papers, JHC; *Viewpoint* #870, June 1, 1964 (second quote); *Viewpoint* #875, June 8, 1964; *Viewpoint* #879, June 12, 1964; "Moore Decides to Ask for Runoff," *Wilmington News,* June 2, 1964 (third quote).

74. Hoover Adams to JH, June 3, 1964, Hoover Adams file, and JH to Paul Kitchin, June 9, 1964, Kitchin file, WRAL-TV Papers, JHC; William Shires, "Around Capitol Square: Preyer Comeback to Moore," *Robesonian* (Lumberton, N.C.), June 11, 1964; William King, "Moore's Victory Seen as a Conservative Swing," *Wilmington News*, June 29, 1964.

75. William King, "Moore's Victory Seen as a Conservative Swing," *Wilmington News*, June 29, 1964; "Thunderous Ovation Given Goldwater and Gavin," *Lexington (N.C.) Dispatch*, September 22, 1964.

76. *Viewpoint* #890, June 29, 1964 (first, second, and third quotes); *Viewpoint* #923, August 27, 1964; JH to Dan Moore, July 3, 1964, and attached statement, Daniel Moore file, and JH to Lenox Baker, October 6, 1964 (last quote), and Baker to Dan Moore, October 1, 1964, Lenox Baker file, WRAL-TV Papers, JHC.

77. Dallek, *Flawed Giant*, 122–84; *Viewpoint* #877, June 10, 1964 (quotes).

78. *Viewpoint* #894, July 3, 1964 (first, second, and third quotes; last quote); *Viewpoint* #895, July 20, 1964 (fifth, sixth, and seventh quotes); *Viewpoint* #907, August 5, 1964; *Viewpoint* #913, August 13, 1964; *Viewpoint* #926, September 1, 1964; *Viewpoint* #936, September 15, 1964.

79. Schulman, *Lyndon B. Johnson*, 62–76; Dallek, *Flawed Giant*, 122–84; *Viewpoint* #894, July 3, 1964 (quote).

80. *Viewpoint* #941, September 22, 1964 (first quote); *Viewpoint* #951, October 6, 1964;

Viewpoint #926, September 1, 1964 (second and third quotes); *Viewpoint* #936, September 15, 1964; *Viewpoint* #907, August 5, 1964 (remaining quotes).

81. Schulman, *Lyndon B. Johnson*, 70–71; *Viewpoint* #863, May 21, 1964 (quotes).

82. The Federal Communication Commission Application for Renewal of Broadcast License, August 1966, Exhibit #6, Public Affairs Programs, Broadcast Station License files, File 173-75-24, box 82, folder WRAL-TV (1966–72), RG 173, NACP; *Viewpoint* #938, September 17, 1964 (first quote); *Viewpoint* #941, September 22, 1964 (second quote).

83. *Viewpoint* #938, September 17, 1964 (first, second, and third quotes); Dallek, *Flawed Giant*, 122–84; JH to Andrew Beck, November 13, 1964, Andrew Beck file, WRAL-TV Papers, JHC (last quote).

84. "Choice of Candidates," *Robesonian* (Lumberton, N.C.), October 28, 1964; "Mountain Man Moore Wins Governorship over Gavin," *Hendersonville (N.C.) Times-News*, November 4, 1964.

85. Joe Hunt to JH, November 1, [1964], Moore file, J. Herman Saxon to JH, September 29, 1964, Republican Party file, JH to Robert Gavin, December 21, 1964, and Gavin to JH, December 17, 1964, Gavin file, WRAL-TV Papers, JHC.

86. JH to Earl Butz, December 4, 1964, Butz file, WRAL-TV Papers, JHC.

87. JH to L. H. Fountain, February 8, 1971, Fountain file, WRAL-TV Papers, JHC.

88. JH to Fred Beard, April 15, 1965 (first quote), Miscellaneous Radio and Television file, and JH to Bill Sharpe, July 21, 1964 (remaining quotes), Sharpe file, WRAL-TV Papers, JHC.

89. *Viewpoint* #998, December 17, 1964.

Chapter 3. "An Uncommon Number of Moral Degenerates"

1. Watson, *Expanding Vista*, 18–35; FCC Public Notice, "Broadcast Licensees Advised Concerning Stations' Responsibilities under the Fairness Doctrine as to Controversial Issue Programming," July 26, 1963, FCC file, WRAL-TV Papers, JHC.

2. FCC Public Notice, "Broadcast Licensees Advised Concerning Stations' Responsibilities under the Fairness Doctrine as to Controversial Issue Programming," July 26, 1963, FCC file, and JH to Thurmond Sensing, August 29, 1963, Thurmond Sensing file, WRAL-TV Papers, JHC (last quote).

3. *Viewpoint* #9, December 2, 1960.

4. JH speech, "Problems in the Procedures of Broadcast Relicensing," Fact Finders Forum, Miami, Florida, April 6, 1967, Speech file, WRAL-TV Papers, JHC.

5. Ibid.

6. Ben Waple to A. J. Fletcher, January 17, 1963, FCC file, JH to William Cheshire, May 21, 1964 (first quote), Chronological file, JH to Clarence Manion, April 28, 1964, Manion file, JH to Lenox Baker, July 20, 1964, Baker file, WRAL-TV Papers, JHC; Ben Waple to A. J. Fletcher, July 29, 1964 (second quote), Broadcast Station License files, File 72A451, box 502, folder WRAL-TV (1961–66), RG 173, NACP.

7. Ben Waple to A. J. Fletcher, January 17, 1963 (first quote), and JH to George Wallace, September 23, 1963 (second quote), FCC file, WRAL-TV Papers, JHC.

8. Ben Waple to A. J. Fletcher, January 17, 1963, FCC file, WRAL-TV Papers, JHC.

9. Ibid.; JH to Clarence Manion, April 28, 1964, Manion file, JH to William Cheshire,

May 21, 1964, Chronological file, and JH to Baker, July 20, 1964, Baker file, WRAL-TV Papers, JHC.

10. *Viewpoint* #659, August 1, 1963.

11. *Viewpoint* #672, August 20, 1963; Ben Waple to A. J. Fletcher, July 29, 1964, Broadcast Station License files, File 72A451, box 502, folder WRAL-TV (1961–66), RG 173, NACP.

12. *Viewpoint* #672, August 20, 1963.

13. Ibid.; Williams, *God's Own Party*, 146–53; Tuck, *We Ain't What We Ought to Be*, 402.

14. *Viewpoint* #672, August 20, 1963.

15. Ben Waple to A. J. Fletcher, January 17, 1963, FCC file, JH to William Cheshire, May 21, 1964, Chronological file, JH to Clarence Manion, April 28, 1964, Manion file, WRAL-TV Papers, JHC; Ben Waple to A. J. Fletcher, July 29, 1964, Broadcast Station License files, File 72A451, box 502, folder WRAL-TV, RG 173, NACP; Robert McFadden, "Mourners Recall Wagner as Man of Subtle Grace," *New York Times*, February 17, 1991.

16. *Viewpoint* #659, August 1, 1963; *Viewpoint* #672, August 20, 1963; Ben Waple to A. J. Fletcher, July 29, 1964 (quote), Broadcast Station License files, File 72A451, box 502, folder WRAL-TV (1961–66), RG 173, NACP.

17. Ben Waple to A. J. Fletcher, January 17, 1963, FCC file, JH to William Cheshire, May 21, 1964, Chronological file, WRAL-TV Papers, JHC; Federal Communication Commission Application for Renewal of Broadcast License Capitol Broadcasting Company, Exhibit 5, Public Affairs Programming (prepared by Jesse Helms), Exhibit 6, Reports of Fred Fletcher to Board of Directors Capitol Broadcasting Company, Incorporated, May 16, 1961, April 1, 1962, June 15, 1963, and August 1963, Broadcast Station License files, File 72A451, box 502, folder WRAL-TV (1961–66), RG 173, NACP.

18. JH to William Cheshire, May 21, 1964 (first quote), Chronological file, WRAL-TV Papers, JHC; Federal Communication Commission Application for Renewal of Broadcast License Capitol Broadcasting Company, Exhibit 5, Public Affairs Programming (prepared by Jesse Helms) (second quote), Exhibit 6, Reports of Fred Fletcher to Board of Directors Capitol Broadcasting Company, Incorporated, May 16, 1961, April 1, 1962, June 15, 1963, and August 1963, Broadcast Station License files, File 72A451, box 502, folder WRAL-TV (1961–66), RG 173, NACP.

19. *Viewpoint* #422, August 9, 1962; Ben Waple to A. J. Fletcher, January 17, 1963, and Memorandum for the files, January 20, 1964, FCC file, WRAL-TV Papers, JHC.

20. *Viewpoint* #422, August 9, 1962 (first quote); Ben Waple to A. J. Fletcher, January 17, 1963, and Memorandum for the files, January 20, 1964 (remaining quotes), FCC file, WRAL-TV Papers, JHC.

21. Lenox Baker to JH, September 11, 1963 (quotes), Baker to Gentlemen (at the FCC) and accompanying notes, September 11, 1963, Baker to J. Q. Mahaffey, September 10, 1963, Baker file, WRAL-TV Papers, JHC. Baker reminded Johnson that his father had been a Texas County Democratic chairman. His letter to Johnson stretched the truth, assuring the vice president that WRAL has "always been most loyal to you and will be so in the future." Others he wrote included Senator Sam Ervin, South Carolina senator Strom Thurmond, and numerous North Carolina congressmen.

22. Ben Waple to A. J. Fletcher, January 17, 1963 (first quote), memo to Jesse, n.d., attached transcript, September 9, 1963, Bill Armstrong memo to Fred, Jesse, A. J. Fletcher, March 4, 1964, and attached transcript, n.d., FCC file, and I. Beverly Lake to JH, January 20, 1964, JH to Lake, January 22, 1964, Lake file, WRAL-TV Papers, JHC.

23. Bill A. to Jesse, n.d., and attached transcript, n.d. (first quote), and Bill Armstrong memo to Fred, Jesse, A. J. Fletcher, March 4, 1964, and attached transcript, n.d. (second quote), FCC file, WRAL-TV Papers, JHC.

24. Memo, Bill Armstrong to JH, January 10, 1964, FCC file, WRAL-TV Papers, JHC; *Viewpoint* #781, January 28, 1964.

25. *Viewpoint* #781, January 28, 1964.

26. Newman Townsend to JH, January 30, 1964 (quotes), and telegrams, Lake to WRAL-TV, January 29, 1964, and Dan Moore to WRAL-TV, January 29, 1964, FCC file, WRAL-TV Papers, JHC.

27. *Viewpoint* #786, February 4, 1964 (first quote); Memos from JH to the Associate Press and United Press International, January 30 and January 31, 1964, press release from David Witherspoon, February 3, 1964, and I. Beverly Lake press release, February 4, 1964 (second quote), FCC file, WRAL-TV Papers, JHC.

28. Memo, Sam Beard to JH, February 24, 1964, FCC file, WRAL-TV Papers, JHC.

29. "Statement by A. J. Fletcher, President Capitol Broadcasting Company," March 26, 1964, FCC file, and JH to William Cheshire, May 21, 1964, Chronological file, WRAL-TV Papers, JHC.

30. Memo for the files, March 27, 1964, FCC file, JH to Landon Lane, April 7, 1964 (first quote), JH to Paul Phillips, April 7, 1964, JH to Chalmers Davidson, April 7, 1964, Chronological file, JH to Bill Sharpe, April 6, 1964, Sharpe file, JH to Thurmond Sensing, May 18, 1964 (remaining quotes), Thurmond Sensing file, and JH to William Cheshire, May 21, 1964, Chronological file, WRAL-TV Papers, JHC.

31. JH to Chalmers Davidson, April 7, 1964, Chronological file, WRAL-TV Papers, JHC.

32. JH's Note on Conversation with Newsom Townsend, April 14, 1964 (quote), and attached telegram, Wally Voigt to Ted Cramer, n.d., and Wally Voigt to Ted Cramer, April 15, 1964, FCC file, WRAL-TV Papers, JHC.

33. Luebke, *Tar Heel Politics*, 108–12, 157–60; "Moore Decides to Ask for Runoff," *Wilmington News*, June 2, 1964 (first quote); *Viewpoint* #875, June 8, 1964 (second quote); *Viewpoint* #870, June 1, 1964; *Viewpoint* #879, June 12, 1964.

34. *Viewpoint* #875, June 8, 1964 (first and second quotes); *Viewpoint* #870, June 1, 1964 (remaining quotes); *Viewpoint* #879, June 12, 1964.

35. Ben Waple to A. J. Fletcher, July 29, 1964, Broadcast Station License files, File 72A451, box 502, folder WRAL-TV (1961–66), RG 173, NACP; JH to William Cheshire, May 21, 1964, Chronological file, WRAL-TV Papers, JHC (quote).

36. Ben Waple to A. J. Fletcher, July 29, 1964, Broadcast Station License files, File 72A451, box 502, folder WRAL-TV (1961–66), RG 173, NACP.

37. Ibid.; JH to Ben Waple, December 12, 1966, and card, n.d., Holtzman Complaint, WRAL-TV Papers, JHC; *Viewpoint* #838, April 16, 1964.

38. JH to Baker, July 20, 1964, Baker file, WRAL-TV Papers, JHC; *Viewpoint* #906, August 4, 1964.

39. History of the Capitol Broadcasting Company, http://www.cbc-raleigh.com/history/history.asp; JH speech, "Problems in the Procedures of Broadcast Relicensing," Fact Finders Forum, Miami, Florida, April 6, 1967, Speech file, WRAL-TV Papers, JHC.

40. JH to George Terry, May 11, 1964 (first and last quotes), JH to Robert Blake, May 7, 1964 (third quote), and JH to David Abbott, April 28, 1964 (fourth quote), Chronological file, WRAL-TV Papers, JHC; *Viewpoint* #849, May 1, 1964 (second quote).

41. *Viewpoint* #848, April 30, 1964 (second quote); *Viewpoint* #851, May 5, 1964 (first quote); *Viewpoint* #852, May 6, 1964 (third quote); *Viewpoint* #853, May 7, 1964; *Viewpoint* #875, June 8, 1964; Furgurson, *Hard Right*, 241–42, 258 (final quote on 258).

42. *Viewpoint* #838, April 16, 1964 (first quote); JH to Hardy Berry, April 28, 1963, Chronological file, WRAL-TV Papers, JHC; *Viewpoint* #1071, April 1, 1965 (last quote).

43. Link, *Righteous Warrior*, 114–20; JH to Earl Butz, January 25, January 31, and March 6, 1957 (quotes), and Butz to JH, February 26, 1957, Personal file, NCBA Papers, JHC; "Cooley Defends Manifesto Stand," *Raleigh News and Observer*, November 1, 1966; Biographical Note (August 1966), Inventory of Harold Dunbar Cooley's Papers Online Guide, Library of UNC Chapel Hill, http://www.lib.unc.edu/mss/inv/c/Cooley,Harold_Dunbar.html (accessed May 20, 2009).

44. Earl Butz to JH, December 3, 1962, and Butz to A. J. Fletcher, February 2, 1963, Butz file, WRAL-TV Papers, JHC; *Viewpoint* #403, July 5, 1962 (quotes); *Viewpoint* #421, August 8, 1962; *Viewpoint* #440, September 12, 1962; *Viewpoint* #742, December 2, 1963; *Viewpoint* #912, August 12, 1964; *Viewpoint* #1084, April 20, 1965.

45. *Viewpoint* #440, September 12, 1962 (first and second quotes); *Viewpoint* #421, August 8, 1962 (third quote); *Viewpoint* #742, December 2, 1963 (last quote); *Viewpoint* #912, August 12, 1964; *Viewpoint* #1084, April 20, 1965.

46. Bob Wood, "1964: Cooley Didn't Know Gardner," *Raleigh News and Observer*, November 10, 1966; JH to Jim Gardner, April 13, November 30, 1964, February 15, April 16, 1965, Gardner to JH, April 10, November 20, 1964, February 10, April 15, 1965, James Gardner file, WRAL-TV Papers, JHC.

47. *Viewpoint* #1148, July 28, 1965.

48. Harold Cooley to A. J. Fletcher, August 6, 1965 (all quotes except last), and n.d. (last quote), and Fletcher to Cooley, August 17 and August 30, 1965, box 107, folders 4336 and 4337, Cooley Papers, SHC.

49. "Cooley Predicts Passage of Farm Production Bill," October 4, 1966, Russell Clay, "Congressional Races Add Some Zip to Nov. 8 Vote," October 30, 1966, "Gardner Hits Farm Policy," October 30, 1966, Jim Lewis, "Cooley and Gardner Clash at Forum," November 4, 1966, Russell Clay, "Survey Shows Cooley, Foe Locked in Dead-Heat Race," November 4, 1966, Russell Clay, "N.C. Spotlight Focuses on 4th," November 8, 1966 (quote), Roy Parker Jr., "Gardner Leaps to GOP Front Rank," November 9, 1966, and "With Harold Cooley, North Carolina Has a Powerful Voice in Washington" (Cooley ad), November 2, 1966, all in *Raleigh News and Observer*.

50. "Plan to See the Famous N.C.S.U. Confrontation" (Gardner political ad), *Raleigh News and Observer*, October 31, 1966 (first quote); Fred Fletcher to FCC Secretary Ben

Waple (response to the complaint of James Maddox, Abraham Holtzman, and Edward Ezell), November 14, 1966, Fred Fletcher to FCC Secretary Ben Waple (response to Allen Paul's complaint), November 14, 1966, Harold Cooley to FCC Secretary Ben Waple (formal FCC complaint), November 18, 1966 (third quote), Transcript of Cooley News Conference, November 7, 1966 (second quote), box 107, folders 4336 and 4337, Cooley Papers, SHC.

51. Fred Fletcher to FCC Secretary Ben Waple (response to the complaint of James Maddox, Abraham Holtzman, and Edward Ezell), November 14, 1966, Fred Fletcher to FCC Secretary Ben Waple (response to Allen Paul's complaint), November 14, 1966, Harold Cooley to FCC Secretary Ben Waple (formal FCC complaint), November 18, 1966 (first and third quotes), Transcript of Cooley News Conference, November 7, 1966 (second quote), box 107, folders 4336 and 4337, Cooley Papers, SHC; Edward Ezell to Chairman of the FCC, December 19, 1966, Holtzman Complaint file, WRAL-TV Papers, JHC.

52. "Gardner's Film Called Distorted," November 3, 1966 (first and second quotes), and Roy Rabon, "Gardner's Film of Debate Becomes Issue in Campaign," November 5, 1966 (third, fourth, and fifth quotes), *Raleigh News and Observer*.

53. "Professors Protest Station's Actions," *Raleigh News and Observer*, November 7, 1966; Transcript of Cooley News Conference, November 7, 1966, Cooley Papers, SHC.

54. *Viewpoint* #1476, November 7, 1966.

55. Fletcher to Waple, November 14, 1966, Fletcher to Ben Waple (response to Allen Paul's complaint), November 14, 1966, Cooley to Waple, November 18, 1966 (quote), Cooley Papers, SHC; Russell Clay, "Gardner Defeats Cooley by 13,000-Vote Margin," *Raleigh News and Observer*, November 9, 1966; *Viewpoint* #1477, November 8, 1966; *Viewpoint* #1478, November 9, 1966.

56. Cooley press release, November 21, 1966 (second quote), Fletcher to Waple, November 14, 1966, Fletcher to Ben Waple (response to Allen Paul's complaint), November 14, 1966, Cooley to Waple (formal FCC complaint), November 18, 1966 (first, third, and fourth quotes), Cooley Papers, SHC.

57. Cooley press release, November 21, 1966 (first quote), Fletcher to Waple, November 14, 1966, Fletcher to Ben Waple (response to Allen Paul's complaint), November 14, 1966, Cooley to Waple (formal FCC complaint), November 18, 1966 (remaining quotes), Cooley Papers, SHC.

58. Capitol Broadcasting Company, Incorporated, for Renewal of License, Memorandum and Opinion, July 5, 1967, Broadcast Station License files, File 173-75-24, box 82, folder WRAL-TV (1966–72), RG 173, NACP; FCC Grants WRAL-TV, Raleigh, N.C., License Renewal, July 7, 1967, Cooley Papers, SHC.

59. Capitol Broadcasting Company, Incorporated, for Renewal of License, Memorandum and Opinion, July 5, 1967, Broadcast Station License files, File 173-75-24, box 82, folder WRAL-TV (1966–72), RG 173, NACP; FCC Grants WRAL-TV, Raleigh, N.C., License Renewal, July 7, 1967, Cooley Papers, SHC; memo, L. E. Casson to Cooley, December 12, 1966, Earl Cox Jr. Affidavit, February 20, 1967, FCC Grants WRAL-TV, Raleigh, N.C., License Renewal, July 7, 1967, and Cooley to Mrs. C. F. Huntting, August 4, 1967, Cooley Papers, SHC.

60. Fred Fletcher to FCC Secretary Ben Waple (response to Allen Paul's complaint),

November 14, 1966 (quote), and FCC Grants WRAL-TV, Raleigh, N.C., License Renewal, July 7, 1967, Cooley Papers, SHC Capitol Broadcasting Company, Incorporated, for Renewal of License, Memorandum and Opinion, July 5, 1967, Broadcast Station License files, File 173-75-24, box 82, folder WRAL-TV (1966–72), RG 173, NACP; FCC Grants WRAL-TV, Raleigh, N.C., License Renewal, July 7, 1967, Cooley Papers, SHC.

61. Capitol Broadcasting Company, Incorporated, for Renewal of License, Memorandum and Opinion, July 5, 1967, Broadcast Station License files, File 173-75-24, box 82, folder WRAL-TV (1966–72), RG 173, NACP; FCC Grants WRAL-TV, Raleigh, N.C., License Renewal, July 7, 1967, Cooley Papers, SHC; Fred Fletcher to FCC Secretary Ben Waple (response to Allen Paul's complaint), November 14, 1966 (quote), and FCC Grants WRAL-TV, Raleigh, N.C., License Renewal, July 7, 1967, Cooley Papers, SHC; James Gardner to JH, March 18, April 27, 1967, and JH to Gardner, March 22, May 18, 1967 (quote), Gardner file, WRAL-TV Papers, JHC.

62. FCC Grants WRAL-TV, Raleigh, N.C., License Renewal, July 7, 1967, Cooley Papers, SHC; Capitol Broadcasting Company, Incorporated, for Renewal of License, Memorandum and Opinion, July 5, 1967 (quotes), Broadcast Station License files, File 173-75-24, box 82, folder WRAL-TV (1966–72), RG 173, NACP.

63. JH speech, "Problems in the Procedures of Broadcast Relicensing," April 6, 1967 (first quote), JH speech, "Meredith College Talk," February 13, 1968, Speech file, WRAL-TV Papers, JHC.

64. Cooley to Mrs. C. F. Huntting, August 4, 1967, Cooley Papers, SHC.

65. JH to Bill Sharpe, July 21, 1964, Sharpe file, WRAL-TV Papers, JHC.

66. James Gardner to JH, April 27, May 24, 1967, and October 15, 1968, and JH to Gardner, March 22, May 18, August 3, 1967, September 9, September 16, and October 11, 1968 (first quote), Gardner file, Butz to A. J. Fletcher, July 28, 1967 (last quote), Earl Butz file, WRAL-TV Papers, JHC; *Viewpoint* #1843, May 10, 1968 (second quote).

Chapter 4. Backlash

1. JH to James Gardner, February 15, 1965, Gardner file, and JH to Clarence Manion, January 21, 1966, Manion file, WRAL-TV Papers, JHC; Joseph Califano Jr., "What Was Really Great about the Great Society: The Truth behind the Conservative Myths," *Washington Monthly*, October 1999, 13–19.

2. Williams, *God's Own Party*, 80–88.

3. JH to Paul Johnston, May 11, 1964 (quote), JH to Landon B. Lane, August 21, 1969, and Lane to JH, August 20, 1969, Chronological file, WRAL-TV Papers, JHC; Williams, *God's Own Party*, 42.

4. Dallek, *Flawed Giant*, 211–21; Branch, *Pillar of Fire*, 586–88, 592–93, 597–600; *Viewpoint* #1056, March 11, 1965 (quote).

5. Dallek, *Flawed Giant*, 211–21 (LBJ quotes on 219); *Viewpoint* #1064, March 23, 1965 (remaining quotes).

6. *Viewpoint* #1059, March 16, 1965 (quotes); *Viewpoint* #1087, April 23, 1965.

7. Dallek, *Flawed Giant*, 211–21; *Viewpoint* #1069, March 30, 1965 (quotes).

8. *Viewpoint* #1086, April 22, 1965.

9. *Viewpoint* #1100, May 12, 1965 (first, second, and third quotes); JH to Alvis Fleming,

May 11, 1964, JH to Mel Warner, May 15, 1965 (fourth quote), and JH to John Parker, May 20, 1969 (fifth and sixth quotes), Chronological file, WRAL-TV Papers, JHC. On the National Council of Churches see *Viewpoint* #808, March 5, 1964, *Viewpoint* #862, May 20, 1964, and *Viewpoint* #1025, January 27, 1965.

10. JH to Gordon C. Hunter, August 17, 1965 (first quote), and JH to H. A. Dartt, March 14, 1966 (second quote), Chronological file, WRAL-TV Papers, JHC.

11. Anderson, *The Movement and the Sixties,* 132–35; Dallek, *Flawed Giant,* 222–25, 322–25; *Viewpoint* #1166, August 17, 1965 (quote). Other commentaries on Watts included *Viewpoint* #1168, August 19, 1965, *Viewpoint* #1169, August 20, 1965, *Viewpoint* #1174, August 27, 1965, and *Viewpoint* #1176, August 31, 1965.

12. *Viewpoint* #1169, August 20, 1965 (first quote); *Viewpoint* #1168, August 19, 1965 (second quote).

13. *Viewpoint* #1166, August 17, 1965.

14. *Viewpoint* #1169, August 20, 1965.

15. *Viewpoint* #1788, February 16, 1968.

16. *Viewpoint* #1168, August 19, 1965 (quotes); Bond, "The Media and the Movement."

17. JH to Gary Powell, August 23, 1965, Chronological file, WRAL-TV Papers, JHC.

18. *Viewpoint* #1375, June 9, 1966. Helms's thrashing of Meredith on *Viewpoint* made it particularly ironic that the activist joined Helms's staff in 1989.

19. Carson, *In Struggle,* 207–21.

20. Ibid. (second quote on 210); Tuck, *We Ain't What We Ought to Be,* 327–29 (first quote on 328).

21. *Viewpoint* #1383, June 27, 1966.

22. *Viewpoint* #1411, August 4, 1966 (quotes); W. F. Alston to JH, March 17, 1966, JH to Alston, March 23, 1966, JH to Gertrude Price Hood, March 29, 1966, Hood to JH, March 25, 1966, and attached *Raleigh News and Observer* clipping, Chronological file, WRAL-TV Papers, JHC.

23. Stokely Carmichael, Berkeley Black Power Speech, October 29, 1966 (quotes), http://americanradioworks.publicradio.org/features/sayitplain/scarmichael.html (accessed June 28, 2010); Carson, *In Struggle,* 207–21.

24. *Viewpoint* #1467, October 26, 1966.

25. *Viewpoint* #1988, December 12, 1968.

26. *Viewpoint* #273, December 28, 1961.

27. Ibid.

28. *Viewpoint* #33, January 6, 1961 (first, second, and third quotes); *Viewpoint* #1757, January 1, 1968 (remaining quotes); Nyerere, "Rhodesia in the Context of Southern Africa."

29. Nyerere, "Rhodesia in the Context of Southern Africa"; JH to Ruth Tompkins, March 16, 1966 (quote), Chronological file, and JH to Mrs. W. M. Ingram, June 29, 1966, JH to Douglas Garner, June 27, 1966, and JH to I. A. E. Dixon, December 11, 1967, and January 19, 1968, Rhodesia file, WRAL-TV Papers, JHC.

30. *Viewpoint* #620, September 27, 1963.

31. *Viewpoint* #908, August 6, 1964.

32. *Viewpoint* #1153, July 29, 1965 (quotes); Herring, "American Strategy in Vietnam";

Herring, "Vietnam"; McMahon, "The Vietnam War—Revisited and Revised"; Hess, "The Unending Debate"; Hunt, "Washington Quagmire."

33. *Viewpoint* #908, August 6, 1964 (first quote); *Viewpoint* #1517, January 10, 1967 (remaining quotes).

34. JH to J. T. Squires, March 14, 1966, Chronological file, WRAL-TV Papers, JHC.

35. *Viewpoint* #1014, January 12, 1965.

36. Schulman, *Lyndon B. Johnson*, 99–102; *Viewpoint* #812, March 11, 1964 (quote).

37. *Viewpoint* #1467, October 26, 1966.

38. *Viewpoint* #1060, March 17, 1965; *Viewpoint* #1072, April 2, 1965 (quotes).

39. *Viewpoint* #1377, June 13, 1966 (emphasis in the original).

40. *Viewpoint* #723, November 1, 1963.

41. *Viewpoint* #267, December 19, 1961.

42. JH to Alexander W. McAlister, January 15, 1969 (first quote), and June 15, 1970 (second and third quotes), Alexander W. McAlister file, WRAL-TV Papers, JHC.

43. JH to Alexander W. McAlister, December 20, 1967, January 8, 1968 (quotes), June 15, 1970, and McAlister to JH, December 28, 1967, McAlister file, WRAL-TV Papers, JHC.

44. Rozella Brower to JH, February 24, 1969 (first quote), JH to A. W. McAlister, March 3 (second quote), March 7 (third quote), March 13, 1969, and McAlister to JH, March 6, March 12, 1969, McAlister file, WRAL-TV Papers, JHC.

45. McAlister to JH, March 6 (first quote) and March 12, 1969 (second quote), McAlister file, WRAL-TV Papers, JHC.

46. Lenox Baker to JH, August 4, 1964, JH to Baker, July 8, 1963, and August 10, 1964 (quote), Baker file, WRAL-TV Papers, JHC.

47. JH to A. T. Spaulding, August 23, 1965, Chronological file, WRAL-TV Papers, JHC.

48. Ibid.

49. Ibid. (quote); JH to A. T. Spaulding, August 30, 1965, Chronological file, WRAL-TV Papers, JHC; Federal Communication Commission Application for Renewal of Broadcast License Capitol Broadcasting Company, August 1969, Exhibit 9, Broadcast Station License files, File 173-75-24, box 82, folder WRAL-TV (1966–72), RG 173, NACP.

50. *Viewpoint* #1636, July 6, 1967.

51. Ibid.

52. *Viewpoint* #1649, July 26, 1967.

53. *Viewpoint* #1798, March 1, 1968.

54. *Viewpoint* #1458, October 13, 1966 (quotes); Rooke, "The Ice House Gang"; Rooke, "If Lost Return to the Swiss Arms"; "The O. Henry Award: Winners List 1919–2000," http://www.randomhouse.com/boldtype/ohenry/0900/winners1919.html (accessed August 18, 2012).

55. Memo, William Friday to Hugh Holman, October 14, 1966 (quote), Raymond Adams, Statement to the English Department, October 26, 1966, English Department Special Committee's handwritten notes, [October 26 to November 9, 1966], Special Committee typed notes of interview with Paull, October 27, 1966, Gary McCown, Analysis of Student Themes, [October 1966], Richard Lyon, Comment on Themes, [October 1966],

Committee Members to Raymond Adams, November 9, 1966, and attached Report of a Special Committee on a Disputed Theme Assignment in a Class Taught by Mr. Michael Paull, English 1 Disputed Theme Case, 1966, box 4, English Department Records (#40081), Subseries 1: Administrative Files, University Archives, Wilson Library, University of North Carolina.

56. English Department Special Committee's handwritten notes, [October 26 to November 9, 1966], Special Committee typed notes of interview with Paull, October 27, 1966 (quotes), English 1 Disputed Theme Case, 1966, box 4, English Department Records (#40081), Subseries 1: Administrative Files, University Archives, Wilson Library, University of North Carolina; Bill Amlong, "Instructor Loses Teaching Duties," *Daily Tar Heel*, October 19, 1966.

57. Raymond Adams, Statement to the English Department, October 26, 1966, English Department Special Committee's handwritten notes, [October 26 to November 9, 1966], Special Committee typed notes of interview with Paull, October 27, 1966, Gary McCown, Analysis of Student Themes, [October 1966], Richard Lyon, Comment on Themes, [October 1966] (last quote), Committee Members to Raymond Adams, November 9, 1966, and attached Report of a Special Committee on a Disputed Theme Assignment in a Class Taught by Mr. Michael Paull, English 1 Disputed Theme Case, 1966, box 4, English Department Records (#40081), Subseries 1: Administrative Files, and Statement of Chancellor J. Carlyle Sitterson, October 18, 1966, Michael Paull Case, box 11, Office of Chancellor Records: Joseph Carlyle Sitterson, 1966–72 (#40022), Series 2, Academic Affairs, 1966–72, University Archives, Wilson Library, University of North Carolina.

58. "English Instructor Reassigned at UNC," *Raleigh News and Observer*, October 19, 1966; "University Professor Reassigned in Furor over Seduction Theme," *Greensboro Daily News*, October 19, 1966; "UNC Reassigns Instructor after Class Misunderstands," *Charlotte Observer*, October 19, 1966; "UNC Class Assignment Seen 'Objectionable,'" *Durham Morning Herald*, October 18, 1966; JH to J. Carlyle Sitterson, October 25, 1966, Michael Paull Case, box 11, Office of Chancellor Records: Joseph Carlyle Sitterson, 1966–72 (#40022), Series 2, Academic Affairs, 1966–72, University Archives, Wilson Library, University of North Carolina.

59. Charles Altieri and 72 others to Carlyle Sitterson, [October 18, 1966], Richard Lyon and 16 others to Sitterson, October 19, 1966, Maeda Galinsky and 8 others to Sitterson, October 19, 1966, Weldon Thornton to Sitterson October 20, 1966, letter from Lynwood Potter and 21 other class members, October 20, 1966, statement of Chancellor's Advisory Committee, [October 21, 1966], Sitterson press release, October 21, 1966, Sitterson press release, November 10, 1966, Michael Paull Case, box 11, Office of Chancellor Records: Joseph Carlyle Sitterson, 1966–72 (#40022), Series 2, Academic Affairs, 1966–72, University Archives, Wilson Library, University of North Carolina; "Who's Afraid of Jesse Helms? The University—That's Who," October 20, 1966; Bill Amlong, "Instructor Removal Subject of Meeting," October 20, 1966; Bill Amlong, "Chancellor Seeking Paull Case Advice," October 21, 1966; Don Campbell, "CFI Asks for 'Due Process,'" October 21, 1966, all in *Daily Tar Heel*.

60. Kate Erwin, "Shift of Paull Reaffirmed at UNC," October 22, 1966, *Raleigh News and Observer*; "Chancellor's Position on Teacher Clarified," October 22, 1966, *Durham Morning Herald*; "'Seduction Theme': Instructor's Case Is Reconsidered," October 21, 1966, *Charlotte Observer;* editorial "Score One for WRAL," October 20, 1966, *Greensboro Daily News*; "Always a New Nit to Pick," October 25, 1966, *Raleigh News and Observer*; "The Seduction Groves of Academe," October 25, 1966, *Charlotte Observer.*

61. *Viewpoint* #1466, October 25, 1966 (quotes); JH was objecting to publication of Rooke's "The Ice House Gang." The story's protagonist recounts his future wife's seduction of him in an ice house on a hot summer day.

62. *Viewpoint* #1466, October 25, 1966; *Viewpoint* #1473, November 3, 1966; "Teacher Who Assigned a Poem about Seduction Is Transferred," *New York Times*, October 23, 1966; "The Coy Mistress Caper," *Life*, November 11, 1966; Elinor Nevins to *New York Times* Editor, December 1, 1966, R. C. Sims to Sitterson, November 12, 1966, Edward Collins to Sitterson, February 16, 1967, Michael Paull Case, box 11, Chancellor Records: Sitterson (#40022), Wilson Library, University of North Carolina.

63. *Viewpoint* #1473, November 3, 1966.

64. Raymond Adams, Statement to the English Department, October 26, 1966, English Department Special Committee's handwritten notes, [October 26 to November 9, 1966], Special Committee typed notes of interview with Paull, October 27, 1966, Gary McCown, Analysis of Student Themes, [October 1966], Richard Lyon, Comment on Themes, [October 1966] (quote), Committee Members to Raymond Adams, November 9, 1966, and attached Report of a Special Committee on a Disputed Theme Assignment in a Class Taught by Mr. Michael Paull, English 1 Disputed Theme Case, 1966, box 4, English Department Records (#40081), Subseries 1: Administrative Files, University Archives, Wilson Library, University of North Carolina.

65. English Department Special Committee's handwritten notes, [October 26 to November 9, 1966], Special Committee typed notes of interview with Paull, October 27, 1966, Gary McCown, Analysis of Student Themes, [October 1966], Richard Lyon, Comment on Themes, [October 1966] (quote), Committee Members to Raymond Adams, November 9, 1966, and attached Report of a Special Committee on a Disputed Theme Assignment in a Class Taught by Mr. Michael Paull, English 1 Disputed Theme Case, 1966, box 4, English Department Records (#40081), Subseries 1: Administrative Files, University Archives, Wilson Library, University of North Carolina; *Viewpoint* #1466, October 25, 1966.

66. *Viewpoint* #1479, November 11, 1966; *Viewpoint* #1480, November 14, 1966.

67. Paul Hasting to Sitterson, December 9, 1966, and R. C. Souder Jr. to Sitterson, November 29, 1966, Michael Paull Case, box 11, Chancellor Records: Sitterson (#40022), Wilson Library, University of North Carolina.

68. JH to Vernon T. Bradley, August 6, 1965, Chronological file, WRAL-TV Papers, JHC.

69. Mrs. P. C. Brown to JH, March 14, 1966 (second quote), W. F. Alston to JH, March 17, 1966, JH to Mrs. Atlas Tant, March 21, 1966, JH to Mrs. Leland Gurley, April 1, 1966, Chronological file, WRAL-TV Papers, JHC.

Chapter 5. Turning Off *Turn-On*

1. Watson, *Expanding Vista*, 18–35; *Viewpoint* #122, May 12, 1961 (quotes).

2. *Viewpoint* #790, February 10, 1964; *Viewpoint* #339, April 5, 1962.

3. JH to Sim DeLapp, January 31, 1969, Chronological file, WRAL-TV Papers, JHC.

4. The Federal Communication Commission Application for Renewal of Broadcast License, August 1966, Exhibit #6, Public Affairs Programs, and The Federal Communication Commission Application for Renewal of Broadcast License, August 1969, Exhibit #16, Part II, Past Programming, Broadcast Station License files, File 173-75-24, box 82, folder WRAL-TV (1966–72), RG 173, NACP.

5. JH speech, "Problems in the Procedures of Broadcast Relicensing," April 6, 1967, Speech file, WRAL-TV Papers, JHC.

6. Ibid.; Brown, *Les Brown's Encyclopedia of Television*, 1–4, 389–90; Gayle Noyes, "American Broadcast Company: U.S. Network," in Newcomb, *Encyclopedia of Television*, 53–54; Phillip Kierstead, "News, Network," in Newcomb, *Encyclopedia of Television*, 1164–68; Report of Fred Fletcher to Board of Directors, Capitol Broadcasting Co., Inc., April 1, 1962, Broadcast Station License files, File 72A451, box 502, folder WRAL-TV (1961–66), RG 173, NACP; A. J. Fletcher to Leonard Goldenson, November 17, 1969, ABC file, WRAL-TV Papers, JHC.

7. JH speech, "Problems in the Procedures of Broadcast Relicensing," April 6, 1967 (quote), Speech file, WRAL-TV Papers, JHC; Brown, *Les Brown's Encyclopedia of Television*, 1–4, 389–90; Gayle Noyes, "American Broadcast Company: U.S. Network," in Newcomb, *Encyclopedia of Television*, 53–54; Phillip Kierstead, "News, Network," in Newcomb, *Encyclopedia of Television*, 1164–68; Report of Fred Fletcher to Board of Directors, Capitol Broadcasting Co., Inc., April 1, 1962, Broadcast Station License files, File 72A451, box 502, folder WRAL-TV (1961–66), RG 173, NACP; A. J. Fletcher to Leonard Goldenson, November 17, 1969, ABC file, WRAL-TV Papers, JHC.

8. JH to Robert Coe, June 25, 1965, ABC file, WRAL-TV Papers, JHC.

9. Ibid.; Elizabeth Bain to Robert Caudle, June 11, 1969 (first quote), Oliver Blackwell to JH, July 24, 1969, JH to Blackwell, June 18 (second quote), July 25, 1969, Katz Television file, WRAL-TV Papers, JHC.

10. JH to Nat Cavalluzzi, June 4, 1965, and JH to Cavalluzi, January 19, 1968 (last quote), ABC file, WRAL-TV Papers, JHC.

11. JH to John Gilbert, September 30, 1968, ABC file, WRAL-TV Papers, JHC.

12. Oliver Blackwell to JH, January 11, 1972, and JH to Blackwell, January 13, 1972, JHC, Katz Television file, and JH to Shirley Stahnke, April 25 (first quote), May 2, and June 20, 1969, Stahnke to JH, April 30, 1969, JH to Barron, May 16, 1969, John Dillon to Del Carty, June 26, 1969, J. Reginald Dunlap to Dear Sir, August 4, 1969, JH to Dunlap, August 8, 1969, and Jane Dowden to JH, July 21, 1969 (last quote), Programs file, WRAL-TV Papers, JHC.

13. JH to A. Hartwell Campbell, December 15, 1958 (first quote), and A. Hartwell Campbell to JH, January 15, 1959, Personal file, NCBA Papers, and JH to Mr. E. W. Muller, August 24, 1965 (second quote), JH to Mrs. J. C. Wootten, August 20, 1965 (last quote), and JH to J. D. Wills, January 6, 1969, Chronological file, WRAL-TV Papers, JHC.

14. JH to Nat Cavalluzzi, November 8, 1969 (second quote), and JH to Sandra Morrow, November 27, 1972 (first and last quotes), Chronological file, WRAL-TV Papers, JHC.

15. JH to John F. Butler, January 14, 1969 (first and second quotes), Mrs. Z. V. Patterson to JH, January 27, 1969 (third quote), and JH to Patterson, January 27, 1969 (last quote), Chronological file, WRAL-TV Papers, JHC.

16. JH to John F. Butler, January 14, 1969 (first and last quote), Ruth Janesick to JH, December 29, 1967 (second quote), JH to Janesick, January 2, 1967, JH to Nat Cavalluzzi, January 2, 1967, Cavalluzzi to Janesick, March 1, 1968 (third quote), Chronological file, WRAL-TV Papers, JHC.

17. Postcard, L. H. Barnes to WRAL, n.d. (first quote), JH to Nat Cavalluzzi, March 18, 1968 (remaining quotes), Mrs. Henry Dennis to A. J. Fletcher, August 12, 1969, and JH to Dennis, August 12, 1969, Chronological file, WRAL-TV Papers, JHC.

18. JH to Lonnie Smith, January 31, 1969 (remaining quotes), and Smith to JH, January 29, 1969 (first and second quotes), Chronological file, WRAL-TV Papers, JHC.

19. JH to Robert Coe, May 6, 1964 (quote), Chronological file, WRAL-TV Papers, JHC; Sue Brower, "*Peyton Place*: U.S. Serial Melodrama," in Newcomb, *Encyclopedia of Television*, 1248–50.

20. Luckett, "A Moral Crisis in Prime Time"; Margaret Mayo to WRAL Television, February 8, 1965, JH to Robert Coe, February 12, 1964 (second quote), Coe to JH, February 26, 1964, and JH to Coe, March 3, 1965 (last quote), Chronological file, WRAL-TV Papers, JHC. Mayo also objected to an early Aaron Spelling effort, *Burke's Law*.

21. Ethel Jones to JH, December 30, 1968, and JH to Jones, January 2, 1969, Chronological file, WRAL-TV Papers, JHC.

22. John D. H. Downing, "Racism, Ethnicity, and Television," in Newcomb, *Encyclopedia of Television*, 1333–39.

23. Mrs. W. B. Knott to JH, May 21, 1969, and JH to Knott, May 21, 1969, Chronological file, WRAL-TV Papers, JHC.

24. JH to Nat Cavalluzzi, December 6, 1968, Cavalluzzi to JH, December 18, 1968, and JH to L. J. Phipps, December 26, 1968, Chronological file, WRAL-TV Papers, JHC; Bodroghkozy, "Negotiating the Mod"; Jeremy Butler, "Police Programs," in Newcomb, *Encyclopedia of Television*, 1264.

25. JH to Nat Cavalluzzi, May 11 (first quote), May 27, 1965 (last quote), and Cavalluzzi to JH, May 25, 1965 (second quote), Chronological file, WRAL-TV Papers, JHC; Terrace, *Complete Encyclopedia of Television Shows*, 152.

26. Harry M. Benshoff, "*Dark Shadows*: U.S. Gothic Soap Operas," in Newcomb, *Encyclopedia of Television*, 461–62 (first four quotes); JH to Nat Cavalluzzi, May 27, 1968 (remaining quotes), Chronological file, and memo, JH to Jim Goodmon and others, August 3, 1970, Memos file, WRAL-TV Papers, JHC.

27. JH to Ruth Janesick, January 2, 1967 (quote), Chronological file, WRAL-TV Papers, JHC; Terrace, *Complete Encyclopedia of Television Shows*, 390; Brown, *Les Brown's Encyclopedia of Television*, 575.

28. Terrace, *Complete Encyclopedia of Television Shows*, 390 (first quote); Brown, *Les Brown's Encyclopedia of Television*, 575; Mrs. Larry Lumley to JH, February 5, 1969, JH

to Lumley, February 7, 1969, JH to Mrs. E. W. Elmore, February 10, 1969 (remaining quotes), JH to Mr. and Mrs. R. L. Carroll, February 10, 1969, Mrs. Max A. Gilmore to JH, February 8, 1969, JH to Gilmore, February 11, 1969, Chronological file, WRAL-TV Papers, JHC; "WRAL, Others Drop Program," *Raleigh News and Observer*, February 8, 1969.

29. JH to Mrs. Larry Lumley, February 7, 1969 (first quote), JH to Nat Cavalluzzi, May 1, 1969 (first quote), March 4, 1968, Cavalluzzi to JH, April 15, 1968, and attached form letter from Grace Johnsen, n.d. (remaining quotes), Chronological file, WRAL-TV Papers, JHC; Terrace, *Complete Encyclopedia of Television Shows*, 361; Brown, *Les Brown's Encyclopedia of Television*, 263.

30. *Viewpoint* #1064, March 23, 1965.

31. JH to Warren Denker, December 15, 1971, and attachment (first quote), Chronological file, WRAL-TV Papers, JHC; JH speech, "Meredith College Talk," February 13, 1968 (second quote), Speech file, WRAL-TV Papers, JHC; "Atlanta's 'Coach Friday': Female Forecaster Hits the Target," *Free Lance–Star* (Fredericksburg, Va.), November 17, 1964.

32. Mrs. Max A. Gilmore to JH, February 8, 1969, Chronological file, WRAL-TV Papers, JHC.

33. JH to Nat Cavalluzzi, May 1, 1969 (quote), March 4, 1968, Cavalluzzi to JH, April 15, 1968, and attached form from Grace Johnsen, n.d., Chronological file, WRAL-TV Papers, JHC.

34. Nachman, "Sibling Revelry" (last quote); Steven D. Stark, "*The Smothers Brothers Comedy Hour* and the Fate of Controversy on TV" (quote of joke on 138; quote of *TV Guide* on 141) and "*Rowan and Martin's Laugh-in* and Acceleration as a TV Style," in Stark, *Glued to the Set*, 137–47; Aniko Bodroghkozy, "The Smothers Brothers Comedy Hour: U.S. Comedy Variety Program," in Newcomb, *Encyclopedia of Television*, 1510–12; Brown, *Les Brown's Encyclopedia of Television*, 516.

35. Nachman, "Sibling Revelry"; Steven D. Stark, "*The Smothers Brothers Comedy Hour* and the Fate of Controversy on TV" and "*Rowan and Martin's Laugh-in* and Acceleration as a TV Style," in Stark, *Glued to the Set*, 137–47; Aniko Bodroghkozy, "The Smothers Brothers Comedy Hour: U.S. Comedy Variety Program," in Newcomb, *Encyclopedia of Television*, 1510–12; Brown, *Les Brown's Encyclopedia of Television*, 516; telegram, Richard Beesemyer to station management, March 20, [1970] (first quote); JH to Beesemyer, March 23 (second quote), April 2, April 24, May 25, 1970, and Beesemyer to JH, March 31, May 21, May 22, 1970, Chronological file, WRAL-TV Papers, JHC.

36. JH to Beesemyer, March 23, April 2, April 24, May 25, 1970, and Beesemyer to JH, March 31, May 21 (first quote), May 22, 1970, Chronological file, WRAL-TV Papers, JHC; Merle Miller, "Review: *The Smothers Brothers Summer Show*," *TV Guide*, September 5–11, 1970; Stark, "*Rowan and Martin's Laugh-in* and Acceleration as a TV Style," in Stark, *Glued to the Set*, 142–47 (last quote on 143).

37. JH to Roy Sisk, March 17, 1966 (first quote), and Sisk to JH, March 14, 1966, Chronological file, WRAL-TV Papers, JHC; A. J. Fletcher to JH, January 12, 1959, and JH to Fletcher, January 14, 1959, with attachment (last quote), Personal file, NCBA Papers, JHC. Capitalization in the original.

38. *Viewpoint* #884, June 19, 1964.

39. Report of Fred Fletcher to Board of Directors, Capitol Broadcasting Co., Inc., April 1, 1962, and Fred Fletcher's Report to Board of Directors, Capitol Broadcasting Co., Inc., for April 1, 1963–March 31, 1964, n.d., Broadcast Station License files, File 72A451, box 502, folder WRAL-TV (1961–66), RG 173, NACP; JH to E. W. Muller, August 24, 1965, Chronological file, WRAL-TV Papers, JHC; Lackmann, *Encyclopedia of American Television,* 256–58.

40. Report of Fred Fletcher to Board of Directors, Capitol Broadcasting Co., Inc., April 1, 1962, and Fred Fletcher's Report to Board of Directors, Capitol Broadcasting Co., Inc., for April 1, 1963–March 31, 1964, n.d., Broadcast Station License files, File 72A451, box 502, folder WRAL TV (1961–66), RG 173, NACP; JH to E. W. Muller, August 24, 1965, Chronological file, WRAL-TV Papers, JHC; Lackmann, *Encyclopedia of American Television,* 256–58; John D. H. Downing, "Racism, Ethnicity and Television," in Newcomb, *Encyclopedia of Television,* 1333–39; Brown, *Les Brown's Encyclopedia of Television,* 1–4; Branch, *Parting the Waters,* 763 (quote); Bond, "The Media and the Movement."

41. Report of Fred Fletcher to Board of Directors, April 1, 1962, and Fred Fletcher's Report to Board of Directors for April 1, 1963–March 31, 1964, Federal Communication Commission Application for Renewal of Broadcast License, August 1966, Exhibit 6, News Programs, Broadcast Station License files, File 173-75-24, box 82, folder WRAL-TV (1966–72), RG 173, NACP. Early in the decade the local news on WRAL was called *Stateline.* "Friday Television" (program listings), *Raleigh News and Observer,* October 28, 1966.

42. JH to John Gilbert, June 6, June 14, 1968, and June 14, 1968 (two letters), Donnie H. Jones Jr. to Frank Reynolds, July 22, 1968, ABC file, WRAL-TV Papers, JHC; Brown, *Les Brown's Encyclopedia of Television,* 389–90, 451, 459, and 515; Lackmann, *Encyclopedia of American Television,* 256–58; Phillip Kierstead, "Network News," and Albert Auster, "Howard K. Smith: U.S. Journalist," in Newcomb, *Encyclopedia of Television,* 1164–68, 1508–10.

43. JH to John Gilbert, June 6 (quote), June 14, 1968, and June 14, 1968 (two letters), ABC file, WRAL-TV Papers, JHC.

44. JH to John Gilbert, June 6 (quotes), June 14, 1968, and June 14, 1968 (two letters), ABC file, WRAL-TV Papers, JHC.

45. Gilbert to JH, June 26, 1968, ABC file, WRAL-TV Papers, JHC.

46. JH to Gilbert, July 1 (first quote), July 26, 1968, A. J. Fletcher to Leonard Goldenson, July 25, 1968, Ernest Wall to JH, January 27, 1969, and JH to Wall, January 28, 1969 (second quote), ABC file, WRAL-TV Papers, JHC.

47. JH to James Pike, November 17, 1969 (last quote), Spiro Agnew file, and JH to Nat Cavalluzzi, August 30, 1968, ABC file, WRAL-TV Papers, JHC.

48. *Viewpoint* #2219, October 21, 1969.

49. JH to Fred, n.d. (second quote), JH to Thomas White, March 31, 1970 (third quote), White to JH, n.d., and transcript of *The Huntley-Brinkley Report,* March 25, 1970 (first quote), NBC file, WRAL-TV Papers, JHC.

50. JH to David Brinkley, October 10 (quote), October 21, 1969, NBC file, WRAL-TV Papers, JHC; Lackmann, *Encyclopedia of American Television,* 256–58; Brown, *Les*

Brown's Encyclopedia of Television, 389–90; Phillip Kierstead, "Network News," in New-comb, *Encyclopedia of Television*, 1164–68.

51. Memo, Oliver Blackwell to JH, January 19, 1968 (quotes), and JH to Blackwell, January 22, 1968, Katz Television file, and A. J. Fletcher to Leonard Goldenson, November 17, 1969, ABC file, WRAL-TV Papers, JHC; "Today's Fare on Television" (program listings), *Raleigh News and Observer*, November 4, 1969.

52. JH to David Brinkley, October 10, October 21, 1969, NBC file, and Daniel Denen-holz to JH, June 30, 1969, JH to Frank Magrid, July 2, 1969, attached "Personalities Ap-pearing on WRAL-TV Locally Originated News Programs," Denenholz to JH, July 14, 1969, JH to Denenholz, July 31, 1969, attached "WTVD, Durham, News Personalities," JH to Oliver Blackwell, August 13, 1969, and attached "Frank N. Magid Associates, Survey Research" (questionnaire for the survey), Katz Television file, WRAL-TV Papers, JHC; Chris Patterson, "News, Local and Regional," and Eric Rothenbuhler, "Frank N. Magid and Associates," in Newcomb, *Encyclopedia of Television*, 1160–64 and 982. I was unable to find the results of the Magid survey at the JHC. The collection was unprocessed at the time of my research, so a systematic search for a single document was difficult.

53. Bill Morrison, "Goings On: Raleigh TV Attends Movies and Morality," *Raleigh News and Observer*, October 27, 1966.

54. JH to Nat Cavalluzzi, April 9, 1968, ABC file, WRAL-TV Papers, JHC.

55. JH to Leonard Goldenson, February 16, 1968 (first, second, and third quotes), Byrnes to JH, March 11, 1968 (fourth quote), JH to Sydney Byrnes, March 13, 1968, JH to Goldenson, June 19, 1968 (last quote), John Gilbert to JH, July 1, 1968, JH to Gilbert, July 5, 1968, ABC file, WRAL-TV Papers, JHC.

56. JH to Nat Cavalluzzi, February 24, July 21 (quotes), August 28, 1969, ABC file, and J. Harold Herring Jr. to JH, September 29, 1969, and JH to Herring, September 12, 1969, YAF file, WRAL-TV Papers, JHC; Lackmann, *Encyclopedia of American Television*, 184.

57. *Viewpoint* #1754, December 27, 1967.

58. Identical letters I. Beverly Lake to Frank Stanton of CBS, Julian Goodman of NBC, and Leonard Goldenson of ABC, all November 14, 1969, Agnew file, and JH to Jo Ann Long, May 19, 1969, Chronological file, WRAL-TV Papers, JHC.

59. Telegraph, JH to Harry Dent, November 4, 1969, Telegraph file, WRAL-TV Papers, JHC.

60. Ryan, *American Rhetoric*, 212–19 (quotes); Brown, *Les Brown's Encyclopedia of Television*, 16.

61. *Viewpoint* #2217, November 19, 1969.

62. JH to Jack Riley, November 17, 1969, Ralph and Lois Todd to Gentlemen, November 18, 1969 (first quote), Mark V. O'Neill to Frank Stanton (CBS president), November 17, 1969 (second quote), Tommy Temple to Vice President Spiro Agnew, November 17, 1969 (third quote), Thomas Adams to the chairmen of the board at each network, November 17, 1969 (fourth quote), Adams to JH, November 19, 1969, Harvey Johnson to Leonard Goldenson, November 14, 1969 (fifth quote), John Lloyd to Sir, November 14, 1969 (sixth quote), and James Pike to Agnew, November 14, 1969 (seventh and eighth quotes), Agnew file, WRAL-TV Papers, JHC.

63. Mr. and Mrs. W. J. Allen to Gentlemen (at WRAL), November 14, 1969 (first and second quotes), James Duncan to Sir (at WRAL), November 15, 1969 (third quote), and Mrs. Ray Bacon to JH, November 17, 1969 (fourth quote), Agnew file, WRAL-TV Papers, JHC.

64. Frances Berger to JH, November 14, 1969 (first quote), R. G. Carson to Fletcher, JH, et al., November 14, 1969 (second quote), and JH to Lake, November 14, 1969 (third quote), Agnew file, WRAL-TV Papers, JHC.

65. JH to Malcolm Quick, November 17, 1969, and JH to Mr. and Mrs. W. T. Allen, November 17, 1969, Agnew file, and JH to Cavalluzzi, November 17, 1969 (first quote), Fletcher to Goldenson, November 17 (first quote), November 28, 1969 (second quote), ABC file, WRAL-TV Papers, JHC.

66. Cavalluzzi to JH, June 9, 1969, JH to Cavalluzzi, November 17, 1969, JH to Howard K. Smith, March 25, 1971, ABC file and JH telegram to Tom White at NBC, January 6, 1971, Telegram file, WRAL-TV Papers, JHC; Lackmann, *Encyclopedia of American Television*, 256–58; Brown, *Les Brown's Encyclopedia of Television*, 389–90; Phillip Kierstead, "Network News," in Newcomb, *Encyclopedia of Television*, 1164–68.

67. *Viewpoint* #2742, January 21, 1972.

68. *Viewpoint* #1137, July 2, 1965.

69. *Viewpoint* #2478, December 14, 1970.

70. *Viewpoint* #2722, December 21, 1971 (quotes); Williams, *God's Own Party*, 146–53.

71. JH speech, "Meredith College Talk," February 13, 1968; Ted Reinhard to JH, February 7, 1968 (first quote), and attached "Tele News," and JH to Reinhard, February 9, 1968 (second quote), NBC file, WRAL-TV Papers, JHC; "Atlanta's 'Coach Friday': Female Forecaster Hits the Target," *Free Lance-Star* (Fredericksburg, Va.), November 17, 1964.

72. *Viewpoint* #2478, December 14, 1970.

73. *Viewpoint* #2530, February 26, 1971 (quotes); Williams, *God's Own Party*, 111–20.

Chapter 6. The Dawn of a Conservative Era

1. Viewpoint #2214, November 14, 1969 (first quote); JH to J. C. Peele, August 24, 1971 (second quote), Peele file, and JH Speech, Future Farmers of America, Princeton, N.C., March 15, 1968 (remaining quotes), Speech file, WRAL-TV Papers, JHC.

2. JH to J. C. Peele, August 24, 1971 (quote), Peele file, Speech file, WRAL-TV Papers, JHC.

3. Hall, "The Long Civil Rights Movement."

4. *Viewpoint* #1929, September 18, 1968.

5. *Viewpoint* #2000, December 31, 1968; Biographical Information, n.d., Biographical Sketch file, and press release, "Jesse Helms Files for Senate," February 18, 1972, Miscellaneous file, and Madeleine O'Malley, April 1, 1966, Chronological file, WRAL-TV Papers, JHC; Furgurson, *Hard Right*, 83–84.

6. JH to Henry Royall, August 27, 1969, Chronological file, and JH to J. C. Peele, August 24, 1971, Peele file, WRAL-TV Papers, JHC.

7. *Viewpoint* #1650, July 27, 1967.

8. *Viewpoint* #1774, January 24, 1968.

9. *Viewpoint* #1814, April 1, 1968.

10. *Viewpoint* #1760, January 4, 1968 (first quote); *Viewpoint* #1790, February 20, 1968 (remaining quotes).

11. *Viewpoint* #1790, February 20, 1968.

12. *Viewpoint* #1818, April 5, 1968.

13. *Viewpoint* #1862, June 6, 1968.

14. JH to Earl Butz, August 1, August 15, November 28, 1967, January 2, February 7, 1969, Butz to A. J. Fletcher, July 28, November 24, 1967, and Butz to JH, July 28, August 11, November 24, 1967, and January 29, 1969, Butz file, WRAL-TV Papers, JHC.

15. JH to Earl Butz, August 1 (first quote), August 15 (second quote), November 28, 1967 (remaining quotes), January 2, February 7, 1969, Butz to A. J. Fletcher, July 28, November 24, 1967, and Butz to JH, July 28, August 11, November 24, 1967, and January 29, 1969, Butz file, WRAL-TV Papers, JHC.

16. JH to Bill Sharpe, October 23, 1968 (first and second quotes), Sharpe file, WRAL-TV Papers, JHC; *Viewpoint* #1842, May 9, 1968 (remaining quotes); *Viewpoint* #1843, May 10, 1968.

17. *Viewpoint* #1842, May 9, 1968; *Viewpoint* #1843, May 10, 1968 (quotes).

18. *Viewpoint* #1900, August 6, 1968.

19. *Viewpoint* #1910, August 22, 1968 (first quote); JH to Bill Sharpe, August 9, 1968, Sharpe file, WRAL-TV Papers, JHC (second quote); *Viewpoint* #1913, August 27, 1968.

20. Anderson, *The Movement and the Sixties*, 214–28 (quotes on 223–25).

21. *Viewpoint* #1915, August 29, 1968.

22. *Viewpoint* #1918, September 3, 1968 (first quote); *Viewpoint* #1920, September 5, 1968 (remaining quotes).

23. *Viewpoint* #1916, August 30, 1968 (quotes); Anderson, *The Movement and the Sixties*, 214–28 (last quote on 223).

24. *Viewpoint* #1918, September 3, 1968.

25. Schulman, *The Seventies*, 35–39; Edsall and Edsall, *Chain Reaction*, 74–81 (quote on 76); Hall, "The Long Civil Rights Movement."

26. *Viewpoint* #1930, September 19, 1968.

27. A. W. McAlister to JH, October 9, 1968 (first quote), and JH to McAlister, October 10, 1968 (second and third quotes), McAlister file, WRAL-TV Papers, JHC; *Viewpoint* #1933, September 24, 1968 (last quote).

28. JH to Bill Sharpe, October 23, 1968, Sharpe file, WRAL-TV Papers, JHC.

29. Schulman, *The Seventies*, 35–39; Edsall and Edsall, *Chain Reaction*, 74–81; Luebke, *Tar Heel Politics*, 159–60; *Viewpoint* #1962, November 6, 1968 (first quote); JH to Bill Sharpe, October 23, 1968 (second and third quotes), Sharpe file, WRAL-TV Papers, JHC.

30. JH to Earl Butz, January 2 (quotes), February 7, 1969, and Butz to JH, January 29, 1969, Earl Butz file, WRAL-TV Papers, JHC. Although Butz lost his race for governor, Nixon would appoint him secretary of agriculture in 1971.

31. JH to Lenox Baker, March 4, 1968 (quote), Baker file, WRAL-TV Papers, JHC.

32. JH to Thomas White Jr., February 28, 1969 (quote), Thomas White Jr. file, WRAL-TV Papers, JHC.

33. JH to Edward Annis, December 4, 1968 (quote), Annis file, and JH to Earl Butz, February 7, 1969, Butz file, WRAL-TV Papers, JHC.

34. *Viewpoint* #2029, February 10, 1969.

35. Hoff, *Nixon Reconsidered,* 147–66, 194–200; *Viewpoint* #2533, March 3, 1971 (quotes).

36. *Viewpoint* #1989, December 13, 1968.

37. JH to Nina Tribble, December 28, 1972 (first quote), JH to Pat Lennon, June 26, 1969 (third quote), and Lennon to JH, June 25, 1969 (second quote), Chronological file, WRAL-TV Papers, JHC; Herring, "American Strategy in Vietnam." Lennon wrote because of *Viewpoint* #2108, June 6, 1969. It described a hawkish letter from a Marine in Vietnam. JH had spoken at his high school graduation in 1967.

38. *Viewpoint* #2450, November 4, 1970 (first quote); *Viewpoint* #2747, January 28, 1972 (second quote).

39. *Viewpoint* #2203, October 29, 1969.

40. Memo, Robert Scott to Presidents, State Supported Institutions of Higher Learning, February 20, 1969 (first quote), series 1, folder 117, Thomas Jackson White Jr. Papers, SHC; JH to Tom Anderson, June 3, 1969 (second quote), Chronological file, WRAL-TV Papers, JHC; *Viewpoint* #2056, March 20, 1969 (last quote); *Viewpoint* #2047, March 6, 1969; Billingsley, *Communists on Campus,* 218–24.

41. J. Harold Herring Jr. to Randall Teague, July 24, 1969, Herring to JH, July 29, 1969, and January 6, 1970, and JH to Herring, September 12, 1969, YAF file, WRAL-TV Papers, JHC.

42. *Viewpoint* #2082, April 30, 1969; "Go to Hell," *Daily Tar Heel,* May 14, 1969 (quotes); J. Harold Herring Jr. to Joe Beard, June 25, 1969, Chronological file, Herring to JH, January 6, 1970, YAF file, WRAL-TV Papers, JHC. Conservatives at UNC were divided into factions including YAF and Young Republicans.

43. JH to Harvey Harkness, May 29, 1969 (quote), and Harkness to JH, May 28, 1969, Chronological file, WRAL-TV Papers, JHC; *Viewpoint* #2104, May 30, 1969.

44. *Viewpoint* #2104, May 30, 1969.

45. JH to Harvey Harkness, August 21, 1969, Harkness to JH, August 20, 1969, Chronological file, J. Harold Herring Jr. to JH, January 6, 1970, YAF file, JH to Thomas White Jr. September 25 (first quote), September 23, 1969 (last quote), White to JH, September 24, 1969 (second quote), Memorandum of Remarks by Thos. J. White to the Board of Trustees, October 27, 1969, Thomas Jackson White Jr. file, WRAL-TV Papers, JHC; *Viewpoint* #2082, April 30, 1969 (third quote). In this *Viewpoint,* Helms focused on the Duke University newspaper. White raised the issue of the *Daily Tar Heel* again at the October meeting of the trustees.

46. JH to Harold Herring, October 3 (first, second, and third quotes) and October 28, 1969, YAF file, and JH to Harvey Harkness, October 8, 1969, Harkness to JH and attachment "Required Texts," October 8, 1969 (fourth quote), JH to Gray Miller, November 26, 1969, JH to Steve Markman and David Boone, November 26, 1969, and JH to Governor Robert Scott, November 5, 1969, and two on November 26, 1969, Textbooks file, WRAL-TV Papers, JHC.

47. *Viewpoint* #2266, February 3, 1970 (first, second and third quotes); *Viewpoint* #2273, February 12, 1970 (fourth, fifth, and sixth quotes).

48. *Viewpoint* #2034, February 17, 1969.

49. *Viewpoint* #2148, August 12, 1969 (quotes); *Viewpoint* #2249, January 9, 1970.

50. Link, *Righteous Warrior*, 114–20.

51. Richard Nixon: "Address in the Alfred M. Landon Lecture Series at Kansas State University," September 16, 1970, online by Gerhard Peters and John T. Woolley, The American Presidency Project, http://www.presidency.ucsb.edu/ws/?pid=2663; *Viewpoint* #2418, September 17, 1970; *Viewpoint* #2419, September 18, 1970.

52. *Viewpoint* #2418, September 17, 1970 (quotes); *Viewpoint* #2419, September 18, 1970.

53. JH to Richard Nixon, September 18, 1970 (first quote), JH to Harry Dent, September 18, 1970 (second quote), and Dent to JH, September 28, 1970, Nixon Whitehouse file, WRAL-TV Papers, JHC.

54. "North Carolina Interview: Jesse A. Helms Jr.: Our New Senator Reviews Campaign and Looks at Issues," *North Carolina*, January 1973, 27; JH to Earl Butz, December 17, December 21, 1971, Butz file, WRAL-TV Papers, JHC; Link, *Righteous Warrior*, 114–20.

55. "North Carolina Interview: Jesse A. Helms Jr.: Our New Senator Reviews Campaign and Looks at Issues," *North Carolina*, January 1973, 27; Link, *Righteous Warrior*, 114–20; press release, JH, January 21, 1972 (quote), press release, JH for Senate, [January 31, 1972], and press release, "Jesse Helms Files for Senate," February 18, 1972, Miscellaneous file, WRAL-TV Papers, JHC.

56. Eugene Price, "Senate Fight Likely to Be a Humdinger," *Goldsboro News*, February 23, 1972; Link, *Righteous Warrior*, 114–29; Luebke, *Tar Heel Politics*, 23–27, 156–60, 164–65; Edsall and Edsall, *Chain Reaction*, 5, 14–15; Furgurson, *Hard Right*, 97–102; Schulman, *The Seventies*, 35–37, 193.

57. Link, *Righteous Warrior*, 114–29; Luebke, *Tar Heel Politics*, 23–27, 156–60, 164–65; Edsall and Edsall, *Chain Reaction*, 5, 14–15; Furgurson, *Hard Right*, 97–102; Schulman, *The Seventies*, 35–37, 193.

58. JH, memo to Sim DeLapp and others, February 29, 1972, Miscellaneous file, Charlie Black to Bobby Guyton, November 16, 1972, JH to Mary Joe Proctor, November 27, 1972 (quote), JH to Ronald Docksai, November 20, 1972, JH to Tim Baer, December 13, 1972, Chronological file, and JH to Harold Herring, August 17, 1971, YAF file, WRAL-TV Papers, JHC.

59. Robert Cullen, "Helms, Galifianakis Differ on Vietnam," October 9, 1972, "Both Galifianakis, Helms Ride Hard on Antibusing Plank," October 10, 1972, "Helms Not as Critical of GOP Foreign Policy," October 11, 1972, "Helms, Galifianakis Agree Economy Is in Mess," October 12, 1972, and "Skim Off Rhetoric and Helms, Galifianakis Aren't Far Apart," October 13, 1972, all in *Greensboro Daily News*; "Candidates Probe Issues," *Raleigh News and Observer*, November 4, 1972 (quote).

60. Leslie Wayne, "Nick, Helms Quietly Shift Strategy," *Raleigh News and Observer*, September 19, 1972; "Nixon, Bowles, Nick Still Ahead," *Greensboro Daily News*, October 8, 1972; Marjorie Hunter, "Major Races in North Carolina Seem Close," *New York Times*, October 28, 1972.

61. Harvey Harris, "Nick Keeps Up a Rigorous Pace in Tour of Area," *Greensboro Daily News*, October 8, 1972; "Nick on Tour Shaking Hands," October 26, 1972, and "Nick

Shops for Votes in 6 Cities," November 5, 1972, *Raleigh News and Observer*; JH to Logan Howell, December 4, 1972 (first quote), Chronological file, fund-raising letter JH to E. R. Van Deusen, July 21, 1972, and Van Deusen to JH, n.d., Miscellaneous file, WRAL-TV Papers, JHC; Link, *Righteous Warrior*, 114–29; Furgurson, *Hard Right*, 97–102 (last quote).

62. Ads, *Cleveland Times*, July 25, 1972, *Kings Mountain Herald*, August 24, 1972, *Andrews Journal*, October 11, 1972, and *TV Guide*, September 16, October 29, 1972.

63. Ads, *Cleveland Times*, July 25, 1972, *Kings Mountain Herald*, August 24, 1972, *Andrews Journal*, October 11, 1972, and *TV Guide*, September 16, October 29, 1972; Leslie Wayne, "Nick, Helms Quietly Shift Strategy," September 19, 1972, and "Senate Vote Drive Centers in the Piedmont," October 29, 1972, *Raleigh News and Observer*; Marjorie Hunter, "Major Races in North Carolina Seem Close," *New York Times*, October 28, 1972; "Jesse Helms Outlines Conservative Views," October 1, 1972, and Robert Cullen, "Skim Off Rhetoric and Helms, Galifianakis Aren't Far Apart," October 13, 1972, *Greensboro Daily News*; JH to Lennox Baker, December 8, 1972, Chronological file, WRAL-TV Papers, JHC; press release, "Helms Backs Farm Supports," November 6, 1972, folder 19, Ernest B. Furgurson Papers, SHC.

64. "Where Was Nick?" ad, *Haywood Enterprise*, September 21, and *Raleigh News and Observer* and *Charlotte Observer*, September 20, 1972 (emphasis in original); "Mr. Helms Must Take the Blame," September 22, 1972, and Paul Clancy, "'Where Was Nick?' Ads Paid For by Helms," September 21, 1972, *Charlotte Observer*; "Tactic May Suggest Helm's [*sic*] Strategy," September 22, 1972, "Nick Goes Handshaking in Charlotte," November 1, 1972, and Leslie Wayne, "Helms Drive Funded Ad Critical of Nick," September 21, 1972, *Raleigh News and Observer*; "McGovern-Galifianakis?" *Greensboro Daily News*, October 5, 1972; Tom Ellis statement, JH for Senate Committee, folder 19, Furgurson Papers, SHC; Furgurson, *Hard Right*, 101–2.

65. Paul Clancy, "Helms Says Ad Attacking Galifianakis Lacked His OK," September 27, 1972 (first quote), and Tom Ellis, "Nick Missed Anti-Drug Votes," September 29, 1972, *Charlotte Observer*; Tom Ellis statement, JH for Senate Committee (remaining quotes), folder 19, Furgurson Papers, SHC.

66. McGovernGalifianakis flyer (first quote), folder 19, Furgurson Papers, SHC; McGovernGalifianakis ad, *Greensboro Daily News*, October 4, 1972 (remaining quotes except busing); "Helms-Ervin" ad, October 30, 1972 (busing quote), *Raleigh News and Observer*; Leslie Wayne, "Nick, Helms Quietly Shift Strategy," *Raleigh News and Observer*, September 19, 1972; "McGovern-Galifianakis?" *Greensboro Daily News*, October 5, 1972. Helms's ads sometimes spelled McGovernGalifianakis as one word without a hyphen.

67. Leslie Wayne, "Nick, Helms Quietly Shift Strategy," *Raleigh News and Observer*, September 19, 1972; "McGovern-Galifianakis?" *Greensboro Daily News*, October 5, 1972 (first and last quotes); McGovernGalifianakis ad, *Greensboro Daily News*, October 4, 1972 (second quote).

68. "Busing 'Undecided'" ad, *Raleigh News and Observer*, October 18, 1972.

69. Remarks of Congressman Nick Galifianakis, October 5, 1972 (second and third quotes), and press release, "Helms Backs Farm Supports," November 6, 1972, folder 19, Furgurson Papers, SHC; "Nixon Needs Helms" ads in *Clemmons (N.C.) Courier*, October

26, 1972, and *Salisbury (N.C.) Evening Post*, October 31, 1972; Galifianakis comparison ad, October 20, 1972 (last quote), "Senate Vote Drive Centers in the Piedmont," October 29, 1972, Leslie Wayne, "Nick, Helms Quietly Shift Strategy," September 19, 1972, Ferrel Guillory, "Nick Aligns Himself with Nixon," October 6, 1972, and Wayne, "Recent, Earlier Helms Views Differ," October 29, 1972, *Raleigh News and Observer*; Ned Cline, "Nixon Needs Helms in Senate—Buckley," October 7, 1972, and Rip Woodin, "Galifianakis Charges Helms Trying to Hide Real Stance," October 6, 1972, *Greensboro Daily News*; Linda Charlton, "Conservative Republican Victor in North Caronia Senate Race," *New York Times*, November 8, 1972.

70. Press release, "Helms Backs Farm Supports," November 6, 1972, folder 19, Furgurson Papers, SHC; "Senate Vote Drive Centers in the Piedmont," October 29, 1972, Leslie Wayne, "Nick, Helms Quietly Shift Strategy," September 19, 1972, Ferrel Guillory, "Nick Aligns Himself with Nixon," October 6, 1972, and Wayne, "Recent, Earlier Helms Views Differ," October 29, 1972 (quote), *Raleigh News and Observer*; Ned Cline, "Nixon Needs Helms in Senate—Buckley," October 7, 1972, and Rip Woodin, "Galifianakis Charges Helms Trying to Hide Real Stance," October 6, 1972, *Greensboro Daily News*; Linda Charlton, "Conservative Republican Victor in North Carolina Senate Race," *New York Times*, November 8, 1972.

71. Wayne, "Recent, Earlier Helms Views Differ," October 29, 1972, *Raleigh News and Observer*; "Trust" ad, November 6, 1972 (first and second quotes), "Helms Scores Nick's Honor," October 25, 1972 (third, fourth, and last quotes), and "Helms Speaks on 'Credibility,'" October 27, 1972, *Raleigh News and Observer*.

72. *Viewpoint* #2756, February 10, 1972.

73. Democrats for Helms, n.d., folder 19, Furgurson Papers, SHC; "Democratic Group Set for Helms," October 29, 1972 (first quote), *Raleigh News and Observer*; "Message" ad (second quote), *Salisbury (N.C.) Evening Post*, November 6, 1972; Luebke, *Tar Heel Politics*, 163.

74. Democrats for Helms, n.d., folder 19, Furgurson Papers, SHC; "Helms-Ervin" ad, October 30, 1972 (first and second quotes), Ervin Endorsing Nick ad, November 3, 1972 (third quote), "Nick Attacks Helms Stance," October 25, 1972, "Helms Blasted for Use of Jim Graham Photo," October 29, 1972 (fourth quote), Ferrel Guillory, "Ervin Not Told about Jesse Helms's Ad," October 31, 1972, "Democratic Chairman Attacks Helms Ads," November 2, 1972, *Raleigh News and Observer*.

75. Various "He's One of Us" ads (first quote), in *Andrews Journal*, October 12, 1972, *St. Pauls Review*, October 12, 1972, and *Raleigh News and Observer*, October 27 and November 6, 1972; "Helms Groups Disclaim Mystery Ad about Nick," October 26, 1972 (second and third quotes), and "Stand" ad, November 6, 1972, *Raleigh News and Observer*; Link, *Righteous Warrior*, 128–29; Luebke, *Tar Heel Politics*, 26–27, 164; Furgurson, *Hard Right*, 100–101; Furgurson interview with Galifianakis in folder 19, Furgurson Papers, SHC.

76. Rip Woodin, "Galifianakis Charges Helms Trying to Hide Real Stance," *Greensboro Daily News*, October 6, 1972 (quote); "Suddenly Jesse Helms Is a Moderate?" October 7, 1972, "Charlotte Observer Backs Nick," November 2, 1972, "Greensboro Paper

Backs Galifianakis," November 2, 1972, "Galifianakis the Clear Choice," November 2, 1972, *Raleigh News and Observer*.

77. Rip Woodin, "Galifianakis Charges Helms Trying to Hide Real Stance," October 6, 1972, Ned Cline, "Nixon-Helms—Odd Couple: Political Expediency Makes for Strange Bedfellows," October 8, 1972, and Cline, "Nixon Needs Helms in Senate—Buckley," October 7, 1972, *Greensboro Daily News*; Leslie Wayne, "Recent, Earlier Helms Views Differ," October 29, 1972, "Suddenly Jesse Helms Is a Moderate?" October 7, 1972, "*Charlotte Observer* Backs Nick," November 2, 1972, "Greensboro Paper Backs Galifianakis," November 2, 1972, "Galifianakis the Clear Choice," November 2, 1972, *Raleigh News and Observer*.

78. "Helms Declares Ad Says It All," October 17, 1972 (quotes), and "Helms Criticizes 'Ultraliberal' Editors," November 3, 1972, *Raleigh News and Observer*.

79. "Helms Declares Ad Says It All," October 17, 1972 (quotes), and "Helms Criticizes 'Ultraliberal' Editors," November 3, 1972, *Raleigh News and Observer*; "Helms Scores Nick's 'Honor,'" October 25, 1972, *Raleigh News and Observer*; Ned Cline, "Nixon-Helms—Odd Couple: Political Expediency Makes for Strange Bedfellows," October 8, 1972 (quote), and "Helms Favors Highest Price for Peanuts," *Greensboro Daily News*, October 8, 1972.

80. "Nixon, Bowles, Nick Still Ahead," *Greensboro Daily News*, October 8, 1972; Marjorie Hunter, "Major Races in North Carolina Seem Close," *New York Times*, October 28, 1972; "Helms: Poll Shows I Lead," October 31, 1972, and "Nick Says Polls Unimportant," November 4, 1972, *Raleigh News and Observer*.

81. "Nixon, Bowles, Nick Still Ahead," *Greensboro Daily News*, October 8, 1972; Marjorie Hunter, "Major Races in North Carolina Seem Close," *New York Times*, October 28, 1972; "Helms: Poll Shows I Lead," October 31, 1972, and "Nick Says Polls Unimportant," November 4, 1972, *Raleigh News and Observer*; Mark Pinsky, "Riding the Airwaves to Washington," *More*, March 1973; "Helms Defends Campaign Costs," October 26, 1972, and Pat Stith, "Textile Money Helping Helms," October 27, 1972, *Raleigh News and Observer*; Link, *Righteous Warrior*, 123–24, 129; Furgurson, *Hard Right*, 102; JH to Roger Milliken, July 31, 1972, Roger Milliken file, JH to Hugh Scott, October 11, 1972, and Scott to JH, September 22, 1972, Hugh Scott file, WRAL-TV Papers, JHC. The *News and Observer* reported that the National Republican Senatorial Committee and the Republican Congressional Boosters Club had given Helms over $75,000 by October 16 and that Helms credited the White House with "passing the word" to big out-of-state donors. Helms also received funds from Richard Scaife of Pittsburgh and Henry Salvatori of California—both known for supporting conservatives.

82. "Nixon Needs Helms" ads in *Clemmons (N.C.) Courier*, October 26, 1972, and *Salisbury (N.C.) Evening Post*, October 31, 1972. Link explains that Helms aide and YAF'er Harold Herring convinced Chatham to endorse the loan. The Helms campaign hired consultants and pollsters associated with James Buckley's 1970 victory in New York State including Clifton White, Phil Nicolaides, and Arthur Finkelstein. Link, *Righteous Warrior*, 123–24, 129.

83. Speech and Notes, "Suggested Presidential Remarks: North Carolina Visit, November 4, 1972," November 3, 1972, President's Speech file, 1969–74, box 82, President's

Personal File, Richard Nixon Presidential Library and Museum, NACP; Ferrell Guillory, "State Candidates Share Nixon Rally," *Raleigh News and Observer*, November 5, 1972.

84. Leslie Wayne, "Helms Beats Nick: Early Margin Grows," November 6, 1972 (first quote), *Raleigh News and Observer*; JH victory speech, n.d., Miscellaneous file, JH to Larry Harding, December 4, 1972, JH to Lennox Baker, December 8, 1972 (second and third quotes), JH to William Loeb, December 4, 1972 (fourth quote), and JH to Grant Ujifusa, December 27, 1972, Chronological file, WRAL-TV Papers, JHC; Luebke, *Tar Heel Politics*, 23–27, 156–60, 164–65.

85. JH to Peter Young, November 16, 1972, Chronological file, WRAL-TV Papers, JHC.

86. JH to Jerry Lennon, December 7, 1972, JH to Richard Nixon, November 21, 1972, JH to John Watlington, November 13, 1972, JH to Larry Harding, December 4, 1972 (second quote), JH to H. F. (Chub) Seawell, November 30, 1972, JH to Ronald Docksai, November 20, 1972 (first quote), JH to Tim Baer, December 13, 1972, Chronological file, WRAL-TV Papers, JHC. Docksai was the national chairman of YAF; Baer was Florida state chairman and a volunteer for the Helms campaign.

Epilogue

1. Link, *Righteous Warrior*, 131–32; JH to William Loeb, December 4, 1972, Chronological file, WRAL-TV Papers, JHC.

2. JH to M. Stanton Evans, November 21, 1972, Chronological file, WRAL-TV Papers, JHC.

3. JH to Frank Ream, February 6, 1974, Alphabetical Correspondence, Senate Papers, JHC.

4. JH to Sidney Proctor Jr., December 19, 1973 (quote), Alphabetical Correspondence, Senate Papers, JHC; Elaine Shannon, "Helms' Conservatism Reflected," May 22, 1973, and Shannon, "Helm Sticks by the President on Crucial Votes," June 24, 1973, *Raleigh News and Observer*; "Senate Confirms Brennan and Lynn for Cabinet Posts," *New York Times*, February 1, 1973; Furgurson, *Hard Right*, 107.

5. Link, *Righteous Warrior*, 135–39; Furgurson, *Hard Right*, 103–11; Paul Scott, "Fighting for the Right to Life," *Indianapolis News*, July 10, 1973 (first quote); "The Filibuster: Senator Helms Is Wrong Again," *Charlotte Observer*, December 24, 1973; "Nominees Stymied by Sen. Helms," *Washington Post*, November 20, 1973.

6. Link, *Righteous Warrior*, 135–39; Furgurson, *Hard Right*, 103–11; Paul Scott, "Fighting for the Right to Life," *Indianapolis News*, July 10, 1973; "The Filibuster: Senator Helms Is Wrong Again," *Charlotte Observer*, December 24, 1973; "Nominees Stymied by Sen. Helms," *Washington Post*, November 20, 1973.

7. Schlafly to JH, December 10, 1973, Alphabetical Correspondence, Senate Papers, JHC; Jack Betts, "Sidebar to Helms Speech," typescript wire service report, August 16, 1973, in Seth Effron Clippings Collection, NCC.

8. Schulman, *The Seventies*, 194–205; Furgurson, *Hard Right*, 109–13, 121–25 (quote on 125); Link, *Righteous Warrior*, 144–47, 178–79, 192–95.

9. Thomas Reese to JH, August 23, 1973 (second quote), and attached, "Helms Showing True Colors," *Hickory (N.C.) Daily Record*, August 22, 1973, Alphabetical

Correspondence, Senate Papers, JHC; Elaine Shannon, "Helms' Conservatism Reflected," May 22, 1973, and Shannon, "Helm Sticks by the President on Crucial Votes," June 24, 1973, *Raleigh News and Observer*; Furgurson, *Hard Right*, 106.

10. Jack Betts, "Sidebar to Helms Speech," August 16, 1973 (first quote), Don Hill, "Helms," November 6, 1973 (third quote), and Don Hill, "Helms Statement," August 6, 1974, typescript wire service reports, Effron Collection, NCC; JH to E. W. Charles, November 27, 1973 (second quote), JH to J. C. D. Bailey, December 19, 1973 (last quote), and JH to Allen Brantley, November 6, 1973 (fourth quote), Alphabetical Correspondence, Senate Papers, JHC.

11. Ken Friedlein, "Jesse Helms: Conservative First, Republican Second" [probably *Winston-Salem Journal*], n.d., Effron Collection, NCC; Ferrel Guillory, "N.C. GOP Drifts without Defined Leadership," February 23, 1975, *Raleigh News and Observer*; Paul Clancy, "Helms Would Create Conservative Party," May 16, 1975, and Howard Covington, "Senator Swings Big Club," December 2, 1974, *Charlotte Observer*; Furgurson, *Hard Right*, 109–13, 121–25.

12. JH, press release, "Memorandum to the News Media," February 14, 1975, and Jack Betts, "Jesse," February 14, 1975 (remaining quotes), and Don Hill, "Interview-Helms," April 16, 1975, typescript wire service reports, Effron Collection, NCC; "Helms Possible Chairman: GOP Conservatives Form Committee," *Greensboro Daily News*, February 17, 1975.

13. "G.O.P. Role Sought by Conservatives," *New York Times*, March 2, 1975; "Broadbased GOP Is 'Hokum,'" *Greensboro Record*, March 7, 1975 (first and second quotes).

14. "G.O.P. Role Sought by Conservatives," *New York Times*, March 2, 1975; "Broadbased GOP Is 'Hokum,'" *Greensboro Record*, March 7, 1975 (first and second quotes); R. W. Apple Jr., "Mixed Impact from Moves Seen," *New York Times*, November 4, 1975 (quote).

15. Furgurson, *Hard Right*, 114–20; Cannon, *Reagan*, 201–26; Viguerie, *The New Right*, 65–66, 173–75 (quote).

16. Furgurson, *Hard Right*, 114–20 (first quote on 120); "'Moderate Alternative,'" August 17, 1976, and "Helms Calls for Kissinger to Back Platform or Quit," September 9, 1976 (second quote), *New York Times*.

17. JH and other Senators to Jimmy Carter, April 22, 1977 (first quote), box PU-1, file PU, and March 18, 1977, box WE-6, file WE3, memo "Breakfast with Republican Senators," from Frank Moore, September 20, 1977 (second quote), box SO-1, file SO-1, telegram from JH to Jimmy Carter, September 28, 1978, box FO-44, file FO6-7, White House Central Office Files—Subject, JCL.

18. JH, press release, "Statement Opposing Panama Canal Treaty," August 11, 1977, Effron Collection, NCC; Ferrel Guillory, "Helms Still Set against Treaties," *Raleigh News and Observer*, January 24, 1978; Link, *Righteous Warrior*, 187–92; Schulman, *The Seventies*, 199–200; Furgurson, *Hard Right*, 119; JH to JC, June 5, 1978, and attached JH floor speech, June 5, 1978, box FO-20, FO 3-1/Panama Canal File, White House Central Office Files—Subject, JCL.

19. Daniel Hoover, "Helms Happy as 'No,'" January 5, 1978 (first and second quotes), and Ferrel Guillory, "Helms Forte: Senator Unafraid to Stand Alone," August 6, 1977,

Raleigh News and Observer; Ned Cline, "Helms: Conservative Lone Ranger," *Charlotte Observer*, November 20, 1977; "Helms Interview" transcript, October 24, 1978, and JH, press releases, "Helms Bill Would Cut Accidents, Save Gas, Stop Forced Busing," May 19, 1977, "Helms Would Reform Federal Desegregation Procedures," August 4, 1977, and "Statement of Senator Jesse Helms on Proposed ERA Extension," October 3, 1978, Effron Collection, NCC.

20. Viguerie, *The New Right*, 76, 81–82; Link, *Righteous Warrior*, 192–201; Furgurson, *Hard Right*, 125–31; Phil Gallery, "Populist Makes Helms Squirm on Fund-Raising," *Washington Star*, October 1, 1978; A. L. May, "Helms's Campaign Tops $6 Million," October 13, 1978, *Raleigh News and Observer*; Bill Peterson, "The Six Million Dollar Man," *Washington Post*, October 31, 1978.

21. Viguerie, *The New Right*, 76, 81–82; Link, *Righteous Warrior*, 192–201; Furgurson, *Hard Right*, 125–31; fund-raising letters, Ronald Reagan to Dear Friend, March 1977, JH to Susan Ballentine, May 6, 1977 (second quote), Phyllis Schlafly to Dear Friend, September 15, 1978 (third quote), and Helms to Dear Friend, October 23, 1978 (fourth quote), Group Research Archives, box 159, Jesse Helms file, Rare Book and Manuscript Library, Columbia University.

22. Viguerie, *The New Right*, 76, 81–82; Link, *Righteous Warrior*, 192–201 (quote on 200); Furgurson, *Hard Right*, 125–31; Phil Gallery, "Populist Makes Helms Squirm on Fund-Raising," *Washington Star*, October 1, 1978 (second quote); A. L. May, "Helms's Campaign Tops $6 Million," *Raleigh News and Observer*, October 13, 1978 (second quote); Bill Peterson, "The Six Million Dollar Man," *Washington Post*, October 31, 1978.

23. Link, *Righteous Warrior*, 203–9; Furgurson, *Hard Right*, 132–37; Mark I. Pinsky, "Helmsman of the Right," *The Progressive*, April 1980; Bob McMahon, "Helms: Shining Light of the New Right," *The Guardian*, September 3, 1979; JH to E. Van Buskirk, August 1, 1979 (quote), Alphabetical Correspondence, Senate Papers, JHC.

24. Mark I. Pinsky, "Helmsman of the Right," *The Progressive*, April 1980; Bob McMahon, "Helms: Shining Light of the New Right," *The Guardian*, September 3, 1979; Link, *Righteous Warrior*, 206–9; Furgurson, *Hard Right*, 194–95; Robert Hodierne, "Jesse Helms Dispatches His Gunslingers of the Right," *Charlotte Observer*, October 15, 1979 (first quote); JH to Fred Waller Jr., December 18, 1979 (second quote), and JH to Mildred Tillman, April 11, 1980, Alphabetical Correspondence, Senate Papers, JHC.

25. Reagan Fundraising Letter, JH to Dear Friend, [June 1980], Group Research Archives, box 159, Jesse Helms file, Rare Book and Manuscript Library, Columbia University (quotes); Link, *Righteous Warrior*, 209–18; Furgurson, *Hard Right*, 137–44; Viguerie, *The New Right*, 82, 174–75; Mark I. Pinsky, "Helmsman of the Right," *The Progressive*, April 1980; "Helms Fund-Raising Arm Supports Reagan Amid Criticism at Home," *New York Times*, April 3, 1980; Bob McMahon, "Helms: Shining Light of the New Right," *The Guardian*, September 3, 1979.

26. Link, *Righteous Warrior*, 209–18; Furgurson, *Hard Right*, 137–44; Viguerie, *The New Right*, 82, 174–75; Mark I. Pinsky, "Helmsman of the Right," *Progressive*, April 1980; "Helms Fund-Raising Arm Supports Reagan amid Criticism at Home," *New York Times*, April 3, 1980; Bob McMahon, "Helms: Shining Light of the New Right," *Guardian*,

September 3, 1979; "Nation: Reagan Gets a G.O.P. Senate," *Time*, November 17, 1980; Luebke, *Tar Heel Politics*, 128; Schulman, *The Seventies*, 199–200.

27. Link, *Righteous Warrior*, 203–4, 216–18; 235–36; "'A Battle of the Titans' Shaping Up in Carolina," September 24, 1983 (first quote), *Washington Post*; Hugh Downs and Sylvia Chase, "The Helms Machine," *20/20* transcript, ABC Television Network, March 18, 1982 (second and third quotes), folder 1, Furgurson Papers, SHC.

28. Link, *Righteous Warrior*, 235–36, 239–51; JH to Ed Tenney, November 17, 1980 (first quote), and JH to Richard Viguerie, November 17, 1980 (second quote), Alphabetical Correspondence, Senate Papers, JHC; Furgurson, *Hard Right*, 201–3; Alan Tonelson, "Battling Modern Diplomacy," *Foreign Service Journal*, October 1981, 18–23; JH, Statement of Senator Jesse Helms of North Carolina: The Nomination of Caspar Weinberger, n.d., Effron Clippings Collection, NCC.

29. Link, *Righteous Warrior*, 216–34 (first quote on 224 and second quote on 226); Furgurson, *Hard Right*, 152–60.

30. Link, *Righteous Warrior*, 216–34; Furgurson, *Hard Right*, 152–60 (quote on 158).

31. Rob Christensen, "Helms, Hunt Prepare for All-out Battle," November 6, 1983, and "Organization vs. Money," November 6, 1983, *Raleigh News and Observer*; "Helms in Trouble?" April 19, 1983, and "'A Battle of the Titans' Shaping Up in Carolina," September 24, 1983, *Washington Post*; Luebke, *Tar Heel Politics*, 27–31, 33–34; Mark, *Going Dirty*, 93–97 (quote on 96).

32. Rob Christensen, "Helms, Hunt Prepare for All-out Battle," November 6, 1983 (first and third quotes), and "Organization vs. Money," November 6, 1983 (second quote), *Raleigh News and Observer*; "Helms in Trouble?" April 19, 1983, and "'A Battle of the Titans' Shaping Up in Carolina," September 24, 1983, *Washington Post*; Luebke, *Tar Heel Politics*, 133–35; Link, *Righteous Warrior*, 197–99, 212–15.

33. Mark, *Going Dirty*, 96–101 (quote on 96); Luebke, *Tar Heel Politics*, 137–55; Tom Wicker, "In the Nation: The Other Jesse," April 17, 1984 (second quote), and Martin Tolchin, "Battle for Helms's Senate Seat Already Strenuous," April 29, 1984, *New York Times*; "Jesse Helms Back on the Offensive in North Carolina Race," *Christian Science Monitor*, May 2, 1984; Mark Starr, Holly Morris, and Gloria Borger, "Toe-to-Toe on Tobacco Road," *Newsweek*, May 28, 1984; "Would Helms Spread Race-Hate to Keep Job?" *Southern Exposure*, July/August 1983, 4.

34. David Garrow, "The Helms Attack on King," *Southern Exposure*, March/April 1984, 12–15; JH, "The Radical Record of Martin Luther King," *Human Events*, November 12, 1983, 953–60 (quotes).

35. David Garrow, "The Helms Attack on King," *Southern Exposure*, March/April 1984, 12–15; JH, "The Radical Record of Martin Luther King," *Human Events*, November 12, 1983, 953–60; JH fund-raising Letter, n.d. (quotes), folder 1, Furgurson Papers, SHC; Tom Wicker, "In the Nation: the Other Jesse," *New York Times*, April 17, 1984 (last quote).

36. Ken Eudy and Katherine White, "Helms Camp Launches Ads in Duel with N.C. Democrats," *Charlotte Observer*, December 3, 1983; Edwin M. Yoder Jr., "Helms v. the Holiday," *Washington Post*, October 6, 1983; *World News Tonight* transcripts, ABC Television Network, October 2, October 5, 1983; "Under the Dome: Helms Fund-raising Letter Cites King Fight," *Raleigh News and Observer*, November 6, 1983.

37. Ken Eudy and Katherine White, "Helms Camp Launches Ads in Duel with N.C. Democrats," *Charlotte Observer*, December 3, 1983; Edwin M. Yoder Jr., "Helms v. the Holiday," *Washington Post*, October 6, 1983; *World News Tonight* transcripts, ABC Television Network, October 2, October 5, 1983; "Under the Dome: Helms Fund-raising Letter Cites King Fight," *Raleigh News and Observer*, November 6, 1983; press release, "Conservative Caucus: Joins in Call to Lift Seal on FBI Surveillance Records before Senate Vote on King Holiday," October 11, 1983, Business Wire; David Garrow, "The Helms Attack on King," *Southern Exposure*, March/April 1984, 12–15; JH, "The Radical Record of Martin Luther King," *Human Events*, November 12, 1983, 953–60.

38. Helen Dewar, "Helms Stalls King's Day in Senate," *Washington Post*, October 4, 1983 (quote); Mark, *Going Dirty*, 96–101; Luebke, *Tar Heel Politics*, 137–55.

39. Mark, *Going Dirty*, 96–101; Luebke, *Tar Heel Politics*, 137–55; Rob Christensen, "Helms, Hunt Prepare for All-out Battle," *Raleigh News and Observer*, November 6, 1983. Luebke argues based on exit polls that Hunt's negative ads were effective but that he did not run enough of them and waited too long to start.

40. Mark, *Going Dirty*, 96–101; Luebke, *Tar Heel Politics*, 137–55; Rob Christensen, "Helms, Hunt Prepare for All-out Battle," *Raleigh News and Observer*, November 6, 1983; Frye Gaillard, "It's Jesse Again," *Southern Changes*, December 1984, 1–3.

41. Schulman, *The Seventies*, 253–57.

Bibliography

Primary Sources and Archives

JESSE HELMS CENTER, WINGATE, NORTH CAROLINA

North Carolina Bankers Association Papers
Senate Papers
WRAL-TV Papers

JIMMY CARTER LIBRARY, ATLANTA, GEORGIA

White House Central Office Files—Subject

NATIONAL ARCHIVES, COLLEGE PARK, MARYLAND

Record Group 173, Records of the Federal Communications Commission

NORTH CAROLINA COLLECTION, WILSON LIBRARY, UNIVERSITY OF NORTH CAROLINA
AT CHAPEL HILL

Seth Effron Clippings Collection

SOUTHERN HISTORICAL COLLECTION, WILSON LIBRARY, UNIVERSITY OF NORTH
CAROLINA AT CHAPEL HILL

Harold Dunbar Cooley Papers, #3801
Ernest B. Furgurson Papers, #4912
Thomas Jackson White Jr. Papers, #4231

Secondary Sources

Anderson, Terry. *The Movement and the Sixties: Protest in America from Greensboro to
Wounded Knee.* New York: Oxford University Press, 1995.
Andrew, John, III. *The Other Side of the Sixties: Young Americans for Freedom and the
Rise of Conservative Politics.* New Brunswick, N.J.: Rutgers University Press, 1997.
Ashby, Warren. *Frank Porter Graham: A Southern Liberal.* Winston-Salem, N.C.: John
F. Blair, 1980.
Billingsley, William J. *Communists on Campus: Race, Politics, and the Public University in
Sixties North Carolina.* Athens: University of Georgia Press, 1999.

Black, Earl, and Merle Black. *The Rise of Southern Republicans*. Cambridge: Belknap Press of Harvard University Press, 2002.

Bodroghkozy, Aniko. "Negotiating the Mod: How *The Mod Squad* Played the Ideological Balancing Act in Prime Time." In *Groove Tube: Sixties Television and the Youth Rebellion*, 164–98. Durham, N.C.: Duke University Press, 2001.

Bond, Julian. "The Media and the Movement: Looking Back from the Southern Front." In *Media, Culture, and the Modern African American Freedom Struggle*, edited by Brian Ward, 16–40. Gainesville: University Press of Florida, 2001.

Branch, Taylor. *Parting the Waters: America in the King Years, 1954–1963*. New York: Simon and Schuster, 1988.

———. *Pillar of Fire: America in the King Years, 1963–65*. New York: Simon and Schuster, 1998.

Brennan, Mary. *Turning Right in the Sixties: The Conservative Capture of the GOP*. Chapel Hill: University of North Carolina Press, 1995.

Brown, Les. *Les Brown's Encyclopedia of Television*. 3rd ed. Washington, D.C.: Visible Ink, 1992.

Cannon, Lou. *Reagan*. New York: Putnam, 1982.

Carson, Clayborne. *In Struggle: SNCC and the Black Awakening of the 1960s*. Cambridge: Harvard University Press, 1981.

Carter, Dan T. *From George Wallace to Newt Gringrich: Race in the Conservative Counterrevolution, 1963–1994*. Baton Rouge: Louisiana State University Press, 1996.

———. *The Politics of Rage: George Wallace, the Origins of the New Conservatism, and the Transformation of American Politics*. New York: Simon and Schuster, 1995.

Chafe, William. *Civilities and Civil Rights: Greensboro, North Carolina, and the Black Struggle for Freedom*. New York: Oxford University Press, 1980.

Clinton, Bill. *My Life*. New York: Knopf, 2004.

Crespino, Joseph. *In Search of Another Country: Mississippi and the Conservative Counterrevolution*. Princeton: Princeton University Press, 2007.

———. *Strom Thurmond's America*. New York: Hill and Wang, 2012.

Dallek, Robert. *Flawed Giant: Lyndon Johnson and His Times, 1961–1973*. New York: Oxford University Press, 1998.

———. *An Unfinished Life: John F. Kennedy, 1917–1963*. Boston: Little, Brown, 2003.

Donovan, Robert. *Unsilent Revolution: Television News and American Public Life, 1948–1991*. New York: Cambridge University Press, 1992.

Edsall, Thomas Byrne, and Mary Edsall. *Chain Reaction: The Impact of Race, Rights, and Taxes on American Politics*. New York: Norton, 1991.

Farber, David. *The Rise and Fall of Modern Conservatism: A Short History*. Princeton: Princeton University Press, 2010.

Furgurson, Ernest. *Hard Right: The Rise of Jesse Helms*. New York: Norton, 1986.

Gerstle, Gary. "Race and the Myth of the Liberal Consensus." *Journal of American History* 82 (September 1995): 579–86.

Goldberg, Robert Alan. *Barry Goldwater*. New Haven: Yale University Press, 1995.

Goldwater, Barry. *The Conscience of a Conservative*. New York: Macfadden Books, 1961.

Griffith, Robert. "Dwight D. Eisenhower and the Corporate Commonwealth." *American Historical Review* 87, no. 1 (February 1982): 87–122.

Hall, Jacquelyn Dowd. "The Long Civil Rights Movement and the Political Uses of the Past." *Journal of American History* 90 (March 2003): 1233–63.

Herring, George C. "American Strategy in Vietnam: The Postwar Debate." *Military Affairs* 46 (April 1982): 57–63.

———. "Vietnam: The War That Never Seems to Go Away." *New England Journal of History* 54 (Spring 1998): 2–10.

Hess, Gary. "The Unending Debate: Historians and the Vietnam War." *Diplomatic History* 18 (Spring 1994): 239–64.

Hoff, Joan. *Nixon Reconsidered.* New York: Basic Books, 1994.

Hunt, David Hunt. "Washington Quagmire: U.S. Presidents and the Vietnam Wars—A Pattern of Intervention." In *A Companion to Post-1945 America,* edited by Jean-Christophe Anges and Roy Rosenzweig, 464–78. Malden, Mass.: Blackwell, 2002.

Kruse, Kevin M. *White Flight: Atlanta and the Making of Modern Conservatism.* Princeton: Princeton University Press, 2005.

Lackmann, Ron. *The Encyclopedia of American Television: Broadcast Programming Post World War II to 2000.* New York: Facts on File, 2002.

Lassiter, Matthew D. *The Silent Majority: Suburban Politics in the Sunbelt South.* Princeton: Princeton University Press, 2006.

Link, William. *Righteous Warrior: Jesse Helms and the Rise of Modern Conservatism.* New York: St. Martin's Press, 2008.

Luckett, Moya. "A Moral Crisis in Prime Time: *Peyton Place* and the Rise of the Single Girl." In *Television, History, and American Culture: Feminist Critical Essays,* edited by Mary Beth Haralovich and Lauren Rabinovitz, 75–97. Durham, N.C.: Duke University Press, 1999.

Luebke, Paul. *Tar Heel Politics: Myths and Realities.* Chapel Hill: University of North Carolina Press, 1990.

Mark, David. *Going Dirty: The Art of Negative Campaigning.* Lanham, Md.: Rowman and Littlefield, 2006.

McGirr, Lisa. "Piety and Property: Conservatism and Right-Wing Movements in the Twentieth Century." In *Perspectives on Modern America: Making Sense of the Twentieth Century,* edited by Harvard Sitkoff, 33–54. New York: Oxford University Press, 2001.

———. *Suburban Warriors: The Origins of the New American Right.* Princeton: Princeton University Press, 2001.

McMahon, Robert. "The Vietnam War—Revisited and Revised." *New England Journal of History* 54 (Spring 1998): 11–23.

Nachman, Gerald. "Sibling Revelry: The Smothers Brothers." In *Seriously Funny: The Rebel Comedians of the 1950s and 1960s,* 445–62. New York: Pantheon Books, 2003.

Nash, George. *The Conservative Intellectual Movement in America since 1945.* New York: Basic Books, 1976.

Newcomb, Horace, ed. *Encyclopedia of Television.* Chicago: Fitzroy Dearborn, 1997.

Nyerere, Julius. "Rhodesia in the Context of Southern Africa." *Foreign Affairs* 44 (April 1966): 373–86.

Pleasants, Julian, and Augustus Burns III. *Frank Porter Graham and the 1950 Senate Race in North Carolina.* Chapel Hill: University of North Carolina Press, 1990.

Phillips-Fein, Kim. *Invisible Hands: The Businessmen's Crusade against the New Deal.* New York: Norton, 2009.

Rooke, Leon. "The Ice House Gang." *Carolina Quarterly* 18, no. 3 (1966): 5–9.

———. "If Lost Return to the Swiss Arms." *Carolina Quarterly* 16, no. 1 (1963): 18–32.

Rusk, David. *Cities without Suburbs.* Washington, D.C.: Woodrow Wilson Center Press, 1995.

Ryan, Halford Ross, ed. *American Rhetoric from Roosevelt to Reagan.* 2nd ed. Prospects Heights, Ill.: Waveland Press, 1987.

Schoenwald, Jonathan M. *A Time for Choosing: The Rise of Modern American Conservatism.* New York: Oxford University Press, 2001.

Schulman, Bruce. *From Cotton Belt to Sunbelt: Federal Policy, Economic Development, and the Transformation of the South, 1938–1980.* Durham, N.C.: Duke University Press, 1994.

———. *Lyndon B. Johnson and American Liberalism: A Brief Biography with Documents.* The Bedford Series in History and Culture. Boston: Bedford Books of St. Martin's Press, 1995.

———. *The Seventies: The Great Shift in American Culture, Society, and Politics.* New York: The Free Press, 2001.

Sitkoff, Harvard, ed. *Perspectives on Modern America: Making Sense of the Twentieth Century.* New York: Oxford University Press, 2001.

Snider, William. *Helms and Hunt: The North Carolina Senate Race, 1984.* Chapel Hill: University of North Carolina Press, 1985.

Stark, Steven D. *Glued to the Set: The 60 Television Shows and Events That Made Us Who We Are Today.* New York: The Free Press, 1997.

Terrace, Vincent. *The Complete Encyclopedia of Television Shows, 1947–76.* New York: A. S. Barnes, 1976.

Tuck, Stephen. *We Ain't What We Ought to Be: The Black Freedom Struggle from Emancipation to Obama.* Cambridge: Belknap Press, 2010.

Viguerie, Richard *The New Right: We're Ready to Lead.* Rev. ed. Falls Church, Va.: Viguerie, 1981.

Watson, Mary Ann. *Expanding Vista: American Television in the Kennedy Years.* Durham, N.C.: Duke University Press, 1994.

Williams, Daniel K. *God's Own Party: The Making of the Christian Right.* New York: Oxford University Press, 2010.

Zelizer, Julian. *Arsenal of Democracy: The Politics of National Security—From World War II to the War on Terrorism.* New York: Basic Books, 2009.

Index

Bryan Hardin Thrift teaches history at Johnston Community College in Smithfield, North Carolina.

The University Press of Florida is the scholarly publishing agency for the State University System of Florida, comprising Florida A&M University, Florida Atlantic University, Florida Gulf Coast University, Florida International University, Florida State University, New College of Florida, University of Central Florida, University of Florida, University of North Florida, University of South Florida, and University of West Florida.

DEC   2016

DEC   2016